THE RIDDLE OF THE JEWS' SUCCESS

Theodor Fritsch

BOOKS FROM CLEMENS & BLAIR
— www.clemensandblair.com —

Triumph of the Truth, by Robert Penman
The Book of the Shulchan Aruch, by Erich Bischoff
For My Legionnaires, by Corneliu Codreanu
Myth and Sun, by Martin Friedrich
Unmasking Anne Frank, by Ikuo Suzuki
Pan-Judah! Political Cartoons of Der Stürmer, by Robert Penman
Passovers of Blood, by Ariel Toaff
The Poisonous Mushroom, by Ernst Hiemer
On the Jews and Their Lies, by Martin Luther
Mein Kampf, by Adolf Hitler
Mein Kampf (Dual English-German edition), by Adolf Hitler
The Essential Mein Kampf, by Adolf Hitler
The Myth of the 20th Century, by Alfred Rosenberg

BOOKS BY THOMAS DALTON
— www.thomasdaltonphd.com —

The Steep Climb: Essays on the Jewish Question
Classic Essays on the Jewish Question: 1850 to 1945
Debating the Holocaust
The Holocaust: An Introduction
The Jewish Hand in the World Wars
Eternal Strangers: Critical Views of Jews and Judaism
Hitler on the Jews
Goebbels on the Jews
Streicher, Rosenberg, and the Jews: The Nuremberg Transcripts

THE RIDDLE OF THE JEWS' SUCCESS

Theodor Fritsch

A New English Translation
by
THOMAS DALTON

Clemens & Blair, LLC
— 2023 —

CLEMENS & BLAIR, LLC

Introduction and English translation copyright © 2023, by Thomas Dalton

All rights reserved. No part of this publication may be reproduced, stored in a retrieval system, or transmitted, in any form or by any means, electronic, mechanical, photocopying, recording, or otherwise.

Clemens & Blair, LLC, is a non-profit educational publisher.
www.clemensandblair.com

Library of Congress Cataloging-in-Publication Data

Fritsch, Theodor (1852-1933)
The Riddle of the Jews' Success

A new English translation from German of *Das Rätsel des Jüdischen Erfolges* (1922), published under the pseudonym F. Roderich-Stoltheim

p. cm.
Includes bibliographical references

ISBN 979-8987-7263-10
(pbk.: alk. paper)

1. Jewish Question, the

Printing number: 9 8 7 6 5 4 3 2 1

Printed in the United States of America on acid-free paper.

CONTENTS

INTRODUCTION by Thomas Dalton   i

CHAPTER 1: Jewish Methods in Economic Life   1
Preface   1
Jews and Modern Capitalism   2
The Hebrew Enhances the Circulation of Money   5
The Hebrew Mobilizes Slumbering Values   8
The Hebrew Presses his Predatory Culture   10
Jewish Interest, Jewish Usury   15

CHAPTER 2: Particular Jewish Business Tactics   19
Securing an Advantage   23

CHAPTER 3: The International Connection and the Secret Hebrew League   29
Playing into One Another's Hands   34
Hebrew Nomadism   36

CHAPTER 4: The Peculiar Morality of Jewry   41
The Kol Nidre   47
Judaism as a State   50
'War Against All'   52

CHAPTER 5: Klatzkin's Confession   55

CHAPTER 6: Toward an Explanation, with Sombart   59

CHAPTER 7: Jewish Successes in Modern Times   63

CHAPTER 8: The Stock Exchange   73
A Mania for Speculation   77
On 'Speculation Banks'   82

CHAPTER 9: Sound Methods are Forced Out by the Jews   85
An Old Story   87
Certain Jewish Tricks of the Trade   89
Lowering the Standard of Production   91
Deviating Mode of Thought   93

CHAPTER 10: Jewish Trade Specialties	**97**
Professional Bankruptcy	97
CHAPTER 11: Moral Principles in Trade	**103**
Deviation in the Trend of Jewish Life	109
CHAPTER 12: Hebrews as Supporters of Capitalism	**113**
1. The Extensive Dispersion	119
2. The "Foreignness" of the Hebrew	127
3. Semi-Citizenship of the Jews	130
4. Jewish Wealth	133
CHAPTER 13: Business and Religion	**139**
Judaism versus Christianity	143
The Separation or Shutting-off of the Jews	147
CHAPTER 14: The Race Problem	**153**
In General	153
The Psychology of the Jews	156
Apparent Jewish Superiority	164
CHAPTER 15: Origin of the Jewish Entity	**169**
Descent of the Jews	169
Development of the Jews as a Commercial Nation	174
Dispersion of the Jews over the Earth	180
CHAPTER 16: Influence of the Jew upon Womankind	**187**
Assaults on Young Girls	191
The Enchanter	201
Spreading Sexual Disease	207
Traffic in Girls	213
CHAPTER 17: The Jews and the World War	**219**
CHAPTER 18: Concluding Words	**225**
Postscript	228
APPENDIX:	231
BIBLIOGRAPHY	249
INDEX	251

INTRODUCTION
THOMAS DALTON

Among the many anti-Semitic writers of late-19th-century Germany, a particular standout was Theodor Fritsch (1852-1933). A self-made businessman and politician, he would eventually come to have an outsized role in promoting critical thinking about the Jews of Germany. By the early 20th century, his books *Handbook on the Jewish Question* and *The Riddle of the Jews' Success* stood as among the most influential such works in all of Europe. These books still resonate in the present day; they form an essential backdrop for understanding the current manifestation of the Jewish Question.

The son of a farmer, Fritsch became a trained mechanic, began his own successful business, and quickly branched out into writing and publishing. He came to maturity at a time when awareness of Jewish dominance in European society was beginning to break into public consciousness. A number of important works on the Jewish Question were published in the 1870s, including Millingen's *Conquest of the World by the Jews* (1873) and Marr's *Victory of Jewry over Germandom* (1879).[1] Such works were surely influential for the young Fritsch, and he evidently felt compelled to add his own contribution to this growing body of literature. Already in 1881, at the age of 29, he published his first short anti-Semitic pamphlet, *Flares*. The following year, he participated in the First International Anti-Jewish Congress in Dresden; though nothing directly came of that event, it allowed him to meet and converse with other like-minded German thinkers. By 1885, he was writing directly to the journalist Marr to discuss the possibility of publishing a journal dedicated to anti-Semitic themes—which would eventually come to fruition in Fritsch's periodical, *The Hammer*. By all accounts, Fritsch had developed a clear and compelling vision of the task before him.

The following year, he and the politician Otto Böckel co-founded the German Anti-Semitic Association, and established a new periodical, *The Antisemitic Correspondence*. They planned to use these as a foundation for a new German nationalist party.

---

[1] For full versions of both essays, see my book *Classic Essays on the Jewish Question* (T. Dalton, ed.; 2022).

Then in 1887, and using the pen name 'Thomas Frey,' Fritsch published the initial edition of his book *The Anti-Semitic Catechism*. It was a three-part work: (1) questions and answers on basic issues of the Jewish Question, (2) anti-Jewish statements from famous figures in history, and (3) a critical analysis of Jewish writings such as the Talmud and the Shulchan Aruch, accompanied by names of prominent Jews in German society.[2] The book proved extremely successful, selling thousands of copies throughout Europe, and going through several editions. (It was later expanded and renamed *The Handbook of the Jewish Question*, in 1907). The work had a notable influence on Hitler, Goebbels, and others of the nascent National Socialist party.

In 1889, Fritsch was instrumental in establishing the new German Social Party, as a successor to his Anti-Semitic Association. But he did not thrive there, and left the party within a few years.

By 1892, at the age of 40, Fritsch got married, eventually having four children. But apart from the ongoing success of his *Catechism*, he had little to show for his various efforts for the next several years. Things changed in 1901, when he established a new periodical, *The Hammer*, which again found a large readership. Six years later, in 1907, the newly-renamed *Handbook of the Jewish Question* was released, in its 26th edition.

Apart from these efforts, Fritsch continued to be active in the business community, serving on several trade boards and business organizations. As with broader society, he was highly concerned about the effect that Jews were having on trade and commerce, especially with respect to unethical and illegal practices that allowed them to dominate certain business sectors and to accrue much wealth, all while degrading the quality of German society. Eventually Fritsch decided to document the many pernicious activities of Jewish businessmen in a new book, titled *The Jews in Trade and the Secret to their Success* (1913), published under the pseudonym F. Roderich-Stoltheim. The book would be later updated in 1923, under the new name *The Riddle of the Jews' Success*—the present work.

Then came World War One, trench warfare, military stalemates, and eventual German defeat, in large part thanks to Jewish activism in the German homeland.[3] After the war, Fritsch played a key role in forming the German Peoples' Protection and Defiance League (*Deutschvölkischer*

---

[2] Portions of this book have also been reproduced in my *Classic Essays on the Jewish Question* (2022). For a good study on the Shulchan Aruch, see Erich Bischoff, *The Book of the Shulchan Aruch* (2023).
[3] For details, see my book *The Jewish Hand in the World Wars* (2019).

Schutz- und Trutzbund), a major anti-Semitic nationalist organization. Though only lasting a few years (until 1924), the League was highly influential within the emerging NSDAP ('Nazi') party. Among the League's symbols was the swastika—a prominent figure in Germany since at least 1871, when archaeologist Heinrich Schliemann discovered several ancient relics bearing that symbol. For the Germans, it was a sign of the continuity of a creative, powerful, northern Aryan race of people across the centuries. In this sense, it was a natural symbol to be adopted by Fritsch and, a few years later, by Hitler.

Fritsch continued to be politically active right until the end of his life. In 1922, at the age of 70, he helped to create the new German National Freedom Party; two years later, he himself was elected to the Reichstag, representing Leipzig. But it was just at this time that Hitler and his NSDAP party were gaining in strength—initially serving as competition to Fritsch's new party, but later absorbing it and earning Fritsch's support. By 1930, Hitler was publicly praising Fritsch's *Handbook*, and other leading figures, including Himmler, Goebbels, and Eckart, were quoting from it in their speeches and writings.

Theodor Fritsch died in September of 1933, at the age of 81. Fortunately, he lived long enough to witness the NSDAP accession to power earlier that year. In a sense, his many years of work to raise anti-Semitism to German national policy had finally been realized; his *Handbook* and *Riddle of the Jews' Success*, along with the journal *Hammer*, surely had an effect in terms of building public sympathy for National Socialist ideas.

On the Text Itself

Jewish power has always been predicated on money. People don't do their bidding because they love them, or respect them, or feel some burning urge to aid their cause; they do it because they have been bribed, or threatened, by Jewish money. Therefore, to trace Jewish power, we need to trace how they acquired their wealth. As famously "non-productive" members of society, Jews have traditionally obtained their money through business, trade, commerce, and finance. They don't individually work the land, or become artisans, or work in factories; rather, they hire people to do such things, and then profit off their labor. Or they simply manipulate financial markets, stock markets, or capital flows in order to gain a profit. This is why Jews are so well-suited to capitalism and why they flourish under its conditions; capitalism places all value on money and the growth of money, to the detriment of all other social or human values. Under capitalism, he who cares most about money and least about people succeeds the best, and consequently grows rich and powerful. For hundreds of years, Jews have proven to be masters at the financial game.

Of course, to some extent, all people engage in business and commerce, and obviously, many non-Jews also succeed in trade and financial industries. But Fritsch recognized that the Jewish method of conducting business was far different, and far more destructive, than the non-Jewish approach. Others have condemned Jewish business practices, but Fritsch was the first to critically analyze this distinction in a comprehensive manner, based on personal experience and on conditions as they existed in Germany and Europe around the year 1900.

Even though Fritsch's analysis is now well over a century old, this in no way invalidates his conclusions. In fact, just the opposite: He exposes age-old tactics of Jewish business that are essentially unchanged to the present day. Furthermore, he had one big advantage: In that simpler time, when trade and finance were far less complex and thus far more transparent, a perceptive observer could rather easily discern what was actually going on behind the scenes—actions that illuminate and explain the infamous "Jewish success" in business.

This, after all, was Fritsch's main objective: to explain "the riddle of the Jews' success"—how it happened that the Jew was able to succeed so spectacularly and so rapidly, and to thus acquire so much wealth and power. To the average man on the street, Jewish success might appear to be due to cleverness, or hard work, or 'business smarts.' If Jews seem to do better than most, some might say, it must be because they are simply better at the game than non-Jews. But as Frisch amply demonstrates, this is far from the truth. Jews "succeed" by all sorts of nefarious, conniving, manipulative, unethical, and outright illegal means. Jews succeed at being better deceivers, better exploiters, and better liars than their non-Jewish competitor; and they do so in conjunction with many like-minded compatriots, and with the cover and support of Jewish-owned or -operated media. Jews can count on an entire network of fellow Hebrews to exploit loopholes, bend laws, find shortcuts, and collaborate on ill-gotten gains. Indeed, for Jews, there is no such thing as an 'ill-gotten' gain; any gain is a good gain, no matter the cost to society.

The net effect of such practices is striking; it drives all of commerce, and thus much of society, down to the "lowest common denominator." If you are engaged in a competition of any kind with someone who resorts to deception, cheating, trickery, lies, back-stabbing, and so on, you are faced with some tough choices. Either you (1) try to expose the scoundrel and his malicious tactics, (2) sink to his level and fight fire with fire, or (3) lose. For at least the past 150 years, option (1) largely fails, thanks to Jewish influence in media and government. Any criticism of an individual Jew is—except in the most obvious and egregious cases—covered up and defended by a sympathetic media; and any criticism of Jews collectively is immediately denounced as anti-Semitism, if not punished by law. This leaves the beleaguered individual with options (2) or (3): he either closes up shop and goes out of business, or degrades himself and sinks to the Jewish level, simply in order to compete. Both alternatives harm society; and in both cases, the Jew prospers.

It is truly remarkable how many common but appalling business practices today have been originated and sustained by Jews. Fritsch documents many of these 'Jewish innovations': selling adulterated products, creating false scarcity, exploiting networks of informants, damaging the landscape, using salacious advertising, showing utter disregard for social well-being, and so on. An entire honor roll of unethical practices were either created, refined, or otherwise exploited by Jews: false consumer claims, manipulating terms of sale, bait-and-switch, lies and slander against Gentile competitors, cheating on taxes, insurance fraud (up to and including arson!), bribery of suppliers or officials, exploiting or abusing employees (including sexually!), and polluting or otherwise abusing the environment. Fritsch offers many examples from his day, and in virtually every case we can see echoes in the present.

Worse still, as Jews accrued ill-gotten wealth, they used it to alter and manipulate government policy and laws to work in their favor—in effect, to *legalize* their malicious, unethical, and formerly illegal tactics. This process was only at the beginning stages in Fritsch's day, but in the past 50 years in the West, it has grown to monstrous proportions. Laws that impede Jewish business practices are routinely altered or rescinded, and new laws are introduced that aid them. Thus the legal and regulatory system itself has been co-opted to serve Jewish interests.

Further, Jewish product and marketing strategies are also deployed in their favor, via manipulation of social values. Commercials today routinely feature minorities, biracial individuals, and mixed-race couples, even when they are irrelevant to the product at hand.[4] Children's toys—especially

---

[4] Jews flourish in multiracial societies, preferably those in which Whites are a narrow majority or even a minority. Jews have an interest in promoting multiracialism as normal and natural, when in fact it is highly problematic on several levels.

those by Jewish-founded producers like Hasbro and Mattel—now embody Jewish-friendly (or Gentile-damaging) characteristics.[5] In general, Jewish-sympathetic products get considerable airtime, and anything even slightly critical of Jews, Israel, or Jewish interests is demeaned or censored.

In fact, when we consider the broader commercialization of modern society, the pervasiveness of advertising, and the marketing and monetizing of virtually everything, we can find the roots of all this in late 19th century and early 20th century Jewish business practices. Everything that is coarse and base about the modern world—the power of money, the all-pervading consumer culture, ubiquitous advertising, the pressure to sell one's life for ever-higher income—can be traced back to Jewish actions. Everything in modern life is oriented toward "making a buck," which is the Jews' guiding principle. It never used to be this way.

Because Jewish trade knows no bounds, governments are compelled to try to introduce legal oversight, protection laws, regulatory agencies, and so forth, simply to mitigate the worst effects of predatory Jewish practices. Such things often fail, however, in large part because Jewish entrepreneurs are masters at finding loopholes and distorting legal wording beyond recognition—which in turn requires a new round of regulation and oversight. The end result is a vast and tangled mess of laws that introduces a horrible complexity into modern life, something which would be all but unnecessary without Jews pressing to exploit every possible opening. Governments could be half the size they are today, if only they did not need to grapple with Jewish manipulators and schemers. This alone is a valuable message for all those 'small government' conservatives of the world: rein in your Jewish Lobbies, and the size of government can shrink dramatically.

*****

In the text to follow, one is constantly struck by the pure audacity of Jewish businessmen: their total disregard and even contempt for tradition, custom, and common decency. One is also amazed at their utter shamelessness. With their inbred superiority complex—stemming ultimately from their biblical standing as "God's chosen" and their God-given dominion over the world—Jews break rules and social norms with impunity. When

---

[5] In Fritsch's day, it was the Jewish firm Gebrüder Bing, one of the largest toy manufacturers in Europe, as well as J. W. Spear. In the US, it was Joshua Lionel Cohen (Lionel trains), the Hassenfeld brothers (Hasbro), Elliot Handler (Mattel), and David Rosen (Sega).

Introduction   vii

caught, they are never embarrassed, never ashamed; rather, they only worry about how it might impede future gains.

The practices that Fritsch exposes ring true to this day. Over and over, one sees attitudes, tactics, and ploys that recur constantly in the present day—only now, with much greater sophistication, cleverness, and deception. And today, of course, the stakes are so much higher, given that Jews in trade and finance deal with billions, even trillions of dollars, on a regular basis. At the federal level, they have the power to influence many aspects of governmental spending, and can positively or negatively affect entire national economies. And through international institutions like the International Monetary Fund (IMF), the World Bank, and the European Central Bank, they can influence the global economic network—all while securing vast personal gain.

Fritsch's humble stories and anecdotes, which appear quaint or humorous at first glance, are today elevated to tragic proportions. The same Jew who fooled a naïve clothes buyer a century ago today fools millions of consumers; the same Jew who exploited a young girl back then today exploits and degrades millions of women and girls; the same Jew who skirted local laws to make $1,000 back then, today skirts national and international law to make billions. What was once a local or regional problem has now become a global plague and a global crisis. Fritsch's lessons are more valuable now than ever.

At the highest level, it is impossible to overestimate the detrimental effect of a society that incessantly panders to our lowest natures. Adverse Jewish business practices affect what we buy, how we work, our financial security, interpersonal relations, quality of life, and even our essential human dignity; if people had even half a sense of the magnitude of the problem, there would be immediate cries for action. Daily life for millions of people everywhere could be vastly better, if only we did not have to deal with the ever-present burden of large-scale malicious Jewish influence over our economic, political, and social lives. Theodor Fritsch was one of the first to grasp this elemental fact, and to address it in a systematic way.

This Translation

The following translation has never before appeared in English. It is based on a 1927 translation of the 1922 edition by British activist Capel Pownall, of whom almost nothing is known; but this version has undergone significant modification and clarification, making for a much more readable and enjoyable text. Section heading have been inserted, quotations highlighted, and chapter structure cleaned up. Of the many footnotes here, about half are Fritsch originals and half are my own (prefaced by "Ed."). Also, a large portion of Chapter 10 has been moved to the Appendix; it is a rather lengthy detour, critiquing the negative impact of the then-new concept of a "department store," and which only indirectly pertains to the Jewish Question.

Much of this book is a response to and commentary on the important 1911 book *The Jews and Modern Capitalism*, written by noted economist and sociologist Werner Sombart (1863-1941). The reader is invited to read this work as well, to get a better understanding of Fritsch's critical analysis. Fritsch finds much agreement with Sombart, but equally he is critical of the latter's inability or unwillingness to follow through on his reasoning to the logical conclusions. Sombart is largely dispassionate and non-critical toward the Jews, whereas Fritsch sees them as a pernicious and malevolent force in economics, and ultimately in broader society. Fritsch's solution to this problem—vaguely, a "Germany for the Germans" and "Germany free of Jews"—is only hinted at here. How, and when, this might happen, he does not say.

It is striking that Fritsch wrote his concluding words in 1922, just a few years before *Mein Kampf* would appear and change the world-order forever. Fritsch is not cited by Hitler in that book, but the broader influence of Fritsch's work was surely present in Hitler's mind in those early years, if only indirectly.

THE RIDDLE OF THE JEWS' SUCCESS

The Riddle of the Jews' Success

Chapter 1
Jewish Methods in Economic Life

Preface

If there are riddles in the history of nations, then the Jews most certainly present one of the chief instances. And anyone who has occupied himself with the problems of humanity, without advancing so far as the great problem of the Jews, has, as far as knowledge and experience of life are concerned, merely skimmed the subject's surface. There is scarcely a field, from art and literature to religion and political economy, from politics to the most secret domains of sensuality and criminality, in which the influence of the Jewish spirit and of the Jewish entity cannot be clearly traced. This influence has imparted a peculiar warp or trend to the affairs in question.

Indisputable as these facts are, it is nevertheless equally certain that science, literature, and the press—which concern themselves, not only in Germany but all the world over, with all manner of valuable knowledge—are very anxious to avoid casting any light onto the secret and mysterious sphere of Jewish influence. It is as if a silent mandate had been issued, that the essential life-relations with Jewry are on no account to be disturbed—that the Jews, in fact, must not be discussed. Thus, one is entitled to maintain that in no realm of knowledge is the ignorance of our learned men so pronounced, as it is in everything connected with the Jews. If, however, the influences and activities that the Hebrews exert on the spiritual and political destinies of the nations are of an extraordinary nature, one must finally supplement this recognized fact by a further recognition: that Jewry avails itself of extraordinary powers and means to produce such results.

It is, in this respect, that the present book presents various revelations. To start with, one point must be made perfectly clear: Religious views and religious motives are excluded from this work. I am completely neutral with respect to religion, and cannot subscribe unconditionally to any one of them. When Jews are spoken of in the course of this book, I am not thinking of a religious community, but rather of a particular people, a *nation*, a *race*. Consequently, whenever it would be advisable to avoid the use of the word 'Jew' on account of its unpleasant flavor or taint, I have frequently used the terms 'Hebrew' or 'Semite.'

Jews and Modern Capitalism

Despite their dispersion among the nations, Jews still believe today that they are a special people and a special race, and that they feel themselves united more by their common blood and race than by their religious creed. This is attested by one of the most illustrious of the people of Israel, Benjamin Disraeli.[1] Disraeli, who later became Prime Minister of England and was named the first Earl of Beaconsfield, published the novel *Endymion* in London in 1844. In it, an influential, elderly Jew speak to a young man as follows:

> No man will treat with indifference the principle of race. It is the key of history, and why history is often so confused is that it has been written by men who were ignorant of this principle and all the knowledge it involves. ... [W]hether you encounter its influence in communities or in individuals, its qualities must ever be taken into account. But there is no subject which more requires discriminating knowledge, or where your illustrating principle, if you are not deeply founded, may not chance to turn out a will-o'-the-wisp. ...
>
> In Europe I find three great races with distinct qualities—the Teutons, the Slavs, and the Celts; and their conduct will be influenced by those distinctive qualities. There is another great race which influences the world, the Semites. ...
>
> The Semites are unquestionably a great race, for among the few things in this world which appear to be certain, nothing is more sure than that they invented our alphabet. But the Semites now exercise a vast influence over affairs by their smallest though most peculiar family, the Jews. There is no race gifted with so much tenacity, and such skill in organisation. These qualities have given them an unprecedented hold over property and illimitable credit. As you advance in life, and get experience in affairs, the Jews will cross you everywhere. They have long been stealing into our secret diplomacy that they have almost appropriated; in another quarter of a century they will claim their share of open government. Well, these are races; men and bodies of men influenced in their conduct by their particular organisation, and which

---

[1] Ed.: Disraeli (1804-1881) was a Jewish politician and writer, who twice served as British Prime Minister, in 1868 and 1874.

must enter into all the calculations of a statesman. But what do they mean by the Latin race? Language and religion do not make a race—there is only one thing which makes a race, and that is blood.

At this point, we will look primarily at the importance of the Jews in *trade*—that domain where they have laid the foundation of their power, and over which they are always extending their influence and authority in the attempt to make it a Jewish monopoly. In his excellent book *The Jews and Modern Capitalism* (*Die Juden und das Wirtschaftsleben*, 1911), Professor Werner Sombart takes great effort to prove nothing less than that the economic destinies of states and nations stand in immediate relation to the wanderings of the Jews. The further conclusion attached to this theory can be summarized as follows: Wherever the Jews set foot, trade and culture blossom forth; but if they withdraw, commerce decays and prosperity disappears. We cannot dispute this fact, but it still seems to me that the reasons, adduced by Sombart to account for this phenomenon, are unsatisfactory. And, as his conclusions also appear to me to be unsound, I consider it necessary to supplement his work—which depends almost entirely upon literary and documentary evidence—with examples and experiences taken from practical, everyday life.

According to the impression that is left upon reading Sombart's book, one might be tempted to believe that he has provided a proof that the Hebrews were the real supporters of modern culture. Sombart speaks of the "culture of capitalism" and endeavors to show that this culture rests preponderantly, or almost exclusively, on the shoulders of the Jews. The perception that humanity is extraordinarily indebted to the Jews with regard to culture has been vigorously and continuously propagated in recent times; it may well have given rise to the opinion that is widely held, that culture and religion have come to us mainly from the Hebrews, and consequently that the other nations owe an everlasting debt of gratitude to this Oriental people. In fact, in many quarters, it is actually maintained that all progress proceeds from the Jews, and that culture without Jews is unthinkable. Such notions are, however, no longer tenable in the present day, owing to our extended insight into the most remote periods of national history.

One must remember that highly developed cultural systems have come into being in lands in which a Jew has never set foot, and that great systems of culture even existed at a time when no such thing as a Jewish nation had yet appeared in world history. The discoveries made at the ancient seats of the Egyptian, Babylonian, and Assyrian nations testify to this. The Aztecs, and the Incas in Peru, attained a high degree of culture, and yet they knew nothing about the Hebrews. The culture of the Chinese and the Japanese gradually unfolded itself for thousands of years without the Hebrews contributing in the slightest degree, and even in the present day, the Jew is only to be found as an isolated individual in China and Japan. The strongly developed racial feeling of these nations knows how to keep him at an arm's length. But above all, what may perhaps be regarded as the highest and most exquisite blossom of culture that humanity has ever brought to maturity—that of ancient Greece—developed at a time when Jewish influence was out of the question.

Thus, to hold up the Hebrew to universal admiration as the supporter of culture is simply not admissible. On the other hand, we must concede that what is so commonly called 'culture' at once acquires an acceleration in pace, as soon as the Hebrews lay hands on it; and that, under the influence of this singular people, the external aspects of culture develop in an astonishing manner.

At this stage, though, we ought to make a finer distinction, and not call 'culture' i.e. constructive work, what is really 'civilization' i.e. a refinement or polishing-up of the mode of living. The increase and enhancement of the forms of life that proceed under Jewish influence affect preponderantly the externals of life. Trade and business increase, production receives a powerful stimulus, and the circulation of money and the amassing of capital become more conspicuous than was formerly the case. Life seems to assume a richer and more luxurious aspect, and an impression is created of universal prosperity and of an augmentation of real property. All this, however, must be included in the conception of civilization, whilst real culture—which is the cultivation and encouragement of the highest human capabilities, the improvement of organic and moral structures, and the deepening of religious feeling—is more or less disregarded.

In fact, it appears that these deeper, cultural values actually suffer injury by the externalization of all existence. The dynamic conformity to law throughout nature cannot be avoided, even in human life; too much on one side always causes a deficiency on the other. It is not possible to develop extraordinary powers externally, without incurring a loss in internal values. We are therefore obligated, in order to treat this matter conscientiously, to throw light upon the highly-praised enhancement of culture by Jewry from other points than Sombart has done. As a result, this obvious phenomenon can then be viewed and comprehended as a whole.

The question as to why economic life flourishes wherever Jews direct their footsteps has not been answered by Sombart in a satisfying way. He is obliged to give us important revelations. I will present these to the best of my ability. The facts and phenomena that must be exposed can be separated into groups, according to the points of observation:

1. The Hebrew enhances and accelerates the circulation of money.
2. He mobilizes slumbering values: lets loose balanced and reposing forces.
3. He practices "predatory culture" (*Raubbau*) at the expense of the stored-up forces of nature and mankind.
4. The Hebrew's "playing into one another's hands" (secret understanding).
5. The strange morality.

I will address each of these in the sections and chapters to follow.

The Hebrew Enhances the Circulation of Money and Enlivens Business

The sound merchant of the old school held the opinion that his duty was satisfactorily discharged by satisfying the actual purchase-needs of his customers. He allowed the latter to approach him of their own accord, and waited until they called upon him. He believed that he had conformed in all respects to his business obligations by procuring for the customer, at a suitable price, the goods that the customer wanted. He regarded it as beneath his dignity to run after customers, or to entice them, by all manner of tricks, to buy from him; in fact, in olden times, conduct of this kind was regarded as unbecoming and quite unworthy of an honorable trader. Far less did it ever occur to him to talk a customer into buying some item that he would not have eventually purchased of his own accord. Thus, trade remained a peaceful, and not unduly exciting occupation, and the customer got what he wanted.

The Hebrew introduced a new tendency and a violent revolution into these relations. Wherever he invaded trade, he refused to adopt this quiet and peaceful method of satisfying needs. He attempted to entice the customers by advantageous offers and promises of all kinds. Above all, he emphasized the cheapness of his goods, and knew well how to delude the purchaser, by suggestion, into imagining that, in this cheapness, the buyer would find an enormous advantage. He recommended his goods, loudly and publicly, by methods that were formerly known and forbidden as being those of a charlatan, and which are now called 'advertising.' Very quickly, the Hebrew brought this practice almost to the verge of an art.

When all these means of attracting customers proved of no avail, he went and looked for them, not only by sending out circulars and price-lists, but personally, via peddlers, agents, and travelers. Thus, he did not wait until the need arose, and the demand set in of its own accord; the Hebrew created an *artificial demand*. He aroused requirement by persuasion, and by other means. In this manner, a new and alien trait was introduced into all business life. Commercial business activity now became a wild hunt for customers, as each tradesman sought to tear away the buyer from his rival.

Certainly, all this resulted in a violent application of the spur to business life, and the exchange of commodities was accelerated and hence increased, but this kind of activity was of less service to political economy, in its higher sense, than it was to another purpose. If the aim of sound economy is solely to satisfy a genuine want, and to direct goods wherever they are really required, the new way of proceeding aimed mainly at gathering up or 'assembling' actual money. Trade, according to the new perception, is no longer a useful link in the chain of calm, steady economic development, but is rather a means to direct the circulating money as quickly as possible again into the hands of the trader. It is not the transfer of goods that is so important but the fact that the transfer of goods gives the opportunity for getting ahold of money. Thus, extraction of money from the pockets of customers instead of satisfactorily meeting the need for commodities, now becomes the main purpose of trade. But this is trade divorced from its proper and honorable character, and from its former reputation as an important contributor to the well-being of the community.

One can only learn to understand this particular Hebrew tendency by considering their peculiar relations to their environment. The old-fashioned merchant was not particularly envious of his trade-competitors; his motto was "live and let live." He knew that if he conducted his business honestly and conscientiously, that if he served his customers honorably and fairly, a portion of the universal volume of trade would come his way, and through which his individual sustenance would be assured. The merchants of olden times did not feel themselves competitors with one another, to the extent that the modern ones do. They were not so numerous as today. And through the guild privilege, each was assured of his particular market or sphere of activity. The mania to supplant one another did not press its way to the fore, and was kept within bounds by the respect felt for the vocation. A feeling of goodwill and of mutual toleration—an attitude corresponding to the Christian view of life—prevailed amongst merchants and tradesmen, just as it did in other circles.

The attitude of the Hebrew towards this state of affairs was quite different. He came as a stranger into this kind of existence. It was a new world to him. He was an 'extra,' one whom no one had summoned, and whom no one desired to see. Moreover, he was not united to the native inhabitants of the land—either by the tie of blood, or by a common history, or by patriotism, or by religious and social views. He felt himself to be an alien, and regarded the others as strangers who did not interest him; but he wanted to force a place for himself amongst them by any and all means. He did not look upon other competitors as being either entitled to live, or as compatriots. His view of life, derived from his religion, had taught him that his nation was something out of the ordinary, that it had been "chosen." His holy books contained the promise that he should possess himself of all the riches in the world in order to rule over all other peoples. The "nations of the world" were represented in Hebrew law as strangers and as enemies. He had neither respect nor tolerance for them. All he cared about was to dispossess them, and to make them pay tribute to him. This is simply what stands written in the books of the Old Testament that we also have accepted as "sacred books." And it stands written still more distinctly in the laws that Jewry teaches within itself, but prudently conceals from the rest of humanity.

We shall return to these facts later on. At all events, the Hebrew was not content to keep step with the other merchants, and to confine his attentions to those customers, who came to him of their own free will. He considered it as his right—yes, even as his duty towards himself and to his nation, to seize for himself as much as possible out of the total volume of trade, and to deprive his non-Jewish competitors of as many customers as he could. He also recognized what a great advantage it was, to attract to himself as much as possible of the money in circulation, in order to obtain, by this means, power and mastery over economic life.

This industriousness grew out of his natural disposition. A sense of gain and the impulse towards self-enrichment have always been very pronounced in the Hebrews. The greed for gold is an ancient and hereditary evil in the tribe of Judah. But one only partially understands the situation, if one believes that the Jew is actuated in his business operations solely by the desire for gain, or by the love of money. Certainty the Hebrew is fond of money; but the mere possession of the metal is not enough for him. He knows that behind the glittering gold lurks the secret that the precious metal gives him power over others. In his case, the possession of money is not solely a means for leading an independent and luxurious existence, but is, at the same time, a means for exercising power. He will, by means of money, rule and oppress.

And through his intense—one might almost say, *artificially* forced—business activity, by which he strives to return all circulating money quickly back into his hands again, he achieves something further. By gathering up money on all sides, by every means in his power, and by retaining it in his possession and allowing it to accumulate, the Hebrew knows how to cause a scarcity of money in the nation. And the scarcity of money brings him a new occupation—not indeed as a merchant, but as a money-lender.

If anyone finds out how to return money that is circulating amongst the people, quickly into his own hands again—by enticing his customers to make purchases (especially for which there is no immediate need)—he thereby withdraws money from the 'market.' Money at once becomes scarce, if unforeseen wants appear. Whoever then finds himself in monetary difficulties is compelled to come to those who know how to attract all the money into their own hands. And in this way, commercial activity that has been so violently stimulated, becomes simultaneously an auxiliary to the loan-monger and usurer. It was not chance, nor was it by any means the pressure of circumstances in former times, that made the Jew into a money-lender, but a carefully thought-out system. Money is a very peculiar commodity, and whoever trades in money has a tighter grip on economic life than he who trades in ordinary goods. For this reason, all trade, as far as Jews are concerned, is, strictly speaking, merely a means for gathering together or assembling money, again and again. The Hebrew "follows the money," which has been lent on loan, with ever-watchful eyes, and he knows well what precautionary measures to take to ensure that it will soon find its way back into Jewish pockets.

It is undisputed that the Jewish method of doing business produces a showy splendor, both in trade and traffic, one in which everyone appears to be prospering. We are often dumbstruck, absolutely dazed by the precipitous development that has overtaken all trade during the last few decades. But—and I labor under no delusion in this respect—this blossom of external life, dazzling in all its splendor, is only produced by a heavy sacrifice on the other side.

The Hebrew Mobilizes Slumbering Values

I once knew a man who could not behold any stately tree, either in a garden or a park, without indulging in an outburst, somewhat on the following lines: "How crazy the people must be to allow a tree like that still to be standing! What an amount of capital is lying there, locked up! What fine beams and planks could be sawn out of it!" The man had Jewish blood in his veins, and gave vent to a feeling that must be keenly alive in many Hebrews, although they do not venture to express it in such a barefaced manner. The Hebrew is incapable of allowing anything to rest in calm peace, especially anything that can be turned to some economic use. An urgent impulse to make everything 'liquid' is instilled into his mind, to convert everything into money, to 'mobilize' everything. And on all sides, we see Jewry driven by this impulse, hard at work in order to scoop up, with greedy hands, the treasures of nature and of human life.

Existence is clearly enriched and broadened thereby, and civilization is enlivened. From the common economic viewpoint, it has the appearance of being highly meritorious when a forest—one that has been standing for a hundred years in peace, slowly and laboriously growing up by virtue of the creative power in nature, and has become a great potential source of value—that someone should set to work with axes and saws to liquidate the reposing capital. Hundreds of men are employed to fell the trees, and to cut up and transport the timber, and thus life springs up. Wages are paid, and sales are the result. Regarded from this viewpoint, the man who 'mobilizes' these sleeping values may well appear to be a benefactor to the neighborhood where he provides useful work for so many hands. But not only will the lover of nature be saddened by what has taken place; the serious economist will also be of a very different opinion. No doubt, the forest is there, reduced at last to a form that can be utilized by the community as building-timber and firewood. The wise forester, however, goes to work with care and restraint, and does not fell any timber without making provision for reforesting an area equivalent to that which has been cleared. Or at any rate, he only allows the mature trunks to be felled, and spares all the younger timber. The Hebrew obeys an entirely different principle—his true commercial principle: he clears the ground to the last sapling. He leaves reforestation to others.

The above is an example of real life rather than of mere symbolism. The Hebrews have actually decimated enormous stretches of primeval forest, not only in our Fatherland, but also in Russia and in Poland. By doing so, they have certainly given a stimulus to business and commercial intercourse, and have caused money to circulate. But the reverse side of this activity will perhaps only be appreciated, to its full and disastrous extent, by future generations. The clear-cut forest certainly brings profit for the moment, but for the more or less distant future, it means nothing less than impoverishment of the land—in many cases, actual devastation. Springs dry up all over the now-bare surface; permanent drought sets in, and when heavy rains do come, they simply sweep away the valuable upper layers of soil. The destruction of great forests means, accordingly, nothing less than the exhaustion of fertility, and the conversion of vast tracts of countryside into desert. Italy and the Balkan States furnish a grave enough warning.

As with the forest, the Hebrew also conducts himself similarly in other spheres of activity. He is forever intent upon mobilizing or stirring up sleeping values, and bringing them into circulation in order to derive an ostentatious and momentary benefit. But an organic breadth of vision is completely lacking in this individual. He does not bother to consider what will be the further consequence of this reckless and predatory mode of action. This is quite in accordance with his nomadic nature. He does not feel himself in any way linked to the soil; he forsakes the devastated territories, seeking fresh profit elsewhere in the world. The conception of the Fatherland is altogether foreign to him. In this respect, he is true to his nature as a member of a desert- and nomadic-race.

The Hebrew Presses his Predatory Culture

Once more, as in the case of the forest, the same fate befalls the treasures contained in the bosom of the Earth. That which has been slowly forming in nature's laboratory, by processes that have taken millions of years, are dragged to the light of day with insatiable greed; it is forced to take its part in enriching and adorning life. At first, this sounds very plausible—but how long can it last? Careful economists are already asking uneasily how much longer the world's supply of coal will suffice to shield the human race against the ever-menacing forces of the cosmic cold. Certain geologists have spoken reassuring words: the world's coal supply is plentiful, and will suffice, at any rate, for many centuries; perhaps even for three or four thousand years. Humanity's foresight should enable it to project its conscience across this timespan, for it will be our descendants who will—even if after the lapse of thousands of years—raise bitter reproaches against us because we have squandered the irreplaceable treasures of the Earth, greedily and blindly.

And there are other treasures of the Earth as well that are not so plentiful as coal. The world's supplies of iron ore—which are nearly all known, given they can be discovered and marked down by means of the magnetic needle—have been subjected to close calculation with regard to their extent and richness. The result is that if we continue to use up iron in the same way as we have been doing for the last few decades, all the iron-ore fields of the world will be exhausted in 50 or 60 years. And then what? Whether such calculations prove true or not, they provide us with a glance into the future, one that must arouse apprehension. This situation must cause us to regard our domineering culture, of which we boast so readily today, in a very questionable light.

The Hebrews are certainly not the only ones who practice predatory culture at the expense of the treasures of the Earth, but it can be justly maintained that it was this class of men who introduced the principle of ruthless mobilization of values and of pitiless money-making into our economic life. And it is precisely this fact which Sombart wishes to demonstrate, or actually does demonstrate, whether he does so intentionally or not. The Hebrew has made the principle of ruthless capitalization supreme in economic life, and it is no wonder if others try to copy him—or rather, are compelled to do the same, in order to withstand the Jewish competition.

Not only do we squander these natural treasures, but we are dissipating another treasure as well, one which finally is the most important of all, as far as culture is concerned. The mobilization of the treasures of the Earth, and the tremendous activity of economic life that has risen to an almost morbid degree, impose a terrible strain upon man and his creative powers. He may, perhaps, feel a pride in the results of his work, in the thousands of roaring and clattering machines, in the boldly-executed constructions with which he spans rivers, inlets, and mountain ravines, and in the ingenious technical appliances that transport him with the speed of the wind across the face of the Earth. But what is his booty or prize at the end of this wild pursuit? Generally, only the loss of his best powers, and an early end to his life. Who can now refuse to recognize the fact that the harassing hunt after business that characterizes modern economic life is rapidly leading to an exhaustion of mankind, and that the race itself, despite all the technical perfections of the external world, is slowly sinking, as far as its personal constitution and powers of accomplishment are concerned—that it is steadily decaying, both physically and spiritually?

In this respect as well, the modern economy is ruthlessly conducting another method of predatory culture. Industrialism entices men from the country into the city, and consumes them. It is a well-known fact that the families born in the cities very soon fade away, and that they seldom extend to more than three generations; the large towns and industrial areas can only maintain themselves by a constant influx of human beings from the rural districts. But even the reserve of human strength in the country, taken as a whole, is not inexhaustible. It already shows an alarming decline. Sixty years ago, two-thirds of the inhabitants of Germany lived in the country, and derived their livelihood from agriculture and from forestry, and only a third of the population lived in the cities. Today, the proportion is almost reversed. The rural population has now shrunk to 37 percent of the total, and will no longer be able to make up the deficiency in the births amongst the 63 percent of the population who now dwell in the large cities and industrial districts.

We see accordingly how the magnificence of modern culture can only be produced by the expenditure of powers that cannot be revived. It requires only a few more decades of this mode of existence, and the German nation will have used itself up; foreign national and racial elements will stream in from all sides, and make themselves comfortable in the bed that we, in our excessive and suicidal diligence, have so carefully prepared for them.

A typical example of the fanatical pressure that impels the Hebrew to mobilize all values, for example, is furnished by his attack upon the *fideicommissum*—namely the indivisible family estates. The land-owning nobility, in particular, has frequently made the arrangement that the family estate will descend undivided to the heir, in order to guard against the breaking-up and dispersion of the estate. It is of incalculable value, both for state and community if, in this manner, strong, independent existences can be maintained. It has the added benefit that community is not harmed by it. Notwithstanding this, the Jewish press has, for many years, fiercely attacked this arrangement, as if it were an offense and an injury against the majority. Parliament is overwhelmed, from the Jewish side, with motions to do away with the *fideicommissum,* as if the eternal happiness of the whole nation depended upon this. The innate hatred felt by the Jew towards the nobility plays, in this respect, no small part. The Jew wishes to destroy this nobility—a nobility that presumes, both by breeding and tradition, to be something out of the ordinary. Meanwhile, "the chosen people," according to his opinion, alone possess a claim to pretensions of this kind. Do not the Jews, with predilection, refer to themselves as "the natural aristocracy of mankind"?

Moreover, this aversion to the *fideicommissum* is only the old Hebrew urgency to mobilize values expressing itself anew. There must not be anything durable or constant; everything must be cut up and handed over to speculation. The new revolutionary government, directed by Jews, has no more urgent policy than that of breaking up all the *fideicommissum* and of prohibiting the formation of any new family estates. Who can calculate today the harm that will be caused by such a policy? The undermining of economic foundations must also make itself felt in the social and intellectual structure of society. Genuine men of nobility will become scarcer and scarcer; the nobility has already, in many respects, degenerated, and become degraded by the intrusion of Jewish money and business-spirit. The Jewish principle of life drags mankind back from the heights that it has scaled. The final result is: universal vulgarization.

We hear the ready reply: "But wealth has increased enormously!" Have we not collected huge quantities of capital that are a sufficient guarantee for the future? In this respect as well, the modern idea of economy arrives at a fateful and most erroneous conclusion. Even Sombart represents the situation as if the Hebrews brought riches with them wherever they went, and were continually producing new wealth. Even if we understand the term 'wealth' as merely the gold and silver treasure of the Earth, it certainly cannot be maintained that these are increased by the Hebrew and his economic activity. We have already seen that his art consists in collecting and re-collecting these treasures into his own hands, as quickly as he can. But gold and silver in their totality form only an insignificant portion of the national riches. What we call 'capital' does not generally consist of coined metal. Today we also consider as capital, landed property, such as cultivated fields, forests, buildings etc. But the Hebrews certainly do not increase this kind of property either.

There is, however, another kind of capital that plays the most important role of all in modern political economy: this is *loan capital*—those sums that are lent out in return for the payment of fated rates of interest. And it cannot be denied that the Hebrew possesses an extraordinary talent for increasing this particular kind of capital.

Let us, first of all, make it quite clear to ourselves of what such capital really consists. Whoever owns a million Deutschemarks that earns him interest, does not possess this million marks in the form of gold and silver coins lying in his safe, but has lent the million marks out on loan. But even the borrower—the debtor to the man who owns the money—no longer holds the actual money; he has passed it on further in the course of his business. All that is left to him is the obligation to pay interest. He has taken over for himself—and generally also for his descendants, for indefinite time—the duty of paying the creditor certain sums of money as interest, at certain stated intervals.

Out of all this, the fact next emerges that an equally great debt, on the other side, faces this sum of loan capital. Whoever is in a position to own a million marks of loan capital, and draws interest from the same, must hold other people as his debtors to the extent of a million marks. And thus arises the peculiar equation: the more loan capital there is here, the more debts there are there. An increase of capital of this nature means, in reality, nothing else than an increase of debt.

Loan capital thus consists of acknowledgment of debt, and of obligation to pay. It takes visible shape in the form of mortgage-deeds, bonds, shares, rent-charges, and similar devices. And if we boast today that the number of rich people has increased enormously, that millions and billions of marks are concentrated in the hands of single individuals, we must not forget that the debts and obligations of other people have increased in equal measure. It is accordingly a bold assumption to maintain that the general welfare of the nations is promoted by the increase of capital of this kind. Whoever speaks of modern *wealth* ought, if he is conscientious, to speak at the same time of the monstrous nature of the modern system of creating *indebtedness*. In whatever direction we look, we see an enormous development of this creation of debt; in the kingdom, in the province, in the parish, in the business, in the family—all are carried on by means of debts. The registered mortgages on land throughout the German Empire are computed at 60 to 70 billion marks. It is a very remarkable and significant fact that we have no statistics whatever concerning this vital question of political economy, while we are overwhelmed with statistics on all other matters.

If the above-mentioned sum of debt is approximately correct, it simply means that the nation has to find something like 3 billion marks every year in order to pay the burden of interest placed upon the Fatherland. Who, in the last analysis, provides this sum of money? It is simply the working and productive class of the citizens: the peasant, the craftsman, and the workman. These are the powers that create productive values, and who must, by the excess of their labor, produce the burdens of interest in order to satisfy the owners of loan capital.

If we calculate that there are 15 million working-men in the German Empire capable of production, a yearly cost of 200 marks is laid upon each of them in order to satisfy the owners of loan capital. That this crushing burden is not consciously perceived is simply due to the fact that it is split up and distributed in such a way that it is almost impossible to check or trace it, and that all kinds of roundabout ways and tricks are utilized that make it quite impossible for the ordinary man to discover the source of his misery. The loan capital that burdens our land sucks in its interest by raising the rents of tenements, workshops, and business premises, by increasing the price of food-stuffs and other necessary commodities, and by other similar indirect methods. Thus, the productive worker is not directly conscious of this cost, but feels only an inexplicable pressure on all his business activity. He sees that, in spite of all his effort and industry, the fruits of his toil disappear out of his hands, without his being able, at the same time, to discover any satisfactory explanation of this. In spite of all his toil, he cannot make any advance and prosper, becomes discontented with his lot, and vents his resentment in all directions—mostly against those who are quite innocent of his hard fate. He complains about the high taxes and rates that form only an insignificant portion when compared with that cost—the interest on loan capital. He grumbles about the increasing cost of living, of rent, of food, of clothing, and of other things, including "bread-usurers" and bad government, and does not seem to have even the faintest idea that it is just this invisible cost of the interest on loan capital that is oppressing him by making everything dear.

Thus, this modern system of creating capital, by casting an intolerable burden on the entire national life, produces universal oppression and consequently discontent. This in turn causes an ever-growing resentment between the various classes that compose the community, without the oppressed people being at all clear as to the actual source of the oppression.

Jewish Interest, Jewish Usury

It is not very probable that the Hebrews invented the loaning-out of capital for interest; it is quite likely that it was known and practiced before their time. It is fairly certain, however, that they first introduced this branch of business to us in Germany and, supported by the prohibition against practicing usury by Christians, promoted and developed it to an extraordinary extent. Owing to their peculiar dexterity in always attracting money back to themselves, they know how to produce a constant shortage of money amongst the people. In this way, they compel the productive classes to borrow, and to continue borrowing. The money that has been gradually collected by commerce and other means, leaves the hands of the Hebrew, for the most part, only as loan capital that continuously creates for him fresh circles of people pledged to pay him tribute.

Is it then really such a great blessing for a nation if it can be shown that the Hebrews, living in their midst, possess billions of marks in the shape of loan capital, for which the productive class has to find the interest? What is the meaning of the saying: "Wherever the Jews turn, there appear new riches, new capital"? Should one not, before all other things, state emphatically: "There arise, to a terrifying extent, fresh debts"? It is not the real wealth of the nations that is increased by the Jews, but their debts and obligations which, under the deceitful name of 'mobile capital,' accumulate until they amount to sums of incredible magnitude. In reality, this is only a phantom possession—an imaginary value.

We read, with aversion, the descriptions of the persecutions of the Jews that are said to have taken place in the Middle Ages. It is an open question if these were, in all cases, as many people imagine. At any rate, one ought to conscientiously explain what led up to these persecutions, and what was their real cause. We can read, in every record, that it was by no means a religious hatred that incensed the citizens against the Jews, because at all times and in all countries, a remarkable tolerance has been displayed towards Jewish religious rites, some of which are of a very peculiar nature. No one has prohibited their noisy method of praying; no one has disturbed their Sabbath and Passover festivals. No one has even prohibited their Purim, their festival of revenge that they still celebrate annually with unquenchable thirst for revenge, in remembrance of the massacre of 75,000 Persian enemies of the Jews at the direction of the minister Mordecai more than 2,000 years ago.[2] What really incensed the people against the Jews was their insatiable hunger for interest and their un-Christian-like usury. By reason of this diabolical greed for money that stopped at nothing, this slinking, alien race became so repugnant to the ordinary German man that he considered the Jews capable of anything.

As I have already stated, during the time when the influence of the Church was predominant—from the 11th up to the 18th century—Christians were forbidden to practice usury. Only the Hebrew was allowed to do this. Thus, it naturally came about that anyone who wanted to borrow money was obliged to go to the Jews. According to the law, the Hebrews were aliens and on sufferance, and their sojourn, in either town or district, was only permitted when a tax ("Jew-tribute") had been paid to the ruling prince or potentate. But it was precisely this arrangement, whereby the mild or stern treatment of the Jews depended essentially on the attitude of the ruling house, that relieved the situation to an extraordinary degree for the Jews living in the Empire—a realm that was, at the time, politically divided. Generally speaking, the legislation was very favorable, allowing the Hebrew to devote himself wholeheartedly to his favorite occupation, vis-a-vis traffic in money, and to claim unheard-of interest rates for his loans. Annual rates of 30%, 50%, even 60%, were already known from the

---

[2] Ed.: From the Book of Esther: "The Jews were to be ready on that day to avenge themselves upon their enemies" (8:13); "Mordecai grew more powerful. So the Jews smote all their enemies with the sword, slaughtering and destroying them" (9:5); "The other Jews who were in the king's provinces…slew 75,000 of those who hated them" (9:16).

12th to the 15th century, and were so well-established during the 16th and 17th centuries that it was regarded as nothing unusual. Under these circumstances, and owing to both the scarcity and the extraordinary fluctuations in the value of money throughout that period, it was an easy matter for the Hebrews to always collect all the money again into their hands, and to force the remaining citizens to raise fresh loans.[3]

A particular trick facilitated the obtaining of an exorbitant interest rate. Even when the rate was moderate, the debtor had, for the most part, to pledge himself to pay back his debt on a fixed date by weekly or monthly payments. In case he was unable to keep to the appointed date, he was bound by the terms of his bond to pay double the rate from that time onward; often, indeed, the whole debt was doubled. The well-meaning debtor, who had the best intention of paying off his debt at the appointed time, entered into such contracts with a light heart, in the certainty that, at the appointed date, he would get the money from other sources. The Hebrew, however, who had a complete understanding with his fellow-tribesmen, and knew accurately what call there was for money, and how much there was in circulation, took good care that his debtor did not get the expected money at the appointed time, and thus he compelled him to accept the new and still more onerous conditions. The Hebrew would only grant an extension of the term on the condition that his claims, both with regard to interest and capital, would be increased. Thanks to the cooperation of Jewish friends, delay in the repayment of the debt was frequently repeated, and the Jew was even more successful in entangling, by means of a comparatively small loan, a whole family in debt bondage throughout their lives—or even in expelling them from their house and land.

---

[3] "At the end of the 14th century, the Jews' social position deteriorated, chiefly on account of their arrogance and usuriousness. Until then, they had been respected, were qualified to own landed property, and were appreciated as being necessary for the development of the towns. They had, in some instances, even found an entry into the municipal bodies, for instance at Cologne and Worms. In many towns, the highest admissible interest rate reached 86 2/3 percent annually! Ludwig of Bavaria (1314-1347) decided, as a particular favor for the citizens of Frankfurt, that the Jewish rate was to be restricted to 32 1/2 percent. Since the canonical prohibition against the lending was enforced sternly and universally against Christians, and the cloisters no longer loaned out money, the money-business remained almost exclusively in the hands of the Jews for a long period." (Dürr and Klett, *Textbook on World History* II, 1899, p. 139). "Thus a regular monopoly of usury by the Jews established itself, which was only broken in the 18th century, to the extent that, towards the close of that century, it was permitted to generally charge a 5% interest rate." (R. Schröder, *German History of Law* II, 1926, p. 15).

Thus, there is nothing strange in the fact that, already from the time of Charlemagne, unceasing complaints about the Jewish usurer were directed to both civil and clerical authorities. The earlier peasant-insurrections also, were not due to the "priests" and the nobility, but to money-lending Jewry—as in the Peasants' Uprisings at Gotha in 1391 and at Worms in 1431. Later, once the Jews had drained the extravagant and quarrelsome nobility of their riches, and the latter had made an alliance with the clergy to oppress the German peasant with tithes and compulsory labor, the peasants turned against all three tormentors. In 1450 the cup-bearer Erasmus von Erbach, an ancestor of the present Princes von Erbach, and who personally was quite prosperous, raised his voice against the Jews:

> The poor man is robbed and flayed by the Jews to such an extent that it has become intolerable, and may God have mercy on him. The Jewish usurers settle down, even in the smallest villages, and when they lend five gulden, they take six-fold security and take interest upon interest, and yet again interest, so that the poor man loses all that he possesses.

The well-founded nature of this complaint is proved by the testimony of contemporaries.

Elsewhere it is stated that, "Jewry sits on the necks of the citizen and of the poor man, and is the cause of the rapidly increasing poverty." Jews are referred to as "vultures [who] do not desist until they have consumed the marrow in the bones, and reduced the citizen to beggary" (Petition of the Frankfurt citizens, 10 June 1612). Sombart also mentions, in his conscientiously-collected material, a number of similar expressions of opinion, taken from the same period that confirm these views. Thus, it was not religious hatred that incensed the people against the Jews, but the actual plundering of the masses by a system of excessive interest rates. The wealth that the Jews "brought into a land" was thus of very dubious value. It was a kind of wealth that had a dazzling appearance in certain places, whilst everywhere else it produced only poverty and misery.

In sum: The Hebrews did not create new value in the shape of goods, and consequently, actual new wealth; they merely understood, in a masterly fashion, how to obtain possession of the prosperity of others. They did not produce any new possession, but only brought about a change of possession. What they produced was merely an appearance of wealth, one that, in reality, consisted only of the debts of those people who were not Jews.

Chapter 2
Particular Jewish Business Tactics

Hebrew commercial practices demand that more light be directed upon them. It is conceded that the Jew, in matters of business, displays great dexterity; he has at his disposal a particular method of operation that earns for him the admiration of extensive circles of people. Many are inclined to ascribe an extremely high degree of cleverness to the Hebrew, because he often knows how to give a particular turn to his business machinations that surprises and confounds all concerned. As soon as we look more closely into the matter, and ascertain the principles upon which these business measures are founded, we learn to think less highly of the renowned cleverness of the Hebrew. It becomes a matter of a number of tricks, carefully guarded and transmitted by tradition amongst the Hebrews, and with which this dexterous race of traders surpasses every man who thinks in a natural manner. A short, real-life story will give us an idea of what occurs in this sphere of activity:

> A well-to-do elderly married couple had decided to dispense with their footman, and consequently with his attire as well. The lady of the house offered the garments for sale. A Jew appeared punctually at the appointed time, in order to inspect the clothing. After carefully examining the items, he made an offer of 50 marks. The lady was astonished that the dealer was able to offer such a high price, as the suit could not have originally cost much more, and was, moreover, a kind of clothing—being a uniform with particular badges—for which there would naturally be very little demand. She thought at once that she could do a good business with him, and hurried away to fetch an armful of discarded clothing that she offered to him as well. The Hebrew examined everything, and offered quite respectable prices. Apparently he could make use of it all.
>
> The lady of the house, delighted with the prospect of unloading her excess items, continued to fetch more clothing. The Hebrew chose out most of this as well, and laid it in a great heap together. The only article that did not suit his

approval was a fashionably-cut, light summer-suit that the master of the house had only worn once, and had then laid aside, as it did not take his fancy. The Jew threw this aside with the remark: "This is out of fashion, and nobody will buy it."

When he had laid all the remaining articles of clothing together, and had offered quite a reasonable price, the old lady asked him again to take the summer-suit; she wanted to be rid of it, given that it annoyed her husband. Finally, the Hebrew agreed to take the suit for just five marks. The lady accepted this offer, because of all the other clothing that she had been able to sell. The entire sale amounted to about 200 marks. "I have not got so much money with me," said the Jew, politely, "because I was not prepared to buy so many things. I will, however have the clothing fetched away shortly, and will send the money at the same time. I will leave a deposit of 5 marks, and may as well take the summer-suit with me so that I do not make the journey empty-handed." With this, the Hebrew took his departure, and up to the present moment, has not returned.

The worthy lady related the episode to me herself, and was quite at a loss for an explanation. The Jew must have been taken ill, or something unforeseen must have happened, as otherwise he would have returned, "for he made such a favorable impression." I am afraid that I hurt the lady's feelings, for I had to laugh in her face, before I proceeded to explain the incident to her as follows: "The summer-suit was the only object of any value to the Jew, and consequently the only thing that he was willing to buy. The other articles of clothing he had never intended to buy; he only offered such good prices in order to gain your confidence. Your confidence once gained, you did not observe how he was overreaching you with regard to the good summer-suit. He accomplished his object, and will take good care not to let himself be seen again."

It took a considerable time before I was able to convince the good lady of all this. She then exclaimed with astonishment and almost with admiration: "Gracious me, what a clever fellow he is!" "No, Madam," I replied, "that is not real cleverness; it is a mode of operation, partly inherited, partly the result of instruction. It is an ancient recipe, according to which the Jews have conducted their operations for centuries—even for thousands of years. It is the 'art' in business of deceiving one's opponent as to the value of the goods, and as to one's real intentions. I will tell you a short story of a similar kind that will make quite plain to you how this mode of operating proceeds, according to a certain pattern and custom." I proceeded to say the following:

> A Jewish lad, who could not have been more that 10 or 11 years old, was accustomed to go from village to village, buying up hare- and rabbit-skins. He was instructed what he should pay for the wares, and soon acquired such knowledge of the business, by constant practice, that he was able to carry it on to the satisfaction of his father. One day, a peasant that had sold him several rabbit skins produced the fur of a marten. The young Jew held it to his nose, and said contemptuously: "This is only the skin of a slinking marten, and is not worth anything." The peasant, who understood little about such matters, urged the young Jew to take the marten fur as well, and finally the little businessman purchased it out of pure compassion—for five half-pence!
>
> As soon as the young rascal had reached home, he called out: "Father, look what a stroke of business I did! I bought a valuable marten-fur for five half-pence!" — and he related what had happened. A neighbor, who had witnessed the episode from the window of a stable, told this to me. Even this diminutive man of business already possessed the "cleverness" to speak disparagingly of the most valuable goods in order to deceive the seller with regard to the real value, and thus to enable himself to buy them up at a very cheap rate.

Anyone who has thoroughly grasped the systematic mode of operation in these cases will not express any great astonishment as to the measure of "cleverness" required. It is always the same trick. The Hebrew, who has lived for thousands of years by dealing, and by overreaching other men, has developed, in this direction, a cunning and superior tactic. He knows that desire—demand—causes the price to rise. Whoever shows that he would like to buy certain wares, or that he is urgently in need of something, will soon tempt the seller to demand a higher price. And on the contrary, whoever offers his wares in a pressing manner, and allows it to be seen that he must get rid of them at all costs, probably because he is in urgent need of money, has to put as cheerful a face on the matter as he can, when advantage is taken of his situation to minimize the price.

The old saying "Supply and demand fix the price" has a certain justification—as long as upright and honest merchants are concerned. Today, we know that supply and demand can be artificially produced, simply to influence the price. And the Jew conducts the most insignificant business in accordance with these sagacious measures, just as if he were operating on a large scale, on the stock exchange. He knows how to deceive the other side as to his real intentions; he pretends that there is demand, when he knows that, in reality, the supply is more than sufficient, and also the reverse. The Hebrew, who goes to a Produce Exchange, under the necessity of buying several wagon-loads of wheat because he has contracted to deliver this amount to a mill, takes very good care to conceal his real intention. He assumes an attitude of complete indifference; and if anyone offers him wheat, he replies, shrugging his shoulders: "Wheat? I have enough wheat. Do you want to buy any?" All the other Jewish businessmen there adopt the same attitude. They also want wheat but, as if by some secret agreement, they all behave as if they have no need whatsoever. On the contrary, they say that they want to sell it, and thus they create the impression that there is a surplus of wheat. They thereby force the price down, and succeed in buying the wheat cheaply.

A simple or honest farmer, on the contrary, who has gone to the Produce Exchange in order to get rid of his produce because he urgently needs the money to pay the upcoming interest on his debt, will at once offer his wheat eagerly. But, strange to say, he encounters cold refusal on all sides. And the same thing happens to all the other sellers. Supply preponderates, and the prices fall. Our farmer now returns to the first Hebrew, to whom he had offered his wheat, and who, in reality, urgently *needs* wheat, and the latter appears at last to relent, and says with apparent generosity: "Now, as you are an old business friend of mine, I will relieve you of your wheat, but only at a price that is two marks below the current price"—that is, two marks cheaper than the official price, quoted for that day on the Exchange. In the end, the farmer is glad to have found a purchaser at any price, and is secretly grateful to the Hebrew for having purchased his wheat out of sheer good nature. Several days later, when the supplies have been mostly bought up by the Hebrews, one sees a marked rise in prices.

Business has been carried on in this manner, at the markets and on the exchanges, for decades and for centuries, without that simple section of humanity—the producers—perceiving what is going on. The producers always have the toil and disadvantage, the Hebrew dealer all the benefit. And this benefit or gain, on occasions, amounts to millions. One example of this will suffice, compared with which, the so-called "bread-usury" of the agrarians that the Jews and their lackeys (especially the Social Democrats) are always crying about, is mere child's play:

> In the year 1892, the corn-merchants Cohn and Rosenberg, supported by God-only-knows how many of their friends behind the scenes, bought up, on a gigantic scale, all the available supplies of rye. They then withheld this from the market, producing such a shortage of this indispensable food-stuff that the price of rye rose, in a few months, from 140 to 290 marks. They then "unloaded," and "earned" by this business, in a very short time, about 18 million marks. Most of our newspapers and of our so-called "liberals"—the friends of the people—had not a single word of abhorrence or even of disapprobation for this "bread usury" that happened according to the Old Testament pattern.

The game is made much easier if the Hebrews have a secret understanding, that is to say, if they have consulted beforehand, amongst themselves, about the condition of the market, and have decided what the attitude of the other side is likely to be. Still, any such understanding is scarcely necessary, for all Jewish businessmen respond to one and the same instinct, are schooled in one and the same tactic, and act as one without any previous arrangement.

Securing an Advantage

There is another mode of operation by which the Hebrews secure an advantage in business, and to which they are indebted for their present dominating position. Again, an instance of this mode of operation will make it clear to everyone.

Take, for example, a town in which there have long existed ten separate businesses of the same kind or trade, and all of about the same size. The owners of these businesses have confined themselves, each to his or her circle of more or less regular customers, in accordance with the principle "Live and let live," and have all been able to make a tolerable, and even comfortable living. Suddenly this old harmony is disturbed. One of these businesses changes hands, and the new owner, a man with a large amount of capital, or with extensive credit, brings a new business principle along with him. He calculates thus: "What has been formerly sold by ten businesses, can be just as well sold by one business. I will make it my task to attract all the customers in the town for this kind of business into my shop. This will not be difficult. I have sufficient money at my disposal to live comfortably, even if I make no profit whatever for several years. I will therefore offer all my goods at prices that show no profit at all, i.e. at cost. The result of this will be that all the customers in the town for this class of business will be attracted to my shop." This businessman with the "new principle" orders a new price-list to be printed, and sends it to every customer in the neighborhood. He has reduced the prices so much below what used to be customary in the trade, that all buyers are attracted without fail to the new shop.

The remaining nine businesses or shops now either lose their customers, or are compelled to reduce their prices correspondingly. Either way, no profit is made, and those who have no means to fall back upon must sooner or later give up the contest. Others, who may possess enough capital to support them for the remainder of their lives, say that it is useless and stupid to continue to carry on a business in which there is no profit. These simply discontinue their business. Yet others try to keep pace with the new competitor, but only see their meager means gradually disappear, and they also, sooner or later, are compelled to retire from the ruinous struggle. Thus, after a few years, the man with the "new principle" remains the master of the situation. Now that he is without competitors, and is practically a monopolist on his own territory, he makes up for the loss that he has undergone by gradually raising the prices, until finally the customers are at a greater disadvantage than they had ever been before.

This is no principle of life. On the contrary, it is a principle of destruction or death. It carries on business for the mere sake of business, that is to make money. It does not ask what becomes of the other people. Here we are, face to face, with a tendency that places acquisition before life itself. In reality, business and political economy are, in the last analysis, only of importance when regarded as a means for preserving life. The supreme law of political economy should always culminate in the question: How can we arrange matters economically so that the people shall secure the maximum benefit in body and mind? A political economy that unquestionably enables riches to be accumulated, but which, at the same time, causes the people to degenerate both physically and morally, cannot be regarded as ideal.

Seen from a purely business point of view, it may appear to be an improvement when material advantages are secured by concentrating all the trade into a single business. Certainly, many purely economic advantages may be attained by the uniting of the scattered individual branches of any trade or business into one large central establishment; at any rate, the concentration of the management yields a saving in space, time, and energy. Any person, however, who does not recognize 'business advantage' as the supreme aim of life, but asks, on the contrary: What becomes of the people concerned? — such a person must have the gravest doubts as to the beneficial influence of such a business development as described above. He would feel himself compelled to ask: What has become of the nine families who have been thrown out of action by the "new principle?" And he will then have to confess that this "new principle," however profitable it may seem at the first glance, leads finally to the expropriation and impoverishment of extensive classes of people, and thus, by its ultimate results, becomes a curse to the national life.

The man with the "new principle" is not necessarily a Hebrew; others can also adopt this business method as their guiding principle. But as a matter of fact—at any rate, in our European affairs—it is almost invariably the Hebrew who has introduced this principle. By doing so, he has certainly created a great deal that corrupts the eyes of many by its dazzling appearance—as, for instance, the great retail shops. But the kind of fruit this sort of development will produce in the more distant future of our nation is a question that is well-warranted, and is also very serious.

Another example, taken out of everyday life, occurs to me at this moment. It illustrates, in an allegorical manner, the action or operation of the Hebrew on the community:

> For a great many generations, there had been a number of small mills on a little river in Posen. There was not always sufficient water in the river at all seasons of the year to keep the mills working regularly; but one of the mills, on the upper part of the river, possessed a reservoir of considerable size, in which water could be stored up for times of drought, when the sluices could be opened according to requirements. When the upper miller had enough water to work the mill for a day, or even for half a day, he started his mill, and thus the water flowed down regularly to all the mills situated below. There was no written law to regulate the use of this water; the practical requirements and common sense of the owners sufficed to maintain this arrangement to the complete satisfaction of all concerned.
>
> One day, however, a disturbing element crept into the harmony that had so long prevailed amongst the milling indus-

try along this particular stream. The upper mill, together with the reservoir, passed into new hands. Whether it was that the new owner did not understand much about his business, or did not make himself agreeable to his customers, I don't know; but in short, the old customers gradually deserted the upper mill, and went to the other mills lower down the stream.

This annoyed the new owner, and he did his utmost to disrupt the business of his neighbors. One means of offense he had always at his disposal was his reservoir. He no longer allowed the water to run off at regular intervals, but stored it up for days, and even for weeks, to the utmost capacity of the reservoir. Then he would suddenly release the water by opening all the sluices, generally at night or on a Sunday, so that the accumulated water rushed down the stream with great force. The mills, on the lower part of the river, could make little or no use of this sudden head of water, and were obliged, as they did not possess any reservoirs for storing the water, to open their floodgates, and to allow this superfluous water to flow uselessly away. Any methodical management of the lower mills was thus rendered impossible. The injured parties complained in vain to the local and other authorities; but nothing happened because there was no law that compelled the miller, on the upper part of the stream, to let the water run off at regular intervals.

The mills on the lower reaches of the stream would most certainly have been ruined by these spiteful tricks, if chance had not put a sudden stop to them. On one occasion, after a heavy rain-fall, the upper miller stored up the water to such an extent, and then let it rush through the sluices so suddenly, that a regular inundation ensued that caused considerable damage to the embankments, dams, and machinery of the lower mills. Now, at last, there was cause to take legal action against this disturber of the peace to force him to desist, and to make him pay compensation for the damage that he had brought about.

Also in this case, it does not necessarily follow that the disturber of the peace was bound to be a Hebrew; but as a matter of fact, he was. And one is entitled to say that the example given is typical of the onslaught made by the Hebrew race upon our economic life. The organic connection of economic examples that results from the love of order, innate in the Aryan element, and from a voluntary adjustment to the harmony of life that instills common sense and is supported besides by a moral feeling of duty and a respect for the other men, collapses immediately when the Hebrew puts in an appearance.

The hitherto quiet and regular development of business relations suffers a considerable disturbance in all directions, as soon as this Oriental stranger, with his strange principles, and in whom the sense for social harmony is completely lacking, interferes with the economic life. He displays an utter disregard for others, and pursues, only and always, his private advantage. By the ruthless manipulation of this principle, he has become everywhere the destroyer of economic life. He checks the even flow of development, creates 'corners,' produces artificial shortage and surplus, and knows how to make profit out of both. Thus, in economic life, he is nothing less than a disturber of the peace, a revolutionary, and an anarchist.

CHAPTER 3
THE INTERNATIONAL CONNECTION AND THE SECRET HEBREW LEAGUE

Among the various causes of the tremendous advance of the Jews, special emphasis must be laid upon one of the most important: the way in which they play into one another's hands internationally. Jewish success can be attributed, in a large measure, to the cooperation of many people in conformity with a principle of unity. The House of Rothschild stands before the eyes of all as the most striking example of this; it is, at the same time, testimony to the avalanche-like growth of the property that is strictly confined to Jewish ownership, and which plays the chief part in sucking dry the national prosperity, not only of Europe, but also of most other countries.

The role of the great millionaires who control American economic life has been played in Europe, until quite recently, and almost exclusively by the House of Rothschild, with its active branches in Paris, London, Frankfurt, Vienna, and Naples.[1] The Rothschilds, however, can only be compared with the American millionaires insofar as their actual riches are concerned, and not with regard to their economic position. The American money-princes are always striving to utilize their gigantic fortunes for the further economic development of their country; the Rothschilds, on the contrary, comprise a cosmopolitan company, without any country of its own, devoted to the mere acquisition of money, and which lives solely from the "financing" of the productive power of others. And in order to ply this business on as great and secure a scale as possible, the House of Rothschild has devoted particular attention to that chronic lack of money that is displayed by the governments of the various countries. For the last 50 years, scarcely a single national loan of any importance has been negotiated and concluded without the Rothschilds. They have their fingers on the

---

[1] The founder of this worldwide house was Mayer Anselm (Amschel) Rothschild (1743-1812). He had five sons, of whom Amschel (1773-1855) took over the management of the Frankfurt House, Salomon Mayer (1774-1855) that of the Vienna, Nathan Mayer (1777-1830) that of the London, Karl (1788-1855) that of Naples, and Jacob (James) Rothschild (1792-1868) that of Paris. [Ed.: Today, Rothschild and Co. is one of the world's largest independent financial groups; with headquarters in Paris and London, it has almost €80 billion under management.]

pulse of every exchange, and no one knows better than they how to skim the cream off all important economic operations.

If one wanted to write an appropriate description of the various influences that the Rothschilds exercise on our economic life and upon our politics, it would fill volumes. Here, a mere indication must suffice, and reference must be made to other books. Even in Sombart's work, there is something on the subject. The so-called "*Germanicus-Broschüren*" (pamphlets) published during the years 1880-1888 by G. Richter at Frankfurt, contain much instructive matter. Also, F. V. Scherb's book *History of the House of Rothschild* (Berlin 1892) is informative. "*Germanicus*" is evidently a well-informed judge of all matters relating to the Exchanges, and particularly so of the Jewish fraternity of Frankfurt; he relentlessly lays bare the fraudulent machinations of the great Jewish firms. But although some of these pamphlets passed through several large editions, the voice that spoke therein faded away, completely unheard in authoritative circles. They have not led to the slightest proceeding against the systematic plundering of the people that takes place on the stock exchanges. This is proof of the terrible censorship that Jewry has already cast over our public life. Nothing that runs counter to Jewish interests can any longer be publicized.

If Social Democracy were a genuine movement of the people, it would find, in this respect alone, its most urgent call to come to grips with the real robbers of the nation. But the genuine 'friend of the people' learns to his astonishment, that the apparent representatives of the proletariat extend their hands protectively over the machinations of the stock exchange, and march, arm in arm, with the very men who determine how the people are to be deceived. The notorious diligence of the leaders of the proletariat has earned them their title, 'The truncheon-guard of the Jews.' This is demonstrated by the fact that, during the incendiary destruction that took place at the time of the Paris Commune in 1870, the only property that remained completely unharmed was that of Mr. Rothschild.

Old Meyer Anselm (Amschel) Rothschild laid the foundation of his fortune in Frankfurt, as is known. William I of Hesse, during the time of the Napoleonic wars (1806-1813), handed over the whole of his fortune, amounting to between 12 and 21 million thalers, to Rothschild, in order to prevent it falling into the hands of the enemy. Rothschild paid almost nothing for this "loan," and yet the clever banker earned 5 or 10 percent interest on it, given the scarcity of money during wartime. And those who held the purse-strings for the German Federation were guilty of the criminal folly of entrusting the huge sums of money paid by France as war reparation, and which had been marked for the erection of fortresses for the protection of the Federation, to the Frankfurt Jews—and in particular to the House of Rothschild.

Thus, the House of Rothschild has utilized the millions of marks belonging to princes and states to make a foundation for its own worldwide power, and to still further extend its usury amongst princes and peoples. It became the money-lender and the money-broker for the governments of all the European states, and from then onwards exercised a fateful influence upon all political proceedings. It is significant that Amschel Meyer Rothschild, the eldest son of the founder of the business, was present at the Vienna Conference in 1815, spoke on that occasion, and was altogether a personality of considerable importance. In 1845, Prince Metternich wrote to the French Ambassador in Paris, "The House of Rothschild plays a far greater role at Frankfurt than any foreign government, with perhaps the exception of the English. There are natural reasons for this that one certainly cannot regard as good, and which, from a moral viewpoint, are still less satisfactory. Money is the great and final tribunal in France."

The fine art of the Hebrew has always consisted in ascertaining, by means of espionage, an approaching shortage in goods and provisions, in buying them up, and then, when they are urgently needed, only parting with them at a profiteer's price. In times of war, it is scarcely possible to satisfy the requirements of the army without the aid of the Jews, as they have already laid their hands on all available stores, and secured them by deeds of purchase and payments on account. That the House of Rothschild is quite at home in this underhanded business is proven by the following passage from a letter from Nathan Rothschild, the third son of Meyer Amschel, to his friend, the politician Thomas Buxton:

> When I had established myself in London, The East India Company sold gold to the amount of 800,000 pounds sterling. I bought it all because I knew that the Duke of Wellington must have it; I had purchased a large number of his loan bills at a cheap rate.[2] The government sent for me, and declared that they must have the money. As soon as they had it, they did not know how to send it to Portugal. I undertook this as well, and sent the money across France. This was the best piece of business that I have ever done.

---

[2] Wellington, who was a spendthrift in private life, was first Lord of the British Treasury from 1820-1833.

The members of this firm that became rich through countless, unclean financial operations have even been ennobled (Amschel Meyer by the Emperor of Austria already in 1815), have been loaded with honors and decorations, and have been entrusted by princes and persons of rank with the management of their fortunes. And princes and persons of rank did not regard it as degrading to maintain relations with these wholesale usurers—indeed, they sank almost to subserviency in their eagerness to help this descendant of a Frankfurt Jew, who dealt in old clothes and who had no other name than that of the house in which he lived, to play a more important part even than that assigned to kings and princes of royal blood. Even the oldest and most illustrious nobility, who desired that everyone should know that their honor was a rare and costly possession, bent their knee before men whose ancestor had adopted as his watchword "My money is my honor".[3] The increase in the wealth of the House of Rothschild is calculated as follows by a writer on political economy—Dr. Rud. Herm. Meyer—in the 1880s:

> The Parisian Rothschild (II) died in 1875, and left 1 billion francs. One is entitled, therefore, to estimate the combined fortunes of the members of the House of Rothschild at 5 billion francs. The Rothschilds make more than 5 percent interest. Let us reckon in the meantime, that this "surplus" is utilized for their maintenance, and that their capital only doubles itself every 15 years. One is entitled to assume this, because it has actually increased more quickly since the founding of the House. If it had only doubled itself every 15 years, it would have amounted to:

1800	156 million francs
1815	312 million francs
1830	625 million francs
1845	1250 million francs
1860	2500 million francs
1875	5000 million francs

---

[3] Mayer Amschel Rothschild writes as follows in a letter to the agent of the Elector Wilhelm II of Hesse: "He who has my money holds my honor, and my honor is my life; he who does not pay me my money, takes my honor away from me." The original letter was sold at auction in Berlin.

Chapter 3 – The International Connection

It may be pointed out, however, that old Rothschild had no fortune whatever to speak of in the year 1800. One is therefore entitled to assume that if a remedy is not found by means of anti-capitalistic, truly economic legislation, the Rothschild fortune will continue to double itself every 15 years.

With this fact in mind, one is quite in order in asking what relation does the income of the remainder of humanity bear towards it. The kingdom of Saxony is one of the richest and most prosperous of the German states. In the year 1876, the income that was assessed for income-tax, of 2.75 million inhabitants, amounted to 459 francs a head, and in 1877 to only 430 francs a head. The 15 percent income derived from the present fortune of the Rothschilds is therefore as large as the combined incomes of 581,400 Saxon citizens in the year 1877. If one assumes that the average income throughout Europe always remained the same as that of the Saxons in the year 1877, and bearing in mind the fact that the Rothschild income doubles itself every 15 years, one arrives at the following result:

The fortune of the Rothschilds amounted, in the year 1875, to 5000 million francs; the income out of this was as great as the combined income of 589,000 ordinary individuals. In 1890 the fortune of the Rothschilds amounted to 10 billion francs; the income out of this was equal to the combined incomes of 1,150,000 ordinary individuals. In 1905 the fortune would amount to 20 billion francs providing an income, from which 2,320,000 human beings—half the population of the kingdom of Saxony in the year 1905—would have to live. In the year 1920, the fortune will have swollen to 40 billion francs, and in the year 1965 the fortune will amount to no less than 320 billion francs, providing an income equal to the sum of the incomes of around 37,120,000 human beings.[4]

---

[4] Ed.: By way of comparison, the current assets of the world's richest Jews today are: Larry Ellison ($125B), Larry Page ($120B), Sergey Brin ($117B), Mark Zuckerberg ($115B), and Michael Bloomberg ($70B). This assumes, furthermore, that Jeff Bezos is not Jewish—an open question. Thus, at a minimum, the five richest Jews—five individual human beings—collectively own more than half a trillion dollars in assets.

This survey, even if not absolutely accurate, nevertheless shows, in a very instructive manner, how a great mass of capital constantly increases by means of compound interest, growing like an avalanche and, like a sponge, sucking up the whole economic life. These huge accumulations of property do not, of course, consist of real money, but simply of the debts and obligations of others; their growth, therefore, indicates a progressive indebtedness of the productive classes, and also of the countries themselves.

The success of the House of Rothschild is entirely attributable to the fact that the firm possessed simultaneously an establishment in each of the five most important countries in Europe. By means of their representatives at these establishments, they maintained a constant news service, relating to all political and economic circumstances, that was utilized to exercise active influence in every direction. The five great banking houses all worked on exactly the same lines, and played into one another's hands. They formed, whenever a crisis arrived, a united power—against which the national governments were all but powerless.

Playing Into One Another's Hands; the Secret Hebrew Understanding

This particular instance is not required to demonstrate how valuable organized collaboration is to business interests. The superiority of the Jewish organization over individual activity is apparent in countless cases of everyday life—from the buying of rags and the operations of the auction-room hyenas, to cattle-dealing and traffic in stock exchange shares. The Hebrew, however, is already quite capable as an individual alone, often outstripping all sound and honest competitors in the business arena. Not only does his innate and trained sense of business give him the advantage but, before everything else, he is enabled to do this by particular tactics and by his unscrupulous procedure. Granted that the Hebrew possesses an eminent talent for commerce and all kinds of remarkable characteristics that enable him to force the average German businessman out of the saddle, these powers increase until they become absolutely irresistible when several co-operate to exert them in the same direction.

The German businessman, as a rule, stands as a single individual, opposed to all the rest; he endeavors to advance his business by his own power and ability. At present, it is quite unusual for him to receive any special help or advancement from relatives or friends. With the Hebrews, it is quite different. The strong "holding together" of this foreign national element is a worldwide historical fact. One hears them extolled in all quarters, because they stand by one another and support themselves. That is certainly a praiseworthy characteristic and, as such, may appear worthy of imitation. In the case of the Jews, this "holding together" does not arise from unalloyed mutual goodwill; it is rather a duty of life, created by tradition, and indispensable for this people. The Hebrew recognizes the fact that, owing to his peculiar behavior and to his peculiar designs that are hostile to the rest of humanity, he would be powerless in the world as a separate individual. The cooperation of kindred powers, in the same direction, appears to him as a necessary law of life. It is solely due to the fact that many of his kind—either by agreement or impelled by the common instinct—incessantly oppose the established regulations of the honest and productive nations, that they are able to produce the confusion in the social order that is so essential to the Hebrews' prosperity.

For this reason, no one finds "holding together" so necessary as the Jews. In all their business, whether it be as agent or middleman in the country, or as wholesale merchant or stockbroker in the towns, the Hebrews are organized everywhere in bands or gangs. Even in the domain of theft where, until a few decades ago, they were considerably more active than at the present moment, they had developed 'theft by gangs,' until it could almost be regarded as an art. Each one had a separate part to play. For instance, there was the "scout" who had to seek out opportunity, the *Schmieren-Steher*, whose business it was to keep a look-out while the theft was being committed, fellow conspirators who received the stolen goods, and all kinds of other people who helped to make 'gang robbery' so successful. One has only to read the writings of the criminal actuary Thiele that were published in the 1840s under the title "The Jewish Swindlers in Germany," to learn on what a magnificent scale the people of Judah showed their skill on every occasion—both in organization and in the assigning of parts that each should play.

In one particular legal case—Rosenthal versus Löwenthal —no less than 700 thieves and accomplices were prosecuted, almost all of whom were Hebrews, and whose communications extended from certain towns in Poland as far as the Rhine, with branches all over Germany. This powerful *"Chawrusse"* carried on burglary, embezzlement, artificial bankruptcy, and traffic in stolen goods, on a truly grand scale. Anyone who reads the account of the trial at the time cannot help being struck by the fact that quite a number of characteristic names of various members of this band of thieves are to be found today amongst the magnates of finance and the matadors of the Berlin Stock Exchange. One gets the impression that the present-day Jewish corporation of the Stock Exchange is a direct continuation of the old swindling *"Chawrusse"*.

One must not, by any means, believe that the connection between thieves and bankers belongs to the past. When four Jewish burglars were captured recently in the vicinity of Paris, a large number of letters were found in their possession, connecting them with some of the leading Jewish firms in London and Antwerp. The public press unfortunately remained silent concerning any other discoveries made in the course of the investigation.

Hebrew Nomadism

Internationality presumes, of necessity, a departure from stationary habits—from the attachment to the soil, to the home, to the Fatherland. Since the Jew knows no Fatherland in our sense of the word, internationality is an essential part of his peculiar disposition, and it impels him, on principle, to assume a hostile attitude towards all national effort. For this reason, the German disposition is especially hateful to the Jew.

Sombart very appropriately represents the Jews as a nation of wanderers—of "nomads," compared with the stationary nations.[5] Out of this fundamental opposition arises a wide divergence in the views taken with regard to life and to economic principles. The stationary individual must, of necessity, favor well-regulated conditions and stability, in order that he may have full scope for his productive and constructive activity. The nomad, animated by the impulse to carry all his possessions with him and to make them as portable as possible, must always desire to make things and values moveable—indeed, to "mobilize" them. Consequently, he is not in love with fixity and constancy of relations and regulations; he desires, on the contrary, to see everything in a state of flux and revolution. The earth, with its topsoil that is the precondition and foundation for all productive and stationary nations, has little meaning for the nomad—if he is not able to convert it into moveable, liquid values. He accomplishes this by the production of "paper values," for which the immoveable goods of stationary citizens are pledged. He therefore sides with mortgages, pledge-papers, stocks and shares, bills of exchange, and all other paper values that can be stuck comfortably in the pocket and carried away.

The Hebrew shows just as little interest in the productivity of the native soil. His instinct for "dealing" drives him to desire that all articles, on their journey from producer to consumer, should travel as far as possible,

---

[5] He was certainly not the first to remark this. At least since 1887, we have the masterly work of Adolf Wahrmund (1827-1913): *The Law of Nomadism and Present-day Jewish Domination*.

Chapter 3 – The International Connection 37

and consequently be made to pass, as frequently as possible, the gateways of his middleman monopoly. The more that goods wander about the world, and the more that nations become dependent upon what they import from foreign countries, so much the better for the Hebrew.

It is on this account that he endeavors, by all means, to restrict and complicate the simple and straight-forward course that the exchange of goods would naturally take. He thrusts himself everywhere between producers and consumers, and strives, wherever it is possible, to so arrange matters that not even the smallest business can be completed without his interference. In countries where the Jews sit close to one another, this system has been amazingly perfected. J. C. Kohl, for instance, relates in his *Journeys in the Interior of Russia and Poland* (1841), that in Poland it is impossible to conclude either an important or unimportant piece of business without the mediation of a Jew.

> The nobleman sells his wheat to the shipper through the Jew, the master of the house engages his servants, his steward, his cooks, yes, even the instructors and tutors for his son through the Jew. Estates are let, money is collected, stores are bought, etc. through the agency of the Jew; in short, one feeds, travels, rides, lodges, and clothes oneself through the mediation of the Jew. Formerly the Jews were also the sole tenants of the Customs, Mines, and Saltworks in Poland.[6]

T. von Langenfeldt, in his 1875 book *Russia in the 19th Century*, gives a picture of the interaction of Jewish business activities and of their far-flung net of aids and helpers:

> At the annual markets where the Jews are permitted to do business, the dealing takes on a certain feverish aspect. They appear in enormous numbers, and sell their goods, both wholesale and retail, from booths and stalls, or hawk them from house to house. Around each Jewish wholesale dealer swarm hundreds of poor Jews, who obtain goods from him on credit, only to sell them retail. One Jew supports another; they have their own bankers, brokers, agents—yes, even

---

[6] This work is still regarded by those acquainted with the conditions as correct and reliable. See also Richard Andree, *National Information Concerning the Jews* (1881), page 213.

their own drivers. Over the whole of western and southern Russia, there is spread an innumerable host of commission agents and factors, employed by rich Jewish wholesale merchants. These form the connecting link between merchants and producers, between the more distant markets and the commercial centers. The duties of these agents consist in purchasing goods, and in writing periodical reports, with which they have to furnish their masters concerning every economic novelty, concerning the prices of every possible product, while imparting at the same time their views as to the advantage of this or that commercial operation.

Besides the commission agents, the brokers are absolutely indispensable for Jewish trade. The business of the broker consists in knowing everything, hunting down everything, bringing the interested parties together, watching the actions of those people who have any kind of relations to the merchant—in a word: to represent all the interests of his principal. The broker is a living price list, in whom the prices, the quantity, the quality, and the location of the goods for sale; in fact, everything that can interest the purchaser is recorded. Almost every Jew is a broker; yes, one is entitled to maintain that he is born to the part.

The brokers in any particular market do not allow any stranger to enter, and do not themselves attempt to enter any strange market, but recommend their clients go to a broker known to them, at the place in question. There are special brokers for the grain, tallow, salt, and timber trades. Where Jews exclusively live, the whole country is covered with a net of brokers, who penetrate into the most remote economic corners of each district. The broker understands how to make himself indispensable everywhere, and to everyone. The estate-owner, and especially the Polish estate-owner, is the born friend of the Jew, who flatters him, abases himself before him, knows always where and how money can be procured, and where he—the estate-owner—can dispose of his produce to the best advantage.[7]

---

[7] See my *Handbook on the Jewish Question*, 27th edition, pages 100-111.

The Hebrew mania to give preference to all foreign goods springs from these characteristic motives. He is always the first to bring novelties from foreign countries, and is an indefatigable advocate of everything foreign. He is always ready with an assurance that the foreign article is better than the native; he even goes so far as to claim that foreign corn is more nourishing than that grown by German peasants. He knows full well that the native product very easily finds the direct road from producer to consumer without requiring his services as middleman; and this sticks in his craw.

He would like to make production just like consumption—dependent upon himself, and thus to get it completely into his power. He therefore tries to separate the two processes, and to thrust himself between them. The business of the middleman has become second nature to the Jew to such an extent that he regards it favorably even when practiced by others, as long as he does not thereby lose any advantage. Manufacturers who deliver exclusively to agents, the agents themselves, as well as the great army of brokers and commission men who do not compete with Jews, are inclined to praise the Jews on account of the punctilious respect that he pays to every kind of middleman business. The Jew's ideal would be to convert Germany into a one-sided industrial country, importing all raw material and food-stuffs from abroad, and compelled to export again the greater part of its industrial products. In this case, both the raw material and the finished article must pass through the hands of the middleman, and his control of the market would be complete. But this could also be accompanied by political control of the state. The nearer that the Hebrew brings this ideal to social-democrat Marxist tendencies, the more it separates him from all representatives of national work.[8]

The Jew is therefore a sworn enemy of agriculture in the home country. He persecutes with fanatical hatred the "agrarian," who, by his diligent production, interferes with the Jew's commercial monopoly. For this reason, the latter is never tired of singing the praises of international free trade, of abusing protective duties, of inciting the inhabitants of towns against the countryfolk, and of endeavoring, as far as possible, to sow discord between the two.[9]

The Hebrew fraternity is favored by yet another circumstance in its control of economic life, and that is: their peculiar morality.

---

[8] Karl Marx (1818-1883) was of Jewish origin, as was Ferdinand Lassalle (1825-1864) and many other notorious social-democratic figures.

[9] Ed.: The parallels to the present day are striking.

Chapter 4
The Peculiar Morality of Jewry

That the Hebrew is not very particular with regard to his moral obligations towards other people is fairly well known. One tends to excuse him much in this respect, and to overlook his lack of conscientiousness with the remark that the Jew has been frequently and unjustly persecuted "in olden times," and thus has been driven, by dire necessity, to the adoption of a lax moral code. In this way too, many "worthy souls" are inclined, out of ill-considered amiability, to speak disparagingly of their own nation by casting blame for the moral deficiencies of the Hebrew on their own Christian ancestors. These fine folk could easily ascertain from the Bible, that the bad ethics of the Hebrew are as old as that nation, and already existed before there were any Christians. The Hebrews were already condemned far and wide, in ancient Egypt, Babylon, and Syria, on account of their questionable morality and business tactics; consequently, Christians cannot be blamed for the moral shortcomings of the Jewish people.

We learn from the Old Testament that their law allows the Hebrews to treat the "non-Jew"—"the stranger"—very differently than those of their own faith and blood. In this respect, the "Chosen People" place themselves in the strongest contrast to all other nations, who are designated as "strangers." It is continually reiterated that it is permissible to do all kinds of things towards a stranger which are forbidden towards fellow-Jews. Thus, for example: "Unto a stranger thou mayest lend upon usury; but unto thy brother thou shalt not lend upon usury" (Deut 23:20, KJV). A sharp distinction is always drawn between the Jews and the rest of the nations. All the moral commandments of the Hebrews extend only to members of their race; all other races are excepted. What is forbidden to be done to Jews is permitted towards those who are not Jews. "You may require payment from a foreigner, but you must cancel any debt your fellow Israelite owes you" (Deut 15:3, NIV). The contempt shown for all those who are not Jews goes so far as to regard unclean food and garbage as good enough for the "stranger": "Do not eat anything you find already dead. You may give it to the foreigner residing in any of your towns, and they may eat it, or you may sell it to any other foreigner" (Deut 14:21).

All the commands made with reference to one's "neighbor" are interpreted differently by the Jew than the Christian, who regards them as referring to all men; the Jew accepts these commands quite literally, and as referring only to the actual neighbor, the member of the same race, the fellow-Jew. When we read in Leviticus (19:13), "You shall not oppress your neighbor or rob him," the Jew considers that he is released from any such duty towards those who are not Jews. The writings of the rabbis express this particular interpretation of the text quite unmistakably.

This peculiar comprehension on the part of the Jews of their particular rights as human beings goes, however, further back still; it rests, in the last analysis, on the fact that the Jews not only separate themselves as a "chosen people" from all other men, but have their own particular god. It is a fatal mistake of our theologians to regard the Jewish God as identical with the Christian. On a closer examination, Jehovah—whom modern writers call Yahweh—is found to be the exclusive God of Jewry, and not, at the same time, that of other men. It is clearly stated in Genesis 17 that this Yahweh/Jehovah made his compact exclusively with Abraham and his descendants, and that this covenant bears a hostile meaning for all non-Jewish peoples. As a sign of the covenant, circumcision is introduced, and Yahweh declares that all who are not circumcised will incur his vengeance, and will be completely destroyed.

It is immediately clear that this covenant between Yahweh and Abraham's seed is a warlike covenant, the point of which is directed relentlessly against all non-Jewish nations—the unbelievers, the heathens (Goyim). In the eyes of the Jews, however, heathens are all those who are not of Abraham's seed, all who are not circumcised, all who have not entered into the blood-pact with Yahweh. Dominion over all other nations is promised to the Jews, and the possessions of the former will be given to them as a reward, if they are true to their pact with Yahweh: "Ask me, and I will make the nations your inheritance, and the ends of the earth your possession. You will break them with a rod of iron; you will dash them to pieces like pottery" (Psalms 2:8-9). Yes, open hostility is declared against all non-Jewish nations, and their extirpation (*Ausrottung*) and annihilation (*Vernichtung*) are to be the life mission of the Jews: "You will destroy all the nations the Lord your God will give to you. You will not pity them or worship their gods, for that would be a trap to you" (Deut 7:16).[1]

---

[1] Hence it was a fatal blunder by Martin Luther to always translate the word 'Yahweh' as 'Lord God,' and thus to help to obliterate the fundamental difference between the particular god of the Jews, and the "Heavenly Father" of Christ.

The oriental scholar Adolf Wahrmund is therefore justified in referring to the journey of the Jews across the Earth as an expedition for the capture of the world—certainly not by open force of arms, but by other means, a plentiful store of which is placed at their disposal by the Talmudic teaching of the Rabbis.

The most important Jewish weapon against non-Jewish nations is money; they therefore attempt to obtain possession of it in every form. For this reason, Jews are allowed to practice usury against non-Jews, and the lending of money, and the receiving of interest are recommended as an important means or instrument for dominating other nations:

> For the Lord your God will bless you, as he promised you, and you shall lend to many nations, but you shall not borrow; and you shall rule over many nations, but they shall not rule over you. (Deut 15:6)

Truly a wonderful compact with God, one that is payable in cash and which promises domination over other nations by money-power—whilst Christ teaches: "Ye cannot serve God and Mammon" (Mt 6:24).

The peculiar Jewish perception of life that results from such doctrines culminates in the Talmud. It would take too much time and space to quote even extracts here from the mystical books of the Rabbis; I can only refer to my previous work, *The Wrong God* (1924), in which I cast a strong light upon domains that we can scarcely glance at here. Thus, the segregation of the Hebrews from all other nations is conscious and deliberate, and is in no sense due to possible dislike on the part of those nations. The holy books of the Jews furnish us with plenty of proof on this point. They are incessantly warned never to make common cause with the foreign nations: "Be careful not to make a treaty with those who live in the land where you are going, or they will be a snare among you" (Ex 34:12).

The boundary-line between the Hebrew and the rest of humanity is sharply defined everywhere, and the peculiar morals of Jewry rest on this separation of interests. They were first set out, however, in characteristic form, by the Rabbis, who established the Jewish system of morals in the Talmud (= 'Doctrine'), from the 2nd to the 5th century AD. "The Talmud— a comprehensive work, divided into many parts—is the real code of laws for Jewry since the time of Christ, and is the foundation of its religious and civic arrangements" (Brockhaus' Conversations-Lexicon). And it is precisely in this book, where the perception impresses itself most forcibly upon the reader, that it is only the Hebrew who is a man in the real sense of the word, and that all the remaining nations stand far beneath him; they are, in fact, comparable to animals.

> The nations of the world are like the baskets in which one puts straw and dung. They have a soul that is only equal to that of the animals.

This is an example of what is to be found in the *Midrash shir hashirim*.[2] A further specimen in the Talmud treatise *Bava metzia* is as follows:

> You Israelites are called men, but the nations of the world are called not men, but cattle.

Jalkut Rubeni expresses itself still more distinctly:

> The Israelites are called men (human beings) because their souls are derived from God, but the souls of those who are not Jews are derived from the unclean spirit, and therefore they are named swine.

But if a believing Jew happens to believe that those who are not Jews are just as good men as the Hebrews because they possess the same "form," *Shenei luchot haberit* is prepared to give instruction upon this point, for it is stated there:

> A human form is only given to those who are not Jews in order that the Jews may not be waited upon by beasts.

With such a perception, we can well understand how all intercourse with those who are not Jews is most strictly forbidden to all true Hebrews. It is a matter of common knowledge that the Old Testament warns the true Jew, in the most emphatic manner, not to marry those who are not Jews, and the Rabbis of the Talmud repeat and accentuate this commandment on many occasions. Consequently, when the suggestion is made that a mutual contempt exists between Jews and non-Jews, it is well to remember, first of all, that *that* side started this; it is in consequence of the racial conceit of

---

[2] Ed.: The following quotations from Talmudic and related literature are unconfirmed. But for a related analysis, see *The Book of the Shulchan Aruch* (2023) by Erich Bischoff.

Chapter 4 – The Peculiar Morality of Jewry

the real Hebrew that he regards his nation as quite out of the ordinary, and especially chosen, and permitted to look down upon other men with contempt. It is certainly no wonder if other nations, in their turn, pay back this aversion in the same coin. And they are more entitled to do so, as, in their case, it is a counterstroke to a brutal challenge.

But whoever regards those who do not belong to his race as no better than beasts cannot possibly recognize that he has any moral obligations towards such inferior creatures. On this fundamental perception rests the entire system of Rabbinic morality; it teaches, with constant repetition, that one has duties only towards one's neighbor, one's race, and towards no one else. The Law states: "Thou shalt do no wrong to thy neighbor," and the discerning Rabbi adds, to make it clearer: "the other people are excepted." Again, one reads in the Talmud treatise *Sanhedrin*: "An Israelite is permitted to do a wrong to a 'Goy' i.e. non-Jew, because it is written: 'Thou shalt not do wrong to thy neighbor, without however, paying any heed to the Goy'." It is no wonder then, when the Talmud draws the following conclusion: "Lost property that belongs to a Goy need not be returned."

But the writings of the Talmud do not confine themselves to such general instructions. Just as business creates, as it were, the soul of the entire Jewish existence, so too is great importance given in the Talmud to all business relations; all manner of good advice is imparted there as to how one should conduct oneself in business matters. This is even an aspect of the Jewish religion. When one recalls how little Christian doctrine concerns itself with money matters and business, and how it, to a certain extent, rejects any concept of money, relying instead on the Word ("Ye cannot serve God and Mammon"), one really feels the divide that exists between Christian and Jewish perceptions of life—across which no bridge could ever be built. How important, by contrast, are all business matters to the Hebrew! Thus we find in the Talmudic writings such directions as this:

> If a Goy holds the pledge of an Israelite, and the Goy loses it and an Israelite finds it, the latter shall return it to the Israelite, but not to the Goy; if, however, the finder desires to return it to the Goy for the sake of the sacred reputation[3] then, thee other (Israelite) shall say to him: "If you wish to keep the reputation sacred, do so with what belongs to you." (*R. Jerucham Seph. mesch.* f.51.4)

---

[3] A mode of speaking that frequently occurs, much to this effect: "In order that our religion and our God do not incur a bad reputation."

It is also taught:

> It is permissible to take advantage of the mistake of a Goy, when he makes a mistake (to his disadvantage). Thus, if the Goy sends in his bill, and makes a mistake, the Israelite shall say to him: "See, I rely upon your bill; I do not know if it really is as you state, nevertheless I give you what you demand."

The Hebrew is furthermore allowed to treat non-Jews differently in non-business matters as well. Rabbinism inexorably extends the sharp division between Jew and non-Jew into all remaining domains of life. The Jew is commanded, when acting as judge in lawsuits, to influence the course of the proceedings in favor of his racial companions. In the book *Bava Kamma* (= 'the first door') we find:

> When an Israelite and a non-Jew come before you in the Court, you shall, if you can, administer justice to him—the Israelite—according to Jewish law, and say to him: "it is so according to our law." When the law of the worldly nations is favorable to the Jew, you shall administer justice to him accordingly, and say to him: "it is thus according to our law." But when this is not the case, use cunning. (113a, paragraph 2)

The following passage, for instance, bears eloquent testimony to the assertion that the despicable doctrines of the Talmud towards the Canaanites, Edomites, and Amalekites refer not only to the peoples of antiquity, but also to the present:

> "The inhabitants of Germany," says Kinchi "are Canaanites, for when the Canaanites fled before Jehoschua, they went into the land Alemannia that is called Germany, and even to the present day the Germans are called Canaanites." (*Obadja* 1,20)

In more recent times, the Hebrews eagerly assume the appearance of possessing a warlike spirit, boast of their participation in the various campaigns, and attempt, through their patrons and press, to even get admitted to the rank of officer. The fact is, though, that they prize safety over valor,

Chapter 4 – The Peculiar Morality of Jewry

which is shown by referring to the passage from the Talmud *Pesachim* 112b:

> If you go to war, go not first but last, in order that you can return home first.

Also, the widely held idea that the Jew was compelled by foreign influence to confine himself to trade because other vocations were forbidden to him—a matter that I will go more deeply into later on—is shown to be fallacious by the actual writings of the Rabbis. They prove that the Hebrew has, from the remotest periods, always displayed a preference for trade because other activities, and especially agriculture, appeared too tedious to him, and brought in too little profit. Thus we read in the Talmud:

> Rab Eleazar has said: "No handicraft is so unprofitable as agriculture," it is said *Ezech* 27-29; "You will 'come down' (grow poor)!" R. Eleazar beheld a field, across which cabbages were planted in beds. He then said: "Even if cabbages were planted for the whole length of the field, trading would still be the best." On one occasion when the Rab was walking through a wheat field, and observed how the wheat swayed to and fro, he said: "Continue to sway, trade is to be preferred to you."
>
> Rab has further said: "He who expends a hundred Sus in trade, can enjoy meat and wine every day, but he who expends a hundred Sus on agriculture, has to be content with cabbage and salt, must sleep on the earth, and is exposed to every kind of misery."

Thus, the preference for trade, and the contempt for handicraft and agriculture, are a very ancient legacy of the Jewish race, and no one has ever found it necessary to compel them to turn to trade.

The Kol Nidre

It would be a fatal mistake to imagine that these ancient views and laws in the Talmud do not possess any validity today. On the contrary: the doctrines of the Talmud form, uninterruptedly, an important item in the Jewish religious education. Every young Jew today receives instruction according to the views expressed in the Talmud—however much he may assure you, later on in life, that such matters are entirely unknown to him. Moreover, the law set out in the Talmud has been modernized by a recent revision—the so-called *Shulchan Aruch*—and the validity of this law is so undisputed that Imperial German legal authorities, in lawsuits in which both parties were Jews, have relied upon the precepts of the *Shulchan Aruch*.[4]

In this more recent law-book of Jewry, one can find a remarkable prayer that is said every year on the Day of Atonement (Yom Kippur), in all synagogues, accompanied by great solemnity: the so-called Kol Nidre Prayer. It is as follows:

> All vows, and prohibitions, and oaths, and consecrations, and *konams* and *konasi* and synonymous terms, that we may vow, or swear, or consecrate, or prohibit upon ourselves, from the previous Day of Atonement until this Day of Atonement and from this Day of Atonement until the [next] Day of Atonement that will come for our benefit. Regarding all of them, we repudiate them. All of them are undone, abandoned, cancelled, null and void, not in force, and not in effect. Our vows are no longer vows, and our prohibitions are no longer prohibitions, and our oaths are no longer oaths.

The contents of this peculiar prayer have often been used as a reproach to the Jews, who usually argue their way out of it by maintaining that the vows, declarations, and oaths that are spoken of in this prayer refer only to religious matters, especially to vows and oaths that the Jew makes or takes to himself, or to his God. It is difficult, however, to see why anyone who regards his oaths to God so lightly should take a more serious view of his affirmations or vows to his fellow men. In any case, the praying Hebrew has the right, when reciting the "Kol," to connect this prayer secretly with his own particular vows and oaths.

It is no wonder, then, if a nation with such a remarkable system of ethics obtains a tremendous advantage over men who possess a more sensitive conscience and a finer sense of justice, and who not only abide by their oaths and vows but adhere punctiliously to their ordinary promises

---

[4] Ed.: The *Shulchan Aruch* was composed in the mid-1500s by a Jewish rabbi, Joseph Karo, as a kind of practical condensation of the vast Talmud. In a day-to-day sense, it is perhaps the most relevant guide to Jewish morals and Jewish action. For a further explanation and critical commentary, see Erich Bischoff, *The Book of the Shulchan Aruch* (2023).

Chapter 4 – The Peculiar Morality of Jewry   49

and assurances. The Talmudic ethical perception that forces the Hebrew to observe his duties towards his racial and religious brethren with almost painful exactitude but absolves him of his duties towards other men must introduce a curious kind of discord into our life. The Hebrews are thus united in a strong union that not only possesses a strong common interest, but directs itself, at the same time, in silent hostility against all other men. And since the Hebrews are forbidden to disclose anything of their secret legislation to those who are not Jews, Jewry adopts the nature of a conspiracy that is aimed at all men who do not happen to be Jews.[5]

The situation is aggravated by the following circumstances: The Rabbinic doctrines and laws are—with few exceptions—only to be found in the Hebrew language; thus, they are practically unapproachable for the rest of mankind. Besides, the written language of the Hebrews resembles a cryptograph, the reading and explanation of which are taught by tradition in the schools of the Rabbis. The Jews are consequently in the position to maintain to the uninitiated that any non-Jewish rendering is "incorrect." As a matter of fact, non-Jewish scholars who have learned the Hebrew language and examined the writings of the Rabbis, and who have then proceeded to translate some of the awkward passages, have become the objects of the most violent hostility on the part of the Jews. In many cases, it has only been possible to ascertain the correct reading with the help of converted Jews.

For centuries, reliable Christian scholars have made translations of the immoral passages; where all agree, it is scarcely permissible to doubt the correctness of the version. One need only mention two figures: the Heidelberg Professor of Oriental Languages, *Johann Eisenmenger* (1654-1704) who produced a translation of extracts from the Talmud in the year 1700—*Jewry Unmasked*; and the Canonical Professor, *August Rohling* (1839-1931), of Prague, who published his book *Talmud Jew* in 1878, and who since then has been made the object of most odious enmity from the Jewish side. Furthermore, the Orientalists Professor Johann Gildemeister of Bonn, Dr. Jakob Ecker of Münster, and Professor Georg Behr of Heidelberg have confirmed the correctness of these same translations of the rabbinical writings when the opportunity presented itself in lawsuits, relating to such matters. Since, however, the Jews always renew their denials, there is an urgent necessity, in the interests of both sides, that the disputed

---

[5] Ed.: There is a two-millennia-long history of Jewish hatred of Gentiles, one that has been noted by many prominent men of history. See the book *Eternal Strangers* (T. Dalton, 2020).

passages in the Talmud should be examined by impartial experts; all conflict about the matter would then be removed in simplest manner possible.

It is, however, a most remarkable fact that the Hebrews oppose any such impartial procedure most emphatically and, strange to say, state officials have also declined to do so when requested. In 1890, a petition was sent from the anti-Jewish camp to a number of imperial and local authorities, containing a request that they should appoint a commission of independent experts, whose duty would be to examine carefully the passages in dispute. Not once was the request granted. The Prussian Ministry of Culture dismissed any such step as being "impracticable." If one compares the thoroughness with which the morality of the Jesuits has been and is still discussed in public, one is forced to accept the view that both the zealous friends of truth and their opponents, who work in an obscure and devious manner, know how to restrain their zeal for enlightenment in a truly remarkable way—as far as the Jews are concerned.

The situation is thus very peculiar. This much is established: German national representative bodies and governments have given the Jews equal civic rights, and have recognized them as a separate religious community, but without making any inquiry into whether Jewish moral instruction is compatible with the welfare of the state. There is, therefore, no surprise if attacks are constantly being delivered by the nationalists against this untenable position. There will be no end to this dispute until the matter has been clarified beyond any possible doubt.

Judaism as a State

Johann Ludwig Klüber, the diplomatist and authority on international law, calls the Jews plainly, "a political-religious sect, under the strict, theocratic despotism of the Rabbis," and "a completely separated society of hereditary conspirators, with certain political principles and commandments for general life and for commercial intercourse" (and thus not merely with religious aims!). And this is, in concise and sober language, the essence of the matter. The Jews do not compose, like the Christians, simply a religious community that depends upon certain moral doctrines, and worships its God according to certain established forms; the Jews' law extends to all manner of practical affairs in life and, under the influence of a peculiar morality, concerns itself particularly with the cultivation of trade and usury. They form, despite their dispersion amongst other peoples, an absolutely distinct nation—even as Fichte expresses it, a separate state.[6] And as they are, at the same time, intent upon preserving the purity of their blood, and intermarry amongst themselves as far as possible, they form also a self-contained race.

Of all the rulers in Germany, no one has recognized this fact more clearly than the greatest of all practical politicians, Frederick the Great. He considered it necessary, even in his political will of 1752, to impress this most strongly upon his successors:

> Moreover, the ruler must keep his eye on the Jews, prevent their interference with wholesale trade, check the growth of their population, and deprive them of their right of sanctuary whenever they commit an act of dishonesty. Nothing is more injurious to the trade of the merchants than the illicit profit that the Jews make.

Jewish racial peculiarity, however, is visible to the eye, so that the Hebrew can be recognized immediately and picked out from all the other peoples of the world. And further, there can be no doubt whatever upon this point: by means of their Talmud and their system of Rabbis, the Hebrews are held together in a rigid caste that carries on a cooperative war against all remaining nations, chiefly by means of material expropriation and the undermining of morality.

Helmuth von Moltke, who had the opportunity to thoroughly study Jewry during his residence in Poland from 1830 to 1832, sums up his observations in the following words (*Description of the Internal Conditions in Poland*, Berlin 1832):

---

[6] Ed.: In 1793, Fichte wrote, "Throughout almost all the countries of Europe there is spreading a mighty hostile state that is at perpetual war with all other states, and in many of them imposes fearful burdens on the citizens: it is the Jews. I do not think, as I hope to show subsequently, that this state is fearful—not because it forms a separate and solidly united state but because this state is founded on the hatred of the whole human race… In a state where the absolute monarch cannot take from me my paternal hut and where I can defend my rights against the all-powerful minister, the first Jew who likes can plunder me with impunity. … Do you not remember the state within the State? Does the thought not occur to you that if you give to the Jews, who are citizens of a state more solid and more powerful than any of yours, civil rights in your states, they will utterly crush the remainder of your citizens?" (in *Eternal Strangers*, p. 78).

Despite their dispersion, the Jews still remain closely united. They are guided consistently by unknown authorities for mutual purposes. As they reject all the attempts of governments to incorporate them in the nations, the Jews form a state within a state, and have become a deep wound in Poland that has not healed, even to the present day. Even now, each town has its own Judge, each province its Rabbi, and all are subordinate to an unknown chief who lives in Asia, and who is bound by their law to travel around continually, from place to place, and whom they call the "Prince of Slavery." Thus, retaining their religion, their government, their morality, and their language, and obeying their own laws, they know how to evade those of the land they live in, or, at any rate, to nullify them for all practical purposes. And, closely united amongst themselves, they resist all attempts to merge them into the rest of the nation, as much on account of their religious belief as on their self-interest.[7]

'War Against All'

It will simply not suffice to complacently ignore, with Christian tolerance and sentimental charity, this singular and firmly organized hostile state of Jewry. This hostile state has declared war on us—war to the death; it is attempting to appropriate our material as well as our spiritual values.[8] It is an error to represent the Jews to oneself as a harmless "concession" that lives peacefully beside us, and is only desirous of serving its God in its own particular way. The most excellent Adolf Wahrmund sees in our Jews an ancient principle of the nomadic desert robbers, who sweep across cultivated places in order to leave the pastures grassless and barren behind them. He says:

> According to the view taken from the Talmud and expressed by the Rabbis, the Jews' path across the world is a warlike expedition for world conquest—nothing else. They regard themselves as soldiers on the march, hiding in secret camps or

---

[7] Ed.: Reprinted in Moltke, *Collected Letters* (vol. 2), 1892, p. 101.
[8] In his *Kunstwart* (1912), Dr. Moritz Goldstein stated that it could no longer be disputed that the Jews ruled over both the material and even spiritual values of the German nation, however much the Germans might deny their capacity to do so.

> concealing themselves under a false flag—in the midst of the enemy, always waiting for the signal to attack and surprise.⁹

None of these facts are altered in the least, if, once in a while, this or that Jew appears to us to be quite a harmless and perhaps even an amiable individual. The Jew undoubtedly possesses many human and social virtues; but who will guarantee that this external aspect of his disposition can be regarded as genuine, mixed as it is with bitterness on account of imagined slights, or imbued with feelings of revenge? The peculiar situation of the Jew, amidst a community that is inwardly foreign to him, compels him to adopt a cautious and discrete attitude. It would be foolish on his part if he openly displayed his pride and his aversion to all who are not Jews. How could he thus accomplish his aims? Slyness commands him to adapt himself, by mildness and pliancy, to his environment and to present the appearance of entertaining good-will and a kindly disposition towards his fellow citizens, in order to captivate them in their artlessness, and to win their confidence. Only thus is he enabled to promote his own business interests, and those other secret aims of Jewry, to the best advantage.

One must not, then, accept the plea that there are also some extremely nice and honest Jews as a proof that they are not dangerous. Exceptions prove the rule, and amiability and apparent harmlessness are amongst the deadliest weapons that the Hebrews employ against those who surround them. If, occasionally, a kind heart may prompt a Jew to act unselfishly, and even to display self-sacrifice where others are concerned—an occurrence which, on account of its rarity, is liable to be trumpeted a hundred times as loudly as it would be in the case of anyone who is not a Jew—the best and most moral Jew still remains a member of a secret society that directs its front against us. And, at the moment when the decision must be made whether to defend Jewish interests against other interests, the noblest and most high-minded Jew will surely take the side of his racial comrades, and will treat every non-Jew as an enemy.

Luther already summed up the situation correctly when he spoke as follows, concerning the Jews:

> But if they do anything good, know that it is not done out of love, nor does it happen for your good; but because they must

---

⁹ *The Law of Nomadism*, p. 41.

have room to live amongst us, and they must of necessity do something. But the heart is, and remains, as I have said.[10]

We are in a state of war with the Jews. If a nation has declared war upon us, and advances with hostile intent into our country, it no longer behooves us to ask: is that particular individual a good or a bad man? Rather, from that moment on, each of them must be regarded as our enemy, one against whom we must defend ourselves.

---

[10] Ed.: Source unknown. But see Luther's *On the Jews and Their Lies* (2020; Clemens & Blair).

Chapter 5
Klatzkin's Confession

Until now, it was only thanks to ingenious minds that we have been able to discover a special, hostile Jewish state hiding behind the deceptive mask of a religious creed. Today we no longer need such intuitive insight. Today, we have confessions from honest Jews who fully admit this fact. It seems that the Jews, via their astonishing success, are now so confident that no longer consider it necessary to hide from us. Or rather, that they have such low regard for the intellect and moral willpower of the Goyim that they feel free to lay all their cards on the table.

The past few decades have brought us confessions from Jews in which it is simply declared: We are only a pretense of a religious community. In reality, our creed has nothing to do with high moral standards. In reality, we are a legal and economic community. Our doctrine is not a moral doctrine of ideas, but one on practical life and customized law. Our doctrine is, in the end, a state constitution that rejects all other constitutions. We only take citizenship rights in non-Jewish states in order to give us secure advantages, even as we remain unshakable citizens of the Jewish state—one that unites all Jews around the world. We dismiss the laws of other states; we have our own legal code and our own jurisdiction. Via an insurmountable wall, we are separated from the rest of humanity. The walls that separate us are not the ghetto walls of our enemies, but the inner walls that we have built ourselves—through our law, our nature, our blood.

We conform to the laws of the state in which we live only to the extent that it is required for outward harmony and our personal advantage. Secretly, we try to circumvent these state laws as much as possible, to eliminate them, in order to destroy the non-Jewish state and replace it with a Jewish state…

That, in short, is the meaning of the explanation offered by Dr. Jacob Klatzkin in the magazine *Der Jude*, No. 9, 1916. To avoid any misunderstandings, the essentials of that piece are reproduced here verbatim.

The question was raised regarding the means by which Jews have succeeded for thousands of years amidst foreign, often hostile peoples, and have preserved their special essence without assimilating anywhere. Klatzkin seeks the solution in the peculiar character of the so-called mosaic religion. He says:

> The answer to the riddle of our duration in exile must be sought in our religion. It is the power that separates us from all peoples and unites us all in the diaspora. The outer ghetto walls erected by our enemies could never have done this. But the inner walls that are founded in our religion, and which we took with us on our wanderings and steadily increased in the settlements have expanded, are the movable 'tents of Jacob' that keep us everywhere secure.
>
> The Jewish religion abounds in fences, ones that mark off our communities and keep away all alien types. The Jewish religion is rich in forms that bind us in both being and appearance, as a unity and a sign. In contrast to other religions, it is not a doctrine of ideas, but a doctrine of the law. In our laws, we have an active right of self-determination. We lost our state,[1] but not our state constitution; we saved it, as if it were a portable state, and which also makes it possible for us to establish a kind of national autonomy for the diaspora.
>
> After the loss of our state, we had to stop applying many laws, even as our legal constitution remained in force, by and large; it got expanded, supplemented, and perfected by more precise individual efforts. Only the Jewish code was left to govern and shape our lives. Only the Jewish jurisdiction was decisive for us. We did not appeal to the national courts and did not recognize their code. If their laws were imposed on us, we viewed them as wrong, and thus have always tried to eliminate and circumvent. They had the character of 'fate of a wicked rule' when we were compelled to use them by the formula: 'The law of government is valid law.' Any Jew

---

[1] Ed.: In 70 AD, when the Romans defeated the Jewish rebellion in Jerusalem.

Chapter 5 – Klatzkin's Confession

opposing this was considered a traitor, denounced by the community, and expelled.

Our exiled princes and Rabbis were not clergymen and pastors—not like modern western Rabbis, turning Judaism into a church, like the Christian clergy. Rather, they were rulers and administrators of our community; they were judges; they were the supreme authorities of our exiled state. Their courts of justice also had the power to pass and execute criminal judgments. Their orders not only had religious authority; disobedience and transgression were answered with exclusion from the church. They were with means of power an exemplary organized and very strict regime that violations were punished very sensitively. We submitted to them in love, however also in fear of the force of the law.

In the diaspora, our legal constitution gave us peculiar religious forms of economy, including many in their functions and institutions sectors of activity—although certain "land-based commandments" could not be applied in exile.

Foreign rule has therefore not been able to wrest self-administration from us, as long as we are under the obedience of our own laws and teachers of law stood. We weren't a religious community; we formed one in ourselves closed legal and economic community. Not a creed, but primarily a statute was the structure of the one people. Not so much that religious and moral doctrinal content of Judaism as the concrete forms of our State constitution separated us from all religions. We did not rest on the days of rest of the host people and did not celebrate his feast days, did not share their joys and sorrows, and were not concerned for the welfare of the foreign state. A strong wall, erected by ourselves, separated us from the people of the country, and behind the wall lived a Jewish State in miniature.

It was to be seen in advance that this confession would make many cautious Jews uncomfortable as soon as it entered non-Hebrew circles; and so Jewish papers quickly dismissed this as the confession of an outsider. Anyone who knows the spirit and essence of rabbinical teachings, of course knows that the statements made so bluntly by Klatzkin are only inferences from the Talmud and *Shulchan Aruch*. In addition, meanwhile, other Jews too have subscribed to these views. Thus said the Zionist Alfred Nossig from Berlin at a conference in Vienna in December 1919:

> Like all Orientals, the Hebrew sages also cultivated their teachings to express veiled imagery... The golden apples of knowledge are surrounded—according to their own parables—with silver nets. The core of our tribal doctrine was esoteric ("intended for the initiated, secret, confidential"). Oral tradition entrusted it to a selection of the people—from person to person. But whoever found the key again tried hard to dig in the cultural rubble and add the word-hieroglyphics who understands to decipher, who recognizes that this doctrine from the very beginning is the deepest world wisdom and at the same time contained admirable political art, wrapped in that harmless garment of a pious faith.

So here, too, we find the confession that it is Jewish political arts to know how to wrap the "harmless garment of a pious faith" around the innocent, to deceive the Goyim. In short: they are playing sleight of hand.

When such insights finally take hold in other strata of the people, the day will come when the spirit of the people, awakened from the sober facts, draws the conclusions. If one even generally recognizes the Hebrews as a business and fraudsters' association, the religious mask is no longer able to protect them. Today, however, everyone is allowed to be an enemy of the people, and an assistant to the schemers is seen to thwart an education about these things, and rather seeks and deceives the state and the people by defending special Jewish rights.

Chapter 6
Toward an Explanation, with Sombart

Now that I have sketched in outline my own attitude to the question that lies before us, the task still remains to follow up and supplement Sombart's work (*The Jews and Modern Capitalism*)—partly by confirming it and partly by offering another interpretation. Sombart himself allows that his book is one-sided, and is meant to be. He has, in fact, supplied a written history of the economic method of the Jews that—although the author obviously has taken pains to keep to the point, and to abstain from all judgements—has nevertheless been written primarily from the optimistic side. Anyone who did not know anything about the history of the world would, on reading this book, easily get the impression that the Hebrews were the sole moving principle in society—not only in political economy but chiefly in culture, and that we are indebted to them alone for all great undertakings, and for all progress. It can scarcely have been the author's intention to create this impression, and he would simply disclaim any such explanation. But we can easily understand that, at a time when so many disparaging remarks were made about Hebrews, the desire might arise to muster everything that could be said in their favor. So, although he wishes to refrain from judgement, Sombart still says, "Israel traverses Europe like the sun; new life bursts forth where it arrives; on its departure, what has hitherto prospered, wastes away".[1]

It is scarcely possible to utter a more pretentious appreciation of a people than the above, and it is certainly opportune to examine in detail whether such a pronouncement is justified or not. Sombart has collected from the literature, and with extraordinary diligence, everything that could possibly throw a favorable light upon the activity of the Jews. He acknowledges that other factors have contributed to the building-up of the modern capitalism—which seems to him to be equivalent to modern culture—but does not discuss them in his book. He is of opinion that one will search in vain throughout his work "to discover in any single passage anything approaching an appreciation of the Jews, their affairs, their performances," and yet, a few lines further on, he says concerning the Jews: "They, above

---

[1] Ed.: Part I, chapter 2.

all other nations, are an eternal nation." That is a frequently expressed opinion, and yet the ancestors of Jewry can scarcely date further back than the ancestors of other races, for it is not recognized that the incarnation of the remaining nations only happened within recorded history. The national existence of the Hebrews is not any older than that of the other nations. It is quite the contrary—for it must not be forgotten that ancient cultures were already known in the history of the world before the Jewish people put in an appearance.

Sombart goes on to include amongst the accomplishments of the Jews, the following: "They have presented us with the one and only God, with Jesus Christ, and consequently with Christianity." This is not only a plaudit, but an extravagant eulogy that, in the face of our modern knowledge of these matters, may even be called frivolity. The contention that the Hebrews invented monotheism—the doctrine of one God—belongs to the domain of thoughtless phrases, all the more as the most ancient Jewish documents recognize a whole line of gods, such as Elohim, El-Shaddai, El-Elyon, Adonai, Tzevaot, Yahweh, etc. It was above all Luther's translation—which is frequently very loose—of these names by the universal designation "God the Lord" that is responsible for this semblance of Jewish monotheism.

Moreover, it has been sufficiently established for many decades that the Jewish God has nothing in common with the Christian Father-in-Heaven, or the universal Father of the Germanic nations. Yahweh, as we have already discussed, is the exclusive tribal God of the Hebrews; he has absolutely no desire to be the God of other peoples, for he persecutes the latter with unappeasable hatred, and assigns to his favorite the task of annihilating the remaining nations—or as Luther translates: "to devour them." It is quite clear in this case that we are dealing not with the one and only God of all nations, but with a tribal or separate and national God. Therefore, Jewry can by no means lay claim to have presented "the" only God to the rest of the world. Indeed, the discoveries of the Egyptologists and Assyriologists have furnished sufficient proof that these ancient, civilized nations already worshipped a single God before the Jewish nation was ever heard of. Our Germanic ancestors also worshipped a single God and universal Father in the form of their Dius, and the Egyptians did likewise with their Ptah, the Indians with their Dyaus (from which the Roman 'Jupiter' originated), the Greeks with their Zeus, and the Persians with their Ahura Mazda, etc.[2]

The way in which Sombart misleads his readers with regard to Christ is still more flagrant. On this point as well, we are sufficiently well-informed today to know that Christ was not of Jewish extraction, but was a heathen Galilean.[3] Jewish enmity towards him shows itself in every chapter of the Gospels. The Jews persecute him incessantly so that he must always seek refuge from them "in the land of the Heathen." Their hatred against him is so fanatical because he speaks of a spiritual world that is strange to them. It is the spirit of another race that here opposes the Jewish nature, for the teaching of Christ signifies, in all respects, a complete reversal of the Jewish system of morality.[4]

Christ had, accordingly, nothing in common with the Jews, neither outwardly nor inwardly. His teaching is the most pronounced contrast—yes, the most emphatic protest—against Jewish morality and the Jewish worldview. The whole life of Christ was a continual fight against Jewry.[5] Paul de Lagarde said: "No nation crucifies its ideal, and whoever is crucified by a nation certainly does not correspond to the ideal of that particular nation." One must read the Gospel of St. John in order to convince oneself how, on every occasion, the racial contrast between the Galileans and the Jews bursts forth. But when the Jews boast of being the children of God, Christ calls them the children of the devil (John 8:44-45).

---

[2] Compare Wahrmund, *Babylonia, Jewry, Christendom*; Lagarde, *German Writings*; Fritsch, *Case Against Yahweh*; the journal *Hammer*, no. 257, "The History of the origin of the Old Testament"; W. Schmidt, *Origin of the Idea of God* (1912); and A. Lang, *Making of Religion* (1909). In my book, I attempt to prove that Yahweh is identical with El-Shaddai, whom I call the "Spirit of Darkness" and the personification of the Principle of Evil. The philological comparisons on this point are striking.

[3] Ed.: This is a highly dubious assertion. All extant evidence argues that Jesus—if he did in fact actually exist—was a Jew. See Dalton (2011, 2020).

[4] Ed.: A far more plausible thesis is that the Jew Paul constructed his "Christian" theology from whole cloth, and did so to undermine support for the Roman Empire by confusing and corrupting the local pagans with his new religion. In truth, Paul's new religion was compatible with Judaism in several key aspects (a Jewish God, a Jewish savior, Jews as "chosen," etc); but it was diametrically opposed to the *Roman* worldview, which was the key point.

[5] Ed.: This is because Paul was in conflict with the orthodox Jews who wanted nothing to do with his rabbi Jesus and his new theology. The orthodox Jews persecuted Paul (and his followers) relentlessly, and they quite naturally returned the favor by calling Jews "children of the devil."

It would scarcely be possible to make a more trivial and thoughtless remark than that "the Jews bestowed Christianity upon us," and therefore that we owe them our gratitude. But when this phrase is heard from the mouths of the Jews themselves, the very peak of senselessness is reached; a fraud is produced, calculated only to deceive those who are utterly incapable of judgement. It is only necessary to ask in return: If the Jews assign merit to themselves on account of Christianity, then why did they pass along this great advance in morality to others instead of enriching themselves? And finally, above all, if the Jews of today, who still harbor the utmost contempt and enmity towards Christ and his teaching, claim merit for themselves by reason of the Christian doctrine, will they not also take partial responsibility for the torturing and martyring of Christ?

CHAPTER 7
JEWISH SUCCESSES IN MODERN TIMES

Sombart points out that when the migration of the Jews took place in the 16th century, a remarkable displacement of the economic center of Europe appeared. The Hebrews were driven out of Spain and migrated, for the most part (some authorities say 90,000), to European and Asiatic Turkey, where they are known today as 'Spanioles.' Another large number (around 25,000) migrated to Holland, Hamburg, and England. The remainder, about 50,000, dispersed themselves amongst the various countries of Europe and America. It is undisputed that, from that time, the economic life of Spain suffered a severe set-back, while in those places where the Jews migrated there was a sudden burst of trade. There is, however, nothing extraordinary in this, and the same thing could have happened if people of another nationality and race had migrated instead of the Hebrews. The immigrations of the Huguenots, for instance, are a distinct proof of this.

Every extensive emigration is bound to produce a set-back in the economic life of a country, whilst, on the other hand, every considerable influx of population, of any sort, will always enliven economic life. We experience this on a small scale almost every day—the removal of a factory, of a garrison, etc. In our case, it must be considered that the Hebrews, for the most part, brought capital with them and brought it to countries that were developing, and thus it would be doubly beneficial from an economic viewpoint. We have already recognized, earlier in this work, the kind of enlivenment which the Jew introduces into the economic life. It is the mobilization of all values and forces, by which he imparts a tremendous stimulus to political economy. But we have also seen how this inflated economic life is, at the same time, highly artificial; it acts, in its final phases, devastatingly and destructively upon the nations.

Still, for the moment, I will concede that the Jews enliven trade and international intercourse. But at the same time, one must not forget that they do not stimulate trade out of love for their fellow men, but in order to make profit for themselves. They produce, in all directions, traffic and exchange, in order to derive the utmost benefits for themselves.

It is breathtaking when Sombart tries to convince us that modern colonial affairs owe their development chiefly to the Hebrews. Certainly, the Jews went out to the newly-opened colonies, just as they go anywhere that business prosperity entices them. And for this reason too, they were certainly among the first in the newly-opened America. Sombart serves up, for our edification, the unproven legend that a number of Jews were present with Columbus (except for the original voyage), and that the first European to step upon American soil was the Jew Luis de Torres. Indeed, he even maintains that the expeditions of Columbus were funded exclusively with Jewish money, and that we have, accordingly, to thank the Jews especially for the discovery of America. Still more audacious is the conjecture that Columbus himself may have been a Jew, simply because some Columbus investigator claims to have discovered a family 'Colon' into which a Jewess married. This half-Jewish family Colon is therefore asserted to be identical with the family Colombo/Columbus. This genealogical feat is not made any the more probable by the fact that the Christian name 'Cristobal' occurs in both families.[1]

One can thus see how anxious some people are to assign everything remarkable in the world to the Jews. And Sombart surpasses himself, calling attention to the fact that already in the period 1820-1830 there were numerous Jewish firms in America, with the audacious assertion: "America is, in all respects, a land of Jews." He mentions with satisfaction that New York today contains nearly a million Jews, of whom the majority

---

[1] Ed.: Recent evidence suggests that most of Sombart's claims are true, and that Columbus was indeed a Jew. In March 1492, Spanish King Ferdinand expelled the 800,000 Jews from Spain, unless they agreed to convert to Christianity. Many Jews, known as 'Marranos,' subsequently feigned conversion but secretly kept to their Jewish rites and religion. Spanish scholars Jose Erugo and Otero Sanchez argue that Columbus ("Colon") was in fact one such Marrano, who hid his Jewish background in order to secure royal blessing for his initial voyage in August 1492. Some of the evidence: Columbus' will of 1506 included at least two Jewish customs (tithing for the poor and providing a dowry for poor girls) and also left money to a Lisbon Jew. The document included a triangular signature of dots and letters, similar to that found on Jewish gravestones. His primary language, 'Castilian Spanish,' was the standard tongue of Spanish Jews. In all his letters to his son, he included at the top the Hebrew letters '*bet-hei*,' which meant "with God's help." Wiesenthal (1972) argues that the voyage was motivated, in part, by a desire to find a safe haven for the recently-exiled Jews of Spain. Delaney (2012) argues that Columbus was also motivated to obtain riches for Spain that would then be used to reconquer Jerusalem and thence to rebuild the Jewish Temple. The actual funding for the voyage came, in large part, from loans from two converted Jews and a rabbi: Louis de Santangel, Gabriel Sanchez, and Don Isaac Abrabanel—just as Sombart claimed. And the Jew de Torres was indeed on the initial voyage, brought along by Columbus as a "translator." All this is circumstantial, of course, but collectively it is highly suggested of Jewish origins for Columbus himself.

certainly have not yet begun their capitalistic careers; and since all Hebrews, according to his opinion, are prospective millionaires, his exaggerated fancy sees in the America of the future a land where there will only be Slavs and Negros to act as servants, and Hebrews ruling over all.[2] With the fantastic imagination of an oriental, he calls the Jews "the golden thread that runs through the texture of American political economy." He then utters the following remarkable words with respect to the colonies in general:

> Their economic body would have bled to death, if it had not been fed from outside with a constant bloodstream in the form of precious metal. Jewish commerce, however, directed this bloodstream into the colonies.

Here again we meet an extraordinary idea, either that all the gold treasure in the world always belonged to the Jews, or that the Jews had, in some way, produced the gold themselves. In this respect, one must always keep in mind that the Jew, in general, produces *nothing at all*—neither goods nor money. Rather, he possesses an extraordinary knack for attracting the goods and money of others into his hands, in order to pass them on further, after making a considerable profit for himself.

And a simple fact arises out of all this: if the Jews had not got the money, other people would have it; and other people would conduct whatever commerce was necessary if the Hebrews were not always at hand to push them aside. Therefore again it is a curious kind of exaggeration when the learned man, who pretends to regard matters objectively, states: "The United States must thank the Jews that they—the United States—exist at all." Is it not most peculiar that these Jews, who are supposed to convey riches and life with them in all directions, are never able to exist alone, by themselves? That they have never been able to create a self-supporting state, and always required other men on whom to live, and of whom to take advantage? If the Jews were really the great cultural nation that they claim to be, they would, for once and all, separate themselves from all other

---

[2] Ed.: Sombart writes, "If the conditions in America continue to develop along the same lines as in the last generation, if the immigration statistics and the proportion of births among all the nationalities remain the same, our imagination may picture the United States of 50 or 100 years hence as a land inhabited only by Slavs, Negroes, and Jews, wherein the Jews will naturally occupy the position of economic leadership" (chapter four). And in truth, the present-day Jewish Lobby in America is remarkably dominant, in diverse fields ranging from government and economics to entertainment and academia. Sombart's "100 years hence" was amazingly prescient.

nations, establish their own colonial kingdom, and thus give proof of their power and productivity.[3]

Very probably a Jew was always on the spot wherever there was a prospect of business—but certainly not to benefit the commonwealth, but rather to seize the opportunity and to lay claim to the best for himself. Sombart himself has portrayed the process of the colonization of North America as follows:

> A body of absolutely reliable men and women—say 20 families—advanced into the wilderness, in order to begin life anew there. Amongst these 20 families, 19 would be equipped with plow and scythe, ready to cut down the woods, and to clear the land by fire and, by the work of their hands, to support themselves by cultivating the land. But the 20th family would open a shop in order to provide their comrades quickly, by means of trade, with the requisite utensils. This 20th family would then very soon busy themselves with the sale of the products that the 19 other families would have won from the soil. This family would be the one that would first have ready cash at its disposal, and thus would be in the position, in cases of need, to provide the others with loans. In many such cases, a "rural loan-bank" would attach itself to the shop, etc., etc.

He thus actually portrays, in clever words, a picture of the part that the Hebrew plays amongst the working and productive nations. It appears to me, however, that the real cultural work is done by the people with the pickaxe and the spade, with the plow and the scythe, and not by the shopman. And there is no doubt that if no Hebrew is present to act as shopkeeper, amongst the 20 other families there will certainly be one ready to act in this capacity as soon as the necessity arises. After all, nothing is so easily learned as this elementary dealing in produce, and the lending of money; and we experience every day and in every direction how people of humble origin and very mediocre ability can take up this kind of business with complete success. That the Hebrew, with his peculiar talent for this branch of business and, we may well add, with his ruthless exploitation of

---

[3] Ed.: The nation of Israel was created in 1947, some 20 years after Fritsch wrote these words.

the situation, generally has more success than other and more ingenuous men, we are quite willing to admit.

Further, Sombart tries to prove to us nothing less than that the Hebrew has played an important part in the formation of the modern state. He acknowledges that the Jews are, by their very nature, a "non-national" or "un-national" people. Actually, with the exception of the former Jewish kingdom in Palestine, they have never been able to found a state anywhere in the world.[4] Nevertheless Sombart wishes to assign to leading Jewish politicians an important share in the modern state. It sounds almost like biting irony when he says:

> But even if we do not find any Jews amongst the rulers of the modern state, we can scarcely imagine these rulers, or the modern prince, being without Jews.

Who, on reading this, does not recall Talleyrand's venomous words: "The financier supports the state in the same way as the rope supports the man who is hanged!" And even Sombart, on referring to the conjunction of prince and Jew, cannot refrain from the ironical observation that if you have a Faust, you must also have a Mephistopheles. He continues:

> I consider that it was the Hebrews, above all others, who placed the material means at the disposal of the state, as it came into being, by which it could maintain itself and develop further.

He certainly does not explain to us where the Jews typically procure these means, namely: if not out of the state treasury, then out of the pockets of the people they have fleeced. Also, he does not explain to us how the Hebrews, above all others, have practiced the art of plunging all countries deep into debt, and again, how these state loans are nearly all negotiated and created by Jews.[5] In this process there lies a rich profit for the broker or agent, as the state becomes, so to speak, a cow to be milked for the

---

[4] Even in this case they did not form, strictly speaking, a separate country, but lived in the midst of the native Edomites, Canaanites, Hittites, Amorites, Philistines, Galileans, and Samaritans, and formed, apparently, only the monied bourgeoisie while the real cultural work fell to the lot of the others.

[5] Ed.: At present, the country with the highest total public debt is also the country with the most dominant Jewish lobby: the United States, with around $22 trillion in total debt. This figure is estimated to hit $29 trillion by 2030.

benefit of the Hebrews. One is entitled to ask the question: Do the Hebrews provide this money out of love for the prince and the State? Or do they rather provide it in order, by this means, to make State and prince dependent upon them, and to create an economic system by which they can, as it were, continuously suck the marrow out of the bones of the nation?

One must repeatedly keep in mind that all the highly-praised services of the Jews do not arise from the promptings of a humane heart, but simply from a mania for profit.

It is equally a matter for amazement when Sombart, with extreme conscientiousness, gathers together all the facts of how the Jews have always acted as military contractors in times of war; he appears inclined to assign great praise to them for having undertaken a most meritorious service on behalf of the state. The Jews certainly had a strong predilection for military contracts, and it is equally certain that they always enriched themselves by this means. In his disclosures about Poland, Sombart shows that the Jews, by means of their widely extended organization, held the whole of the grain and cattle trade in their hands; thus there is nothing remarkable if, in times of war, they are the first on the spot—and are the best able—to undertake military contracts. No one should believe that they do this out of self-sacrifice for the state, and that they actually give something away. It is a specific Jewish tactic to represent sly profiteering as kindly acts undertaken for the good of the community.

I concede the following: the non-Jewish nations, and especially the Germanic people, are somewhat simple and awkward as far as economic matters are concerned. Rather, there are excellent, highly spiritual natures, in whom all matters of money and accounting arouse an inward repugnance. And it is just this weakness—that one is equally justified in regarding as a strength, and which certainly has its foundation in a lofty and spiritual constitution—that the Hebrew has always known so well how to exploit. He was always ready to encourage this dislike of all money and commercial transactions, as one would naturally expect in aristocratic circles, and offered his services as obsequious assistant and agent. Sombart says of a Court Jew, Moses Elkhan, who lived in Frankfurt about 1700:

> The industrious man, who procured jewelry for the Princess, cloth for the livery of the head-chamberlain, and delicacies for the head-cook, was also quite ready to negotiate loans.

This would constitute in itself a meritorious beginning, and would allow the Hebrew to appear as a useful member of society, if he had confined himself to taking a moderate remuneration for his work, and had not mixed himself up in other affairs. But the Hebrew has no time and no inclination for the simple discharge, for a moderate remuneration, of such duties as have been mentioned; for him they are rather the opportunity to make other people dependent upon him, and to acquire a determining influence over affairs. Everywhere he plays the role of Joseph in Egypt, whom Potiphar placed in authority over all his property, and who soon lulled his lord and master into such a state of comfortable indolence that it is said of the latter: "He made everything over into Joseph's hands, and no longer took interest in anything except eating and drinking." This was the first step for Joseph towards the all-powerful position of the finance-man of Egypt, by which he fleeced country and people of the shirts off their backs (see Genesis 37-41).

Thus we see that the Hebrew does not aim merely at profit; he desires to exploit, to rule, and to subjugate. He soon finds out how to place the yoke of compulsion onto his confiding clients, and to keep a tight hand over them. He is unfamiliar with the maxim: "Live and let live." He releases nothing until he has seized all for himself.

But it does not matter what the Hebrews do; Sombart always knows how to direct a ray of sunshine upon their deeds. Speaking of our time, he mentions boastfully that, at the present day, the Court Jew has been done away with, and that the loaning of money—we could also say usury—to princes and states is no longer the business of one individual, but that all opulent Jewry takes part cooperatively in the business. And Sombart regards this also as a virtue on their part. He says:

> And now again it is the Jews who have helped to perfect this modern system of loans. It is they who have made themselves superfluous as monopolizers of money-lending and, by so doing, have contributed so much more to the founding of the great states.

What nobility of soul!—or so one might exclaim. But one really does not know if it is supposed to be praise or blame, when Sombart ascribes the "commercialization of economic life" to the Hebrews, understanding thereby, the reducing of all economic events into sheer commercial transactions. He discerns, as the final accomplishment of capitalism, the "transmutation of political economy into a series of Stock Exchange operations." He says:

First of all, a process is completed that one might call 'the manufacture of credit,' and the materialization of it in the shape of paper securities. Closely connected with this is the occurrence, known under the name of 'mobilization' or, if one prefers a German word, the marketing of these claims.

We have accustomed ourselves, in modern times, to understand by the word 'credit' something full of value, and precious in the highest degree. In plain English, sober-minded people call it "begging for a loan economy." One might just as well call it "objectifying claims" or the "conversion of all values into paper form"—which is to say: the transformation of all objects of value into easily transportable promissory notes. I admit the creative part that the Jews play in this transformation of economic life; it is quite another question whether this is wholesome for mankind.

I don't deny that objects of value, when transformed into paper (shares, mortgage bonds, bills, etc.) are a commercial convenience, and facilitate the flow of business on the various markets. But in this mobilization of all values lies also a great economic danger. Imagine, for instance, that a millionaire acquires the power of buying an unheard-of quantity of such paper securities, including the title deeds to a considerable portion of our Fatherland, which he then sticks into his pocket in order to take up residence in some foreign country. In every case, everything, including even the land itself, is thus easily made an object for speculation. And in all this, the Hebrew pursues, if not a conscious calculation, then solely his racial instincts. The nomad, in whom a sense of constancy and of a desire for a permanent habitation is lacking, wishes to make everything transportable, so that it may easily be carried with him wherever he goes—just like the silver and golden vessels that were taken out of Egypt.

The forerunner of paper security—namely, the salable or negotiable promissory note—is already found in the Bible and in the Talmud, as Sombart points out. The loaning of money and commercial business are actually the twin suns around which the whole essence and being of Jewish life revolve. Hence, there is nothing to wonder at if these two conceptions find an important place in the religious writings of the Jews. One can learn from a certain passage taken from the Rabbi Shabtai Cohen, and whom Sombart quotes, that the activity of the Rabbis extends also into business organization. The passage cited speaks of regulations introduced by the Rabbis for the extension of commerce. The Rabbi in question regrets that the trade in promissory notes cannot be very large on account of the amount of detail involved in a transaction of this kind; he boasts, on the other hand, that in his time (in the 17th century) the turnover in notes or paper acknowledgments was considerably greater than in actual property, and he states therefore that the decrees of the Rabbis for the extension of trade deserve the closest consideration.

One can see from this that the role of the Rabbi in Jewry is something quite different from that of a Christian pastor or clergyman. The Rabbi is not only priest and guardian of the soul, but he is also adviser on business matters,[6] and—as we will learn later on—political organizer and leader of his congregation.

The conversion of all economic values into paper arises, in the case of the Hebrew, still more from the mania for creating continuously fresh material for trade. Trade appears to him to be an end in itself—as the real object of life, and all his thoughts are concentrated on the extension of trade. To us, trade is only a necessary kind of evil, a servant, as it were, to production and consumption; the Hebrew, however, regards the world as having been created for the sole purpose of being turned into a huge shop full of goods. Whilst we regard each promissory note, each paper security, simply as representing a receipt for a loan or value received, the Hebrew makes 'trade-material' out of it. Sombart says, "The effect (paper security) is intended, by its very nature, for traffic, and if it is not traded, it has failed to perform its function." This is a specifically Jewish perception that requires further explanation, and we read at once that it is grounded upon the nomadic worldview:

> Any peculiarity that our economic life experiences from the perfection of paper security is derived exclusively from its mobility—something that makes it extraordinarily well-adapted for quick transfer.

We ask: is "quick transfer" of possession necessary for a healthy economy? Is it indispensable for a settled and productive nation? Do we accomplish anything constructive by the continual 'shoving-about' of values in all directions? Sound, economically-productive circles have no interest in such a constant change of owners; steadiness and certainty of duration are far more desirable. But the Hebrew combines this easy salableness of values with yet another purpose: The traffic in paper securities, owing to the

---

[6] This is made clear by the fact that the Stock-Exchange prices from Berlin are announced by telephone to the provincial Rabbis at the same time as they are announced to the provincial banks.

perpetual shifting in values on the Stock Exchange, means a constant opportunity for profit-making. And we shall learn later on how this profiteering is carried on at the expense of the honest and productive section of the community.

Examining such matters, we see a contrast between two worldviews. The settled man desires continuance and steadiness, the nomad desires rapid change and mobilization. Sombart admits that this strange principle of easy change of ownership, and of constant alteration of values, was foreign to both German and Roman law, and that it likely had its origin in Jewish mentality.[7] This is consistent with the fact that the law of mobilization is the law of sudden change and revolution. Sombart calls the Jewish law "traffic-friendly"—but this is only a circumlocution for the idea of mobilization and the shifting of values.

While we would like to see trade confined to what is necessary, the Jew strives to extend it beyond all limits, and into every conceivable domain. The Hebrews are constantly trying to attain the utmost freedom from restriction for trade. Under the phrase "protection for the market," they demand an unconditional recognition of, and sanction for, all trade customs. They go so far as to demand that stolen articles found in the hands of Jewish "receivers" not be reclaimed by the lawful owner. This principle has already been enunciated in the Talmud, and it has been repeatedly corroborated, especially in the Middle Ages, by the privileges given to the Jews. According to Jewish perception, the *right to buy* ranks higher than the *right to own*, and legislation aims almost at giving privileges to receivers of stolen goods.

---

[7] See Richard Schröder, *History of German Law*.

Chapter 8
The Stock Exchange

The Jewish world of trade and mobilization achieves its greatest triumph on the Stock Exchange. The Stock Exchange might well be considered—although Sombart does not claim this on behalf of the Jews—a Hebrew invention in every respect.

Originally it was merely the meeting place for merchants, where they bought and sold their goods. All trade on the Exchange related originally to "effective" goods, that is to say, to goods that actually existed, and which could be physically produced on demand. Even today, business of this kind is still transacted on the Exchange, but the extent of trade there has increased considerably. Not only are goods bought and sold there that are really warehoused somewhere else, but also goods that can only be produced later—yes, goods even that do not exist and which never will exist. It is justifiable, under certain circumstances, to secure in advance, delivery of goods for a future date, and therefore purchase-contracts on the Exchange that refer to a future delivery of the goods. The manufacturer who has pledged himself for months in advance to supply certain of his customers with certain wares at regular intervals is naturally also interested in securing the necessary raw material in advance. He accordingly buys "on term," that is to say: he enters into contracts today at fixed prices that shall only become "effective" at a future date or "term."

Trade of this kind is not intrinsically objectionable, although it was simply forbidden in the sound mercantile exchanges of olden times. But at any rate, this method of doing business opened the path to unlimited speculation. By this means, large quantities of goods can be bought and sold that are never delivered, and which are never intended to be delivered. Buyer and seller make a bet, so to speak, as to whether a commodity at some future date will cost more or less than at the present moment. Settlement is effected on the idea that one party has to pay out, on the appointed date, the difference between the arranged price and the price quoted, for the day in question, on the Stock Exchange list.

Thus, this "term trading" becomes simply a business of differences, and does not rank any higher than gambling and betting. This game of "differences" might appear harmless if it were a private affair, and did not exert its influence upon the genuine fluctuation in the prices of goods. But when business in "differences" is undertaken to a far greater extent than the real business purchases, the basic price at which the business in "differences" has been concluded must, of necessity, influence the price of the actual goods. The fixing of the daily price results from the general average of the prices at which the purchases have been concluded and, generally speaking, one is not able to say whether the latter represent genuine sales of goods, or merely a gamble in "differences." It can also be the case that someone buys himself free from his contract to deliver the actual goods, by paying the price-difference. Accordingly, there is no hard and fast line between genuine purchases and mere speculations in prices.

The essence of the so-called "speculation" consists in making sham purchases on the Stock Exchange so as to create an artificial influence on the movement of real prices. Apart from the fact that this gambling in "differences" ruins many a person, it is thoroughly repugnant to the sense of sound political economy. Strictly speaking, every purchase that does not aim at satisfying the requirement of the moment, but has rather the object of utilizing the occasion to secure cheap goods for a future date, is of a speculative nature. It is more usual, however, to understand "speculation" on the Stock Exchange as sham purchases and trading with imaginary values, as opposed to trade in real values.

The machinations connected with unsound business on the Exchange, and which first appear on the produce markets, assume a more pronounced character on the Stock Market. Here, along with national loans, it is particularly railway stocks and shares in industrial undertakings that form an important object of trade. The computation of the value of the share depends, generally speaking, upon the rate of interest paid during recent years; but that is not by any means an infallible guide as to future returns.

The art of steering events on the Stock Exchange consists in creating, above all things, a favorable atmosphere. Reports are inserted in the newspapers in order to cast a more or less favorable light upon an undertaking, and to anticipate a higher or lower dividend as the case may be. The public is thus seduced into buying or selling the securities in question. Certainly, a pre-condition to the success of this maneuver is that the public press puts itself at the disposal of the powers in question. This is easily managed. Some of the matadors of the Stock Exchange are themselves owners of newspapers, or are connected with them as secret partners. Yet others, through the agency of influential banking firms, procure favorable notices from the press by making considerable payments to the latter in the form of costly advertisements. By far the largest portion of the public press, in all countries, is actually under the influence of the magnates of the Stock

Exchange, and to this extent Sombart is correct when he states that the Jews took a substantial part in the development of the modern Stock Exchange.

But business on the Stock Exchange only yields a sure result when it is transacted by secret collusion—that is to say, by gangs or bands. If individual always opposed individual on the Stock Exchange, the formation and quotation of prices would pursue an even and reliable path, and profit and loss would be more or less dependent upon chance; it might then well happen that what was lost one day might be regained on another. Matters take a very different course when a secret organization of certain brokers exists, and when all the partners, who have a mutual understanding, operate simultaneously according to a prearranged plan. In a case of this kind, the price is like a ball that can be tossed around at the pleasure of this organized clique.

Consider the following: the number of shares actually on the market are limited. One knows, for instance, the exact number of shares in any undertaking. If now, several of the larger banking firms and stock brokers are working in conjunction with one another, they can very easily ascertain what number of the shares of any undertaking are held by the public, and what number are in the hands of the operating banks and brokers. The aim and object of the secret confederates—and here I will make use of a Jewish expression and call them the "*Chawrusse*"—consist, as one can easily understand, in buying up paper securities at a low price, and in selling at a high price. And this business is effected in the simplest way possible. As soon as any particular paper security is extensively held by the public, all that is necessary to do is to arouse suspicion about it. The view is spread abroad, by means of suitable and cleverly-worded press notices, that the security in question has no prospects, and that only a poor dividend can be expected. At once, a number of the holders attempt to get rid of the shares in question, and the price steadily falls as the shares are offered for sale. The large stock brokers help in the process by instructing their agents on other stock exchanges to offer whatever they hold of the security in question, at declining prices. They do not run any risk by doing this, for no one wants to buy the discredited shares. Thus, by reason of these carefully planned and continued influences, the price of the paper security in question falls, day by day.

Then, and only then, after a heavy fall in the price has set in, does the Chawrusse begin, in all secrecy, to carry out their purchases. They buy up the shares, at the greatly depreciated price, and know how to maintain it at this low level until they hold the greater number of the shares in their own hands. Then the page is at last turned over. All at once, the "well-informed" financial press announces that the former suspicions regarding the prosperity of the undertaking were without any foundation, and that it promises, on the contrary, to pay an excellent dividend very shortly. Immediately the price of the shares begins to "recover," to use a stock exchange expression. But for the time being, the Chawrusse withholds all the "material" i.e. the shares. The tension due to the growing demand and the scanty supply contributes to a further rise in the price, and it is only when the Chawrusse consider that their profit is large enough that they begin to unload their stored-up shares at the enhanced price. If, after the course of several weeks or months, as the case may be, they have relieved themselves of enough of their treasure, they turn the point of the spear in the opposite direction. They suddenly make a forced sale of the remainder of their shares, and arrange that the financial press publishes corresponding articles; the price gives way, and the old game begins once more. It is instructive to note that, in these transactions, it is invariably the Chawrusse who gain, and the dear Public who are duped.

Some simple-natured people look up with respectful awe to the ingenious heads who direct our stock exchange affairs, and who, in spite of all fluctuations on the market, always manage, with "miraculous certainty," to secure the advantage. The people imagine that an almost superhuman capability is requisite to survey the situation on the money market aright, and to grapple with the circumstances as they alter. Good, trusting folk! If they only knew how it was done, they might well say, to paraphrase an old saying: "One cannot believe what little understanding is required to rule over the stock exchanges of the world."

The indispensable condition for success, however, is concerted action: the Chawrusse. He who ventures into combat on the Stock Exchange as a freelancer must not be surprised if he emerges from the struggle stripped of all his feathers. Success is assured only to organized bands. It is a well-known fact that, in every game, if two or more of the players have a secret understanding with one another, they always gain the advantage, and "let the others in." They know how to communicate by secret signs, and play into one another's hands. On this account too, one of the conspirators can even attach himself to the losing side without the least apprehension, for he knows that he will receive his share of the profits eventually from his fellow conspirators. This is the secret of the Stock Exchange. And it is only the elect of the people of Israel who form the conspirators of the Chawrusse. The transactions of the Stock Exchanges today are *nothing less than swindling*; artificial quotations are made by the Chawrusse, supply and demand are artificially created, and all this takes place with the sole object of fleecing the unsuspecting, productive nations by the continual rise and fall of the Stock Exchange prices and of adding incessantly to the wealth of Israel.

A Mania for Speculation

This important secret, of which Sombart has unfortunately revealed nothing,[1] is the secret combined action of the Hebrews; it extends over many other domains as well. This secret hand-in-hand working has always been the chief strength of the Jews, and has naturally always given them an advantage over all sound, straightforward traders. We are not at all astonished when we read in Sombart: "Already in the year 1685, the Christian merchants of Frankfurt were complaining that the Jews had gained possession of the entire broker- and bill-discounting business." And that in the year 1733, the Hamburg merchants lamented that: "The Jews were entirely masters of the bill-discounting business, and had outstripped our people."

Let us then grant to the Hebrews the glory that Sombart claims for them; i.e. of being inventors of trading in "futures" and of being the fathers of speculation on the Stock Exchange. And this questionable practice is introduced by the Hebrews wherever they settle. During the 13th and 14th centuries, when they were present primarily in northern Italy,[2] Sombart informs us that stock speculation was, at that time, in full swing in Genoa, and that speculation in the form of "futures" and "differences" was carried on to a considerable extent at Venice—so much, in fact, that a prohibition had to be issued in 1421 against trading in bankers' bills.

The mania for speculation accompanied the Hebrews to Holland as well, where, in the course of the 17th century, the shares of the East India Company furnished the material for a malevolent bit of stock speculation—which Sombart identifies as the source of modern Stock Exchange speculation. Here also was issued a proclamation of the States General in the year 1610, forbidding "the sale of more shares than one actually possessed." This prohibition was followed by many others—but "naturally without having the slightest effect," writes Sombart.

Sombart boasts that the Jews invented dealing in shares. A questionable glory indeed, for, in a report from the French ambassador at the Hague to his government in 1698, the former expresses himself in an extremely

---

[1] Anyone who desires further information on this subject will be enlightened by Kolk's *The Secret of Stock Exchange Quotations* (1893).
[2] The business of loaning paper securities (Lombardising?) which takes its name from the Lombards, dates from this period.

outspoken manner: "the Jews have control of the entire business in paper securities on the Stock Exchange, and regulate it as they see fit." And according to the same report,

> the prices of shares fluctuate so incessantly that they give rise to transactions several times in the course of the day, a kind of business that rather deserves the name of gambling or betting—all the more, as the Jews, who are at the bottom of all this activity, carry out masterstrokes of artifice, by which the people are again and again 'let in' and made fools of.

Sombart informs us, with reference to the activity of the Hebrews in England during the reign of William III (1689-1702), that the chief negotiators of the first loan were Jews; they were ready at hand with their advice when the king began his reign. A rich Hebrew, Medina, was banker to the English Commander-in-chief, Marlborough (1650-1722), and paid the commander a fixed yearly salary of £6000, for which he (Medina) acquired the right to receive all war intelligence direct from headquarters.[3] Sombart explains:

> The victories of the English army brought as much profit to him [Medina] as they reflected glory on the soldiers of England. All the tricks of raising and depressing prices, false news from the theater of war, the pretended arrival of couriers, the secret coteries on the Stock Exchange, the entire hidden machinery of Mammon, were well-known to the first father of the Bourse, and were utilized by them to the utmost extent.

We then learn, concerning Roderigo Lopez (1517-1594), Queen Elizabeth's physician, that he made a large fortune by circulating a false report that the Queen was dead, and by buying up the public funds that consequently fell in value.[4] Nathan Meyer Rothschild received reports in Brussels from Jewish spies concerning the Battle of Waterloo, so that he could travel back with the news to London by express post and special ship. On his arrival, he circulated a false rumor concerning the result of the battle which was the immediate cause of a tremendous drop in the prices of English and German paper securities. He bought up the depreciated securities

---

[3] Ed.: Solomon de Medina (1650-1730) was the first Jew to be knighted in England.

[4] He ended on the gallows, a fate that he incurred for betraying English interests to Philip II of Spain (Drumont, *Jewish France*).

secretly in enormous quantities. Then, 24 hours later, the London Stock Exchange learned the true issue of the battle, and at the same time, that Rothschild had made fools of them, but by then he was many millions richer.

Sombart admits that John Law (1671-1729), the author of the notorious fraud in the shares of trading companies, may have been a Hebrew, and that his real name was probably Levi.

Of kindred spirit to these Jewish "statesmen" was the notorious "Demon of Württemberg:" Süss-Oppenheimer (hanged 1738).

The Hebrews also introduced the trading in shares into Hamburg in the 18th century, and carried it on to such an outrageous extent that the Hamburg Council issued a proclamation in 1720 prohibiting the practice. Today, it is represented as being the narrow view of reactionary circles to speak of business on the Stock Exchange with anything but the most profound respect; but as Sombart himself confesses, this view of those who are called today "provincials" and "agrarians" was, in the 18th century, the settled opinion of the sound merchant. During the debate upon John Bernhard's Act in the English Parliament in 1733, the "infamous practice of stock speculation" was condemned unanimously by all the speakers. See what our Hebrews have accustomed us to in the meantime!

Of this time period, Sombart has already said:

> Public debts were regarded as the shameful side—"*Partie honteuse*"—of national life. The best men saw, in the rapidly advancing indebtedness, one of the worst evils that could be inflicted upon the community.

The extension of the market in shares from 1800 to 1850 is regarded by Sombart as being of equal significance as the expansion of the House of Rothschild:

> The name of Rothschild means more than the firm; it means all of Jewry, as far as the Stock Exchange is concerned. Only with the help of their compatriots could the Rothschilds reach their position of power that dominates all others, and obtain entire mastery of the Stock Exchange.

This is a complete confirmation of the "playing into one another's hands" that characterizes the Jews, and which I have emphasized; this is the

"Chawrusse" and its secret; this is organized Jewry that has used the Stock Exchange to bleed the nations. Sombart says further:

> If, in this way, the sphere of the money-lender was considerably extended, the Rothschilds also took good care to adopt further measures for squeezing the last penny out of the community. This was brought about by skillfully utilizing the Stock Exchange for the purpose of emission or issuing into circulation.

This step on the part of the Rothschilds soon brought into this kind of activity other followers and imitators, in the shape of "banks of issue or emission." These deflect German 'spare' capital abroad to an incredible extent (but not to our colonies!),[5] thereby depriving the home country of the money required for economic purposes, and depressing the value of our national paper securities, upon which countless citizens depend for the proper and regular payment of their interest. These "banks of issue" secure enormous profits for themselves by their activity that is absolutely destructive to all national economy, and which is either inadequately taxed, or escapes taxation altogether. Only a severe legal restriction and even, from time to time, an absolute prohibition of the issue of foreign securities by means of the Stock Exchange could remedy this nuisance.

Sombart then continues:

> "Create a favorable atmosphere" was the watchword that, from this moment, dominated all traffic on the Stock Exchange. "Creating a favorable atmosphere" was the aim and object of the unceasing fluctuations in the market-prices, caused by the systematic sale and purchase of shares as the Rothschilds maneuvered when they were about to "launch an issue." In order to obtain command of the Stock Exchange and the money market, they used all possible means at their disposal; all paths that might lead to the attainment of the desired object were traversed; every conceivable trick of the Stock Exchange, and of anywhere else, was practiced; all levers were put into motion; money was sacrificed both in large and small sums. The Rothschilds practiced "*agiotage*"

---

[5] The amount of German "working" capital invested abroad was estimated in 1912 at 35 billion marks.

Chapter 8 – The Stock Exchange

(speculation) in the narrower French sense of the word. Until then, the great banking houses had never done this, at least openly. The Rothschilds employed the expedient of artificially influencing the market by "creating a favorable atmosphere," a practice introduced by the Amsterdam Jews for a new objective, namely, the launching of shares.

This is a literal quotation from Sombart; and it is the same thing that the wicked anti-Semites have been saying for 30 years. This great banking house placed golden fetters upon governments in order to compel them to create more public debts. The Rothschilds have made it their business to burden the different countries with the necessary public debts; with this object in mind, they understood how to artificially create the occasion for making a public or national debt. According to the latest reports (1913), they have reached Ecuador with their "opening-up activity." Soon we shall hear the press rise up, bursting into hymns of praise concerning this "land of promise."

In addition to the fabrication of public bonds and obligations by the gentlemen who manufacture stocks and shares, the "Flotation and Mortgage" business soon appeared. The industrial undertakings were "financed" and "discounted," on a miniature scale, in just the same way as the various states were on a large scale. In order to provide new trading values for the Stock Market, it became necessary to buy up the sound businesses of private people, and to convert the same into shareholder companies; that is to say, to "float" them. Otto Glagau has bequeathed to us a valuable book about the Flotation Swindle in Berlin in the years 1870-1873.[6] It shows that, in this case as well, the Hebrews were always the active spirits, and that it was only to conceal this fact, as far as the public was concerned, that a number of more or less innocent Germans—aristocrats, whenever it was possible to procure them—were pushed to the front as dummies. What Jews, and the companions of Jews, brought to pass on this occasion, belongs to the most impudent of political comedies.

When, according to their opinion, they had sufficiently plundered the masses at the time of the Flotations, and saw their swindles on the verge of collapse, they put up their tribal companion, Eduard Lasker, the then-leader and particular star of the National Liberal Party, in the Reichstag, to play the part of the suppressor of "flotations." With a great uproar, he proceeded to unearth several members of the Conservative Party whom, he

---

[6] *The Stock Exchange and Flotation-Swindle in Berlin* (1877).

asserted, were implicated in "flotations"; but he let the chief culprits, who were his tribal brethren and Liberal Party friends, escape unharmed. Thereby he secured the double advantage of diverting public resentment from the real culprits to the opposing political parties, and of posing, at the same time, as the guardian of public morality. The Jew-controlled press also helped, for all it was worth, to promote universal indignation against the unfortunate scapegoats in the Conservative camp.[7]

On 'Speculation Banks'

Our professional political economists unfortunately do not report any of these ugly facts, any more than they mention the baneful effect that the Stock Exchange game has on national wealth and on the entire economic and public life. They even lift up their voices in praise of the beneficial development of the Stock Exchange, and everything connected with it. Glagau says that the learned political economists are the chief allies of the "flotation" gang, because they so disgracefully neglect their duty as instructors and guardians of the people. He regards it as beyond doubt that many of these political economists are directly paid for their opinion and instruction by the Stock Exchange.

Sombart then proceeds to speak of the "commercialization of industry." It would be better to use plain English and to call it "converting industry into material for speculation and huckstering." Industry thus becomes a mere object of speculation for the Stock Exchange; actual production is a matter of secondary importance. "In the speculation banks," says Sombart, "capitalist development reaches its highest point.[8] With their help, the commercialization of economic life is carried to the extreme, and Stock Exchange organization becomes complete." He then says, concerning these speculation banks:

> They take part, to a very considerable extent, in speculation, either directly or else by way of the "report" business that has become, at the present moment, the mightiest and most

---

[7] The Jewish statistician Ernst Engels estimated the losses on the Berlin Stock Exchange alone, during the "Flotation Years," at 700 million Thalers; Glagau estimated twice as much.

[8] Ed.: A 'speculation bank' is today called an investment bank. The top five such banks in the world today are 1) Goldman Sachs, 2) Morgan Stanley, 3) JP Morgan Chase, 4) Bank of America, and 5) Rothschild & Co. Leadership in all these companies are heavily Jewish.

important lever of speculation. By means of loaning speculative securities, the banks are thereby placed in a position to create the impression that money is plentiful and is accompanied also by a desire to buy. Thus, on the one hand, a power of creating an upward movement in prices is easily acquired, and this power can be reversed just as easily to depress prices, by depreciating the store of available securities. The great banks accordingly hold the handle that controls the machine called the Stock Exchange literally in their hand. ... The heads of the banks, who control the Stock Exchange, tend more and more to become entire masters of economic life.

Sombart refers to the notorious Crédit Mobilier company in Paris as nothing more than a speculation bank. This "bank" was founded by two Portugese Jews, Isaac and Emil Pereire; other large shareholders in this undertaking are Torlonia of Rome, Salomon Heine of Hamburg, and Oppenheim of Cologne. Sombart also includes in the species of speculation banks, the Berlin *Diskonto-Gesellschaft*, founded by David Hansemann, and the Berlin *Handels-Gesellschaft*, which stands in close connection with the Darmstadt Bank, and the Berlin banking firms of Mendelsohn, Bleichröder, Warschauer, and the brothers Schickler. Sombart also adds: "The Jewish elements also preponderate amongst the founders of Deutsche Bank."

Thus, the international character of the speculation banks is proven, and so is the part they play in world trade.

CHAPTER 9
HOW SOUND BUSINESS METHODS ARE FORCED OUT BY THE JEWS

Sombart recognizes the Jewish influence upon the mental attitude of the capitalist towards the economy. He acknowledges that, owing to the peculiar Jewish spirit, something of an alien nature is introduced into our life, and he understands why Gentile merchants resent these conditions and display a deep sense of injury. He sees in all this a "quite natural reaction against the Jewish disposition, one that is of a fundamentally different order." He refers constantly to the pages of history in order to establish how a sound commercial spirit has protested for centuries, in a similar manner, against the disorder caused by the Jews in trade. It is everywhere and always the same complaint. Thus, the various trades and professions in Brandenburg, in the year 1672, complain "that the Jews take away the food from the mouths of the other inhabitants of the land." The mercantile community of Danzig, in the year 1717, expressed themselves in almost identical terms. In 1740, a petition to the Prince Bishop of Mainz complains "that it is a matter of common knowledge that the Jews are the cause of ruin and destruction to the rest of the community."

And it is the same story in every country to which the Jews come. In England also, the sound mercantile community resists the intrusion of the Jewish spirit with similar expressions of concern. The business people of Toulouse in France complained in the year 1745: "We implore you urgently to check the progress of this nation, as there is no doubt whatever that it will wreck the entire trade of Languedoc." In Sweden, in Poland, everywhere the same picture. A moralist of that period reports with reference to the Jewry of Berlin: "They support themselves by means of robbery and deceit that, according to their ideals, are not regarded as crimes." The behavior of the Jews was universally felt to be an offense against the good customs of the commercial community.

Sombart concedes that, in all this, there exists a battle between two antagonistic views or perceptions of the world. In the settled organization of society as it used to be, in what are called "the olden times," man was the center of interest, and the object of all regulations and laws was to render the honest worker's existence as secure as it could be. The production of goods was proportioned to the actual need, and, in the sound development of all businesses, each honest worker and trader received his fair share. Struggling to obtain unlimited profit was regarded as improper and un-Christian; nobody deliberately tried to enrich himself by damaging, or at the expense of, another. A spirit of social harmony pervaded all; each found his own path, and could exist honestly.

The Jew stepped into this state of social harmony with his entirely different mind and irreconcilable disposition. He had nothing to give—neither productive talents nor capacity for honest, straightforward work; consequently he had to secure an existence by cunning. To him, trade was not only the willing companion of, or the necessary complement to, production and consumption, but rather a way and means also for the enrichment of the individual, and to obtain mastery over others. A moderate profit meant nothing to him; he desired great surpluses that would enable him to heap up capital and thereby become a despot with the power to oppress.

This new tendency naturally brought a very disturbing element into the organic nature of society. Up until that time, all business life and all social cooperation had been based on goodwill and trust; now a hostile element stepped between, an element that did not lay claim to be trusted, and did not offer trust in anyone. The Hebrew considered that he was quite within his rights in abusing the confidence of others; he even despised them on that account, and designated trustfulness as sheer stupidity. This is the bottomless chasm that separates the Hebrews' view of life from ours, and across which no bridge will ever be constructed. The contest has always been an unequal one for the two antagonists. The Hebrew arrived as conscious opponent, with no respect for those who were not Jews. The artless Christian Aryan, however, took pains, in accordance with the teachings of his religious instructors, to see in the Hebrew a fellow man who was to be met with trust and love because he belonged to the nation that allegedly gave birth to our Savior. Thus, heart and home were opened up in all directions to the foreign intruder. The latter knew well how to profit splendidly by this, but not without sneering to himself at the confidence granted to him—something that he regarded as nothing less than stupidity. And as a matter of fact, it is fit material for derision that the Aryan nations, even to the present, fail to grasp the situation.

Certainly there has been a silent conspiracy for centuries on the part of school and church, on the part of the law and the press, to mask this situation. But once in a while, common sense perceived instinctively that the crime that the ancient Jews committed against the Savior outweighed ten times any merit that their successors might claim, on account of their descent. And then the contemporary Jews were taken for what they really were: mysterious beings, alien in blood and country, usurers, dabblers, spies, cheats, and voluptuaries.

An Old Story

The complaints from olden times are all pitched in the same key—rather like the reluctant admissions of the clergy concerning the spoliation of the departing crusaders in the 13th century, whom the Jews deprived of everything they possessed in exchange for bad equipment and faulty weapons. Thus we read—very significant with respect to the mania for dealing that dominates the Jews—in a complaint from the tradespeople of Hannover in the 18th century:

> The trade in manufactured goods has fallen completely into the hands of the Jews. The Jew, by preference, stocks his shop with foreign hats, shoes, stockings, leather, gloves, furniture, and readymade clothing of all kinds, and on the other hand, they prefer to export all raw material out of the country.

And again: "The Jews entice away the customers of their neighbors. They lie in waiting everywhere, both for the buyers and the sellers," a practice that was regarded hitherto as a gross offense against commercial etiquette. In 1685, the gold workers in Frankfurt complained that the Jews had secretly bought up, under their very noses, and carried off by means of their numerous spies, all the available scrap gold and silver. In 1703, the furriers at Königsberg expressed a similar complaint, to the effect that the Jews Hirsch and Moses, together with their followers, overreached them in the purchase and sale of furs, and caused them great loss. "When troops are quartered in the town, the Jews run after the soldiers and officers, and try to entice them into their shops, in order to take away the custom from the other tradespeople."

Under their influence also, the peddler or hawker business develops into a real nuisance. In 1672 the various trades and professions in Brandenburg complained that "the Jews run from village to village, and around the towns, hawking their wares, and forcing the same upon the inhabitants." In Frankfurt on the Oder, the complaint was "that the Jews pursued possible customers in all directions—travelers in their hotels, the nobility in their castles, and the students in their lodgings," because they are not content, like the other tradespeople, to lay up goods in their storerooms, but attempt to force the sale of their wares and thereby to deprive the other business people of their share of the local trade. On the occasion of the great fairs also, the Jews overrun all the restaurants and inns, in order to entice all possible customers to themselves. It is reported from Nikolsburg in Austria that the Jews have acquired for themselves all the trade, all the money, and all the material. They lie in wait for customers outside the town, force themselves upon the travelers, and try to keep them away from the Christian establishments. They listen to every conversation, keep watch for the arrival of strangers, and know how to derive benefit immediately from every kind of disaster, by hastening to the homes of those concerned with their offers and quotations.[1]

Indeed, their pestering is sometimes carried so far that it becomes physical compulsion; they attempt to drag reluctant customers by force into their shops, a mode of operation—the so-called "tearing" at a person—that was in full swing on the Mühlendamm in Berlin during the 1870s and 1880s. The Hebrews lay in wait at their shop-doors, like spiders in their webs. They stopped any passerby who appeared to show the slightest interest in their goods that were spread out even up to the pavement, and tried either to entice, or to tug him by force into the shop. This offspring of Jewish business enterprise has been called "vermin-picking" business, a fact also cited by Sombart. Yes, the Jewish street-dealers even went so far as to erect their stalls, or to push their barrows, straight in front of the shop of a Christian competitor in order to deprive him of his customers.

Attracting customers to himself, by any and all means, is the sole aim and object of the Jewish dealer. In doing so, he does not allow any consideration of decency or shame to stand in his way. The Hebrew was the first to force hostility, as a principle, upon our business life—that pernicious principle that asserts that the most important task in trade is to alienate the customers of other men, and to regard any and every means as permissible that can be utilized for trampling underfoot all business competitors.[2]

The Hebrew has also carried advertising and soliciting in the newspaper to a degree where it is not only offensive to good taste but outrages public decency as well. Some years ago, the phrase "Down with all competition!" was the favorite cry of the Jewish advertisers. The degeneration of

---

[1] Ed.: A remarkable anticipation of the modern-day "ambulance-chasing lawyer."
[2] If only there was some way of making all this known throughout all classes of our community! Then one might indeed expect that the displeasure of all honest people would be directed against such conditions, and that the pernicious stranger would be driven out of our national life once and for all. But in this respect, the public press fails completely; in fact, it places its services, with preference, at the disposal of the Jews.

newspaper advertising brought yet another disadvantage in its wake: the public press became more and more dependent upon Jewish charlatans and quacks. In order not to lose the advertisements, the press placed itself completely at their service. And today no public newspaper of importance dares to publish anything derogatory to Jewry, if it does not wish to lose all Jewish advertisements on the spot, and to be boycotted by the whole Jewish community—a consequence of the unholy alliance.

Thus, under Jewish influence, trade has completely lost its original, sound motive of acting as intermediary between producer and consumer, and has degenerated into laying cunning snares for customers. And it is on this account that the complaint of all sound business people, in all ages, bears always the same refrain: *the Jew ruins trade because he disregards all rules and refuses to recognize any principle except the acquisition of money.*

Certain Jewish Tricks of the Trade

An especially questionable kind of trade tactic practiced by the Jews consists in taking undue advantage of the difficulties that beset the producers of goods. Thus, the Jews know well how to utilize the occasional embarrassments, both of workman and manufacturer, to force the goods out of them at exceptionally low prices; indeed, they also know how to *create* a difficult situation for the producer, and to lead him into it by all manner of tricks. This complaint is an ancient one. Hence, Sombart recounts a report of the wholesale traders of Augsburg in the year 1803, which reads as follows:

> The Jews endeavor to profit out of universal distress; they force goods out of the man who happens to be in urgent need of money, at scandalously low prices, and upset and ruin normal trade by selling these goods again at absurdly inadequate prices.

Unfortunately, ever since the decline of the trade guilds at the beginning of the 18th century, even the authorities have been shortsighted enough to support this fundamentally Jewish policy. They allowed themselves to become corrupted by the cheap offers of the Hebrews, and never asked by what means the Jew came into possession of the goods that he could offer so cheaply. A memorandum of the Chancery of the Court of Vienna, dated 12 May 1762, states bluntly: "it is advisable to make military contracts with the Jews, as their quotations are much lower".[3] It is a remarkable fact that, despite this, the Jewish military contractors have always become rich. It stands to reason that they must have swindled someone, whether it was the State, or the unfortunate manufacturers.

The ways and means by which the Hebrew obtains possession of cheap goods are many; we have already mentioned the spoliation of the producer who happens to be in difficulties. But the Hebrews also utilize the collapse of business concerns to get hold of parcels of goods very cheaply; they even know how to *bring these collapses about purposely*, by scheming amongst themselves in order to transfer the goods from one to the other at a very low price. An example: Levi, who has just opened a new business, knows how to obtain goods on credit. For several times in succession, he conscientiously fulfills his obligations to the merchant who supplies him, and by so doing, gains the latter's confidence. Gradually he increases the quantity of goods ordered, and keeps on taking longer and longer credit. The supply merchants, obviously impressed by the apparent development of the business, are loath to lose such a good customer, and continue to give longer and longer credit. Levi, however, with the help of his compatriots, sells the goods far under the proper price—which is to say, he becomes the middleman for other Jewish businesses that "cut" prices. He sells the goods to these businesses at a price that is actually lower than what the factory charges him; when he has stretched his credit as far as he dares, he declares himself bankrupt. The supply merchants, who have been under the impression that their customer held a large stock of goods, discover an empty nest, and have to satisfy themselves by agreeing to accept from the debtor a meager percentage of what he really owes them.

There is no particular skill or art in delivering goods, or in other words, selling cheaply, if such means are adopted. The Hebrew, who knows only too well how to reverse the order of things, has, in this case also, reversed the normal business principle: sometimes he does not try to make a profit out of his customers, but makes his gain at the expense of the manufacturers and supply merchants. He sells the goods actually cheaper than he buys the same, and ends by never paying for the greater part. Ironically, this peculiar method of carrying on business has actually procured for the Hebrew the reputation of being a philanthropist, because he "helps"

---

[3] We know only too well, from our experiences in mobilizations since that time, the result of following this advice. Hundreds of thousands of soldiers, belonging to the various European powers, have sacrificed their lives or their health in order to satisfy the profiteering greed of Jewish contractors, who supplied clothing of inferior quality, and adulterated food and medication.

poor people to obtain cheap goods. But only a few are aware that he does this out of other people's pockets. Since time immemorial, the Hebrew has been a master of the art of doing good at someone else's expense.

It is a matter of common knowledge that he is always ready to receive goods that have been acquired in an underhanded and illegal manner. He buys pledged, attached, and stolen goods whenever the opportunity presents itself. He prefers to acquire wares that are cheap, either because they have flaws or because they have been rejected for some other reason—the so-called "job-lots," which genuine business people will not accept on account of small imperfections. The Hebrew reckons on the shallow nature and general lack of any expert knowledge on the part of the public, and knows well how to dispose of such articles to his customers under the guise of genuine wares that are worth every penny of the price.

Lowering of the Standard of Production—Cheap and Bad

Sad to say, due to the influence of Jewish machinations, the manufacture of many products has degenerated. Any notion of quality in goods has, for the most part, disappeared; and a great demand has sprung up, by contrast, for the production of cheap and trashy goods. The genuine business people do their best to protect themselves against this unclean traffic, and try to take action against the "cutter" when he tries to pass off his inferior wares as being equal in value to those of better quality. The trade protection associations have frequently brought suits against the "cutters" with satisfactory results; but in many cases, trade experts have been obliged to concede that differences in the quality of the material, and of the labor, are extremely difficult to establish, even when they are responsible for a reduction of 10% or 15% of the value of the genuine article. And thus the Hebrew is allowed to keep on reducing the quality of the goods, and to injure the producers as well as the purchasing public.

Our average public consumer of today is unfortunately far too frivolous to attach value to genuine goods. The Hebrew has carefully trained the consumer, above all, to seek for and find its satisfaction in "modernity" and "appearance," instead of insisting on appropriateness and durability. Most people want to possess what glitters and dazzles for the moment, quite indifferent as to whether it soon loses its value and has to be thrown away, only to be speedily replaced by some new and equally cheap and showy trash. Thus, not only does the national economy enter upon a dangerous road, but so too the national mode of living; and national morals follow. The glitzy lights of the great department stores are not only destructive to genuine business but are ruinous to the nation itself.

As Sombart concedes, the Jew is the author or originator of the "replacement" in its most extensive sense. In plain English: the Jew is the author or originator of adulteration and falsification in trade.

Many inferior goods that have been produced according to the Jewish principle have actually received the name "Jewgoods." Thus, one speaks of "Jew-linen," "Jew-cotton," and other "Jew-stuff." A particular trick in Jewish business circles consists in giving less than the proper weight or measure, especially in the case of goods where weight and measure are difficult to check.[4] When the new [metric] system of weights was introduced, purchasers, according to custom, still demanded an extra "quarter of a pound," or whatever the extra amount might be, and the Hebrew knew only too well how to utilize the opportunity by giving only a fifth instead of a quarter. It is also a matter of common knowledge that a "Jew's gross" is only about 100 instead of 144. If it was formerly maintained that the Jewish method of trading was justified because his lifestyle was humbler and he could subsist on very modest means, this argument is no longer valid. It is notorious that the Hebrews of the present day maintain a most luxurious existence, and their womenfolk especially endeavor to surpass all other classes—even royalty and the aristocracy—in luxury and ostentation.

I concede one point to the Jews; that by increasing cash sales to the utmost possible extent, they accelerate turnover. A fast turnover, at any rate, makes it possible for the merchant to content himself with a smaller profit and yet maintain his standard of living. It is the methods by which the Hebrew procures the quick turnover that are, for the most part, questionable, and which lead to damage in other branches of economic life. In the last analysis, trade is not the sole aim of trade; the mission of human life is not to produce as much as possible; enhanced consumption can be injurious to the individual and to the community. Just as excessive nourishment and excessive enjoyment are detrimental to the individual, so too are excessive stimulation and enhancement of economic functions.

The Hebrew happily lives by the maxim: "Fast turnover and small profits," and utilizes it as an advertisement for his particular methods. It is essentially a matter of discovering a means by which he can dazzle and infatuate.

---

[4] Women, in particular, are victims of this practice. They accept, for instance, "English thread" which is measured by the yard instead of by the meter.

Deviating Mode of Thought

The nature of the Jewish mode of thinking is such that it functions quite differently than the normal one. The Hebrew thinks, as it were, around the corner; his thoughts travel by the opposite path to the natural one. Whereas the Aryan intelligence directs itself towards production and building up, the Hebrew is meditating everywhere on confusion and exhaustion, on ruin and dismemberment. He seeks his advantage in the injuries of others, his advancement in the oppression of his fellow men who do not happen to be Jews. Jewish thought is always of a negative nature; *the Hebrew is the born bacillus of decomposition.*[5] Hence it is that a healthy human mode of thinking has great difficulty following Jewish speculative machinations; and for the same reason, the Hebrew remains an incomprehensible being to the majority of mankind. The Jew is well-acquainted with our mode of thinking and feeling, but we know nothing of his. The Hebrew reckons with certainty upon our straightforward conclusions, but we are quite unable to keep step with his crooked thoughts.

The Jew, therefore, seldom makes a miscalculation when dealing with a German, but the German is almost always mistaken when dealing with a Jew. The Hebrew tries to guide our thoughts into a direction where he can follow their sequence closely—so closely that we are bound to fall into the trap laid for us. He has learned to think the thoughts of other men in advance; we, however, have not practiced the art of following the zigzag workings of his mind. And thus, the Hebrew has acquired an apparent superiority over us which, however, in the final analysis, is only based on a habitual perversion of the natural way of thinking and feeling. His whole endeavor has but one aim, namely, to direct the impulses and activities of others in order to misuse them. The Hebrew is not a natural being with straightforward impulses; everything in him is diverted and perverted. His warped mind is simply a machine for provoking and harassing. Anyone who has not gradually learned to know the eccentricity and subtlety of the Jewish mode of thinking by long personal interaction with Jews themselves—and naturally very few Christians have had this opportunity—is

---

[5] Ed.: In original, *geborene Zersetzungs-Bazillus*. The 'biological' imagery is notable here. Also, the use of the word 'decomposition' recalls a famous phrase by German historian Theodor Mommsen, who wrote "Also in the ancient world, Judaism was an effective ferment of cosmopolitanism and of national decomposition" (*History of Rome*, 1856). A later historian, Heinrich von Treitschke, reiterated this view in 1898: "The Jews have always been an 'element of national decomposition.' They have always worked toward this."

quite incapable of pursuing the Jewish train of thought, unless he has obtained insight into the true Jewish spirit by reading the Rabbinical writings. Everything there—based on a rejection of reason and morality—is turned topsy-turvy, and is directed against the natural feelings and disposition of humanity. He who has not studied, in some measure, the books of the Talmud will never come to a right understanding concerning the Jews.

All the motives and activities of the Jewish brain are directed towards obtaining advantage and material gain. And despite this, the Hebrew imagines that, especially with regard to morality, he is a very exalted being. No one speaks more effusively about ethical values than the Jews. But whoever takes the trouble to examine what they understand by that expression, discovers that they mean the art of seeking their advantage, under the pretext that they are engaged in some praise-worthy and unselfish effort. If one wished to sum up Jewish morality in one concise phrase, it would read as follows: "Anything that brings advantage is moral." The Jew is incapable of applying a higher standard to the values in life than that of advantage or profit.

The Jewish perception can be formulated in yet another way: "Morality is the art of overreaching other people, and of creating, at the same time, the impression of a benevolent disposition—in fact, of representing what is in reality an *offense* against others as an act of *charity*." During the recent war [WWI], we had ample opportunity of admiring the masterly skill of this doctrine as put into practice by the English statesmen, who had graduated from the Talmudic school.[6]

Sombart quotes one passage from the Universal Treasure-house of Commerce, which presents the sound morality of an old-school merchant, and which stands in the most striking contrast to the present-day Jewish perception:

> If you happen to be the sole possessor of a particular class of goods, you are entitled to a fair and honest profit—that is to say, your conscience must be satisfied that you have not exceeded what is Christian-like, and your mind must be at rest upon this point.

The Hebrew is incapable of understanding a moral summons like the

---

[6] Ed.: There was indeed a large "Jewish hand" in World War One, especially on the British side. For an examination of this, see *The Jewish Hand in the World Wars* (T. Dalton, 2019).

above; it would, in fact, excite his derision. The religious and moral command always had top consideration in all Christian business in olden times. It remained for the Jew to chase all morality out of the economic world. He regards everything that brings profit as permissible. He has made the Mammonistic idea the dominating influence in our life, with his dogma: "He who serves Mammon pleases God." For the real God of the Jew is Mammon, a fact which Karl Marx, himself of Jewish descent, openly admitted.[7]

---

[7] Ed.: In 1843, Marx wrote, "What is the profane basis of Judaism? Practical need, self-interest. What is the worldly cult of the Jews? Huckstering. What is his worldly god? Money. ... Money is the jealous god of Israel, beside which no other god may exist" (*On the Jewish Question*).

CHAPTER 10
JEWISH TRADE SPECIALTIES

Professional Bankruptcy

For the sound tradesman, bankruptcy is the severest misfortune that can befall him. In most cases, it spells for him not only economic, but also social and moral ruin. The German tradesman, therefore, devotes all his energy, and all his reserves, to avert this calamity. Just as an honorable captain does not desert his sinking ship so long as he is alive, many German merchants have considered themselves unable to survive the disgrace of bankruptcy. In any case, a genuine German tradesman emerges from his bankrupt business as poor as a church mouse, and must conceal his public disgrace.

In this respect also, Jewish morality and mode of thinking are of quite a different kind; they have brought about a change which, unfortunately, has exercised a demoralizing influence upon the conceptions of honor that were prevalent in the German commercial community. In the Hebrew's eyes, there is nothing dishonorable about bankruptcy; it is something to be regarded, in any case, purely as a business accident, and which, on that account, may evoke the sympathy of kindred souls, but which otherwise hasn't the slightest effect on one's social standing. No, indeed: the Jewish mode of thinking regards bankruptcy as a stroke of good luck, bringing rich profit in its wake. This idea is far from being some invention of the comic papers. This is in accordance, not only with the peculiar Jewish morality, but also with the entire tactic of the Jewish business system or entity.[1]

The Hebrew knows well how to begin a business with someone else's money. According to his solution—which is often thoughtlessly echoed by non-Jews—"credit is equivalent to hard cash." He sets to work to obtain credit from other firms and banks—preferably from non-Jews—assisted in this respect by his racial brethren, who extol his business capacity and reliability with all their might. If the business succeeds, and reaches the stage where a quick and profitable turnover is assured, the Hebrew meets his engagements punctually, and perhaps, works himself up into the position of a truly sound business man. If, however, the shop location has not been well-chosen, and the right type of customer does not appear, the owner

---

[1] In an article written in the year 1816, it is stated that "the Jew forces trading to a height that would make a sound Christian merchant dizzy."

alters his tactics; he now steers a straight course for bankruptcy, one that shall be as profitable to him as possible.

He succeeds in this by the following maneuver: Instead of reducing, or even entirely withdrawing his orders, so as to allow for the deficiency in the sale of his goods, he actually increases them. As long as he still enjoys credit, he intends to make the utmost use of it. By a steady increase in his orders, he creates the impression that the business is in a healthy state. He pays punctually for part of the goods received, but lays claim, at the same time, to more and more credit; and this is willingly enough granted to him because the merchant or manufacturer who supplies him is loath to lose such a good customer. The Jew now disposes of the goods that he has obtained on credit, partly below cost. In the process, he can always find some of his racial colleagues ready to lend a helping hand, either by relieving him of large quantities of goods at half the original price—in order to sell them at extraordinarily cheap prices in their own shops—or by selling the goods again as "job-lots" to others who profess the same faith.

The pending bankruptee takes care to lodge part of the proceeds where it will be safely guarded, and utilizes the remainder to continue his payments to the manufacturer or merchant in order to retain the confidence of the latter, and to gradually drive up credit to its utmost limit. If he succeeds in all this, and is satisfied with the amount of plunder, he finally suspends payment—with the "profoundest regret" that bad times and unanticipated losses no longer allow him to carry on what was formerly a lucrative business. Creditors find scarcely any stock and no cash, and have, moreover, the trouble and expense of the investigation. The man is practically safeguarded against any legal proceedings. The books are apparently in order. The selling-off at low prices of the "job-lots" is justified by the argument that the goods, in order not to become old-fashioned, had to be sold at any price. The considerable sums that ended up in his private account are again justified by heavy expenditure in the household under the plea that, in the interest of the business and its inseparable social connections, it was necessary "to cut a dash." Briefly, it is impossible to get hold of the man.[2]

Burned by similar experiences, the creditors, for the most part, avoid costly bankruptcy proceedings, fearing that, in the end, they will have to content themselves with less than five percent. They prefer to conclude a

---

[2] One frequently reads in the newspapers that Jewish businessmen who have long been in a state of bankruptcy, still continue to live a very expensive lifestyle, and continue to move in a very exclusive social set, until they are finally declared bankrupt to the extent of several millions.

negotiated settlement, meager indeed, but which will leave them with 25% or 30% of the value of their claims. It frequently happens that a special "bankruptcy sale" is arranged that is kept going as long as possible, and by which means large quantities of goods, specially ordered for the occasion, are disposed of in the manner described above; in this way, the whole circle of "business friends" benefits to the utmost by the favorable opportunity.

Recent legislation has made some progress in slowing this unsavory practice that developed during the last decades, but it has by no means put a stop to it. As little as the Hebrew may have invented in other realms, he is a true master in the invention of new ways to circumvent or evade the laws. The fortunate bankruptee knows well how to start business again—if necessary, in another place—and probably on still more lucrative terms; if he considers it advisable, he will carry it on under the name of his wife, or one of his children, in order that his former obligations not become a source of trouble for him. And if the new business fails once again to become a success, the ingenious fellow knows how to arrange for a second, and even a third bankruptcy. The money that is lost in the process never belongs to him, but always to other people—which is to say, it is invariably the property of the confiding Goyim.

Wholesale merchants and manufacturers have been systematically plundered in this way for years by Jews, who have made it a profession or business of becoming bankrupt. This particular species of crime has contributed in no small measure to the enrichment of many Jewish families, and at the same time, to the impoverishment of many honest Germans. Those who suffer from this kind of robbery are not only the merchants who actually deliver the goods, but also the sound tradespeople who are squeezed out of existence by this unclean kind of competition. The Hebrew who has obtained his goods by evil tricks like those described, or who has, perhaps, not paid anything at all, can well afford to sell them more cheaply than the sound tradesman. And thus the "cutting" of prices and unsavory competition is promoted and sustained by those Jews who have become professional bankruptees.

If complaints concerning these abuses have been less frequent in recent years, this improvement is only partly to be attributed to the increased severity of the laws; rather, it is mostly due to great mercantile organizations of all kinds endeavoring to protect themselves against these abuses by uniting to form trade protection societies.

The Jews of today, however, no longer find it so necessary to enrich themselves by such comparatively clumsy methods of deceit; they have acquired enough money in the last few decades, and, to use the words of one particular Hebrew, they "can permit themselves the luxury of trading respectably"— with exceptions, of course!

This task has been made easy for many a Jewish businessman engaged in such practices as those just described, by the absolutely irresponsible and ridiculous ease with which one's name can be legally changed in Germany. The official announcement that, for instance, Hirsch Levi intends to call himself 'Hermann Winter,' or that Aaron Jeiteles wishes to be known as 'Arnold Krause,' appears only in the *German Imperial and Prussian State Advertiser*, a paper that is not read by anyone outside official circles. As a result, those interested seldom learn anything about what has taken place until unpleasant consequences bring it to their notice. A further advantage is taken by those with Jewish names that can be used for either given name or surname. Thus, Moses Meier Aaron, after his first bankruptcy, can reconstruct the firm as 'Aaron Meier Moses,' to be followed, when necessary, by a third reconstruction as 'Moses Aaron Meier'; he is thus in a position to escape more easily the eyes of his old creditors.

Equipped with principles of this kind, together with a complete lack of even the slightest sense of honor, the Hebrew can engage in any business undertaking with a far lighter heart than a man of another race. It is scarcely possible to find a business opening anywhere, even of the riskiest nature, that a Hebrew has not already taken in hand. A costly shop in the newly-erected premises at the junction of two streets; a questionable invention; some speculation relying on the folly or curiosity of the public—all are quickly taken up by Jews, while conscientious businessmen are still carefully considering and weighing the merits and drawbacks of the concern. A decision is actually far easier for the Hebrew than for anybody else because, in event of a failure, the conscience of the former does not trouble him in the slightest. At the very start, he says to himself: "you are not risking your own money."

The Jews certainly have the reputation of possessing great enterprise—one could also say: of possessing great audacity in business. It cannot be denied that they occasionally help to promote a sound undertaking and that many an inventor would have waited in vain if the Jews had not come to his assistance. And one may well wish that occasionally our German merchants and capitalists displayed less reserve where new plans and ideas are concerned, and did not leave this field of enterprise so completely at the disposal of the Hebrews. One must, however, take into consideration that the German promoter of any such undertaking not only risks his own money, but very often his own good name as well, whereas, in the case of the Hebrew, neither of these two all-important considerations enter into the question at all. Moreover, one must not forget a fact that has already been mentioned: In all business undertakings, the Hebrew is assured of the open (if not secret) support and cooperation of his racial friends, whereas the German, in such matters, in most cases has to rely upon himself. Even when peculiar and hazardous enterprises are concerned, the German has to reckon with the opposition of good friends and relatives that arises from denseness of perception, and a dislike of novelty. The Hebrew, on the contrary, sets to work with a light heart and in a very different frame of mind: "Risk it! — if you are not successful, well, it is only someone else who is the loser!"

And further, one must take into consideration that not only the business world but that all of public life, for the last 40 years [since 1880 or so], has been infected with the Jewish spirit, and has taken on a Jewish aspect. Jewish tendencies are supreme everywhere, and Jewish ideas and views rule the mass of the population—at least, in the cities. Everything that is born of the Jewish spirit and pursues Jewish aims, is, on that account, readily assimilated into the current of public life, and blends with it. The genuine German is completely out of the running; he is as a stranger in this new world; he cannot make himself at home amidst such surroundings. Even his best ideas do not seem to fit into this altered world; he is swimming against the stream. This holds good, not only for business, but in equal measure for art, stage, literature, and press. Jewish work is in accordance with the disposition of the times, and the factors of public life that come under the same influence promote Jewish enterprise. Thus, it is far easier for the Jewish businessman, just as it is for the Jewish author and for the Jewish artist, to "make a name for himself" than it is for the more conscientious and, for that reason, more awkward German.

The surrounding world is now estranged in many respects from the German mode of thought and action. It is therefore harder for a German to get by than it is for the eel-like Hebrew, concerning whom Franz von Dingelstedt ("Song of a Cosmopolitan Watchman") sang in 1840:

> *He forces the farmer out of his farm,*
> *He scares the shopkeeper away from the market,*
> *And partly with gold, and partly with his servile wit,*
> *Purchases the password from the Spirit of the age.*

If the German does not possess the power to create an environment for himself, suitable for his mode of thought and action, he will be lost in this Judaized world. In that case, Christian Hebbel's words will come true:

"The German possesses every qualification to gain heaven, but none to maintain himself upon Earth; and thus the time may well come when this people will disappear from the Earth".[3]

---

[3] Ed.: The remainder of this chapter has been moved to the Appendix. It focuses primarily on a critique of "department stores" that is interesting but largely tangential to the main thrust of the book, especially given that there are few references to Jews.

Chapter 11
Moral Principles in Trade

Many people consider themselves very clever when they impart advice to the merchant who complains that he is unable to hold his own against the Jews: *Do the same as the Jew!* In reality, this amounts to the following: Do not recognize any spiritual motives whatever in your mode of doing business, and descend to the level of a low money-grubber and voluptuary. The Jewish economic principle threatens to trample under foot, in our time, all other higher principles of life. That, however, is no evidence of its superiority, but of the contrary—its moral inferiority. The supposition that, if all forces have free play, the better and the nobler must win, is erroneous. On the contrary, what Goethe said remains true for all time:

No one should complain about what is base.
For it remains all-powerful, whatever people may say...

As far as ordinary, everyday life is concerned, what is low and devoid of scruple inevitably wins if it is allowed free play—just as surely as the manners of a brute prevail over those of the civilized man if both are compelled to live in the same room, and to feed out of the same trough. The task for anyone who desires to promote real culture, consists in subduing or eradicating what is vile, in order that it may not smother what is noble. Whoever desires rearing choice plants in his garden must wage incessant warfare against weeds and insect pests. Unfortunately in our time, morality belonging to the higher culture, has been neglected and forgotten—namely, the *will* to control, and the *right* to control that is the prerogative of all that is noble. When one no longer dared to think and to act like an aristocrat, everything became vulgar and plebeian; and the Hebrew is the leading dancer in the dance of vulgarity. He calls this descent into vulgarity "progress," and declares, on the other hand, that everything of an aristocratic or noble nature is out-of-date or reactionary.

In former days, society possessed an organic structure. It separated itself, practically automatically, into classes, whose rights and duties were conscientiously defined and graduated. Thus, a genuine social and moral order came into being that offered to each man such prosperity as he was entitled to, and assigned to him his due share of rights, as well as duties.

The Hebrew has shattered this ancient moral order to pieces. He has absolutely no perception for a moral structure of this kind; to his eyes, it appears merely a jumble of disconnected fragments; he is incapable of understanding the purpose of all this regulated coherence. He regards every restraint as a fetter, and as an interference with his liberty. In addition to his greed for gain, the Hebrew is, for this reason, driven by an irresistible impulse to dissolve all old-established associations and to break up all arrangements that are the outcome of social organization. *He calls for "freedom" and "equality," but whether he does so out of pure calculation, or reacts in response to some dark instinct, it is difficult to say.* At any rate, he knows for certain that, on the dissolution of all social bonds, he and his fellow conspirators will gain the upper hand in the ensuing chaos. Thus, it is that he demands—loudly and incessantly—"free play for the exercise of every kind of power!" which, in reality, amounts to: "privilege for unscrupulousness, and domination by those who conspire in secret!"

There is no doubt whatever that the phrase "freedom and progress" has provided the Hebrew with a slogan of his own. It is certainly not to procure freedom for others but to procure license for himself, and to unsettle and seduce others to desert the firm union of time-honored organization, so that, disorganized and isolated, they may all the more easily fall into his power. In spite of this, it is his constant boast that, by breaking down the old restrictions, he has introduced a "desirable and beneficial freedom" into the economic life. To a superficial observer, this may well appear to be true. But in reality, a ruthless campaign of all against all has been instituted that has certainly produced, as its first and immediate result, a release of all kinds of forces, and a stimulating and goading of economic life to an alarming extent. Now, however, it must eventually exhaust the most valuable activities of a nation, and end in complete victory for those who are most ruthless and most dishonest.

In former times, there was also no lack of stimulating competition; it was, however, of quite a different kind. The competition then was in the good quality of what was produced; whoever sold the best goods secured the most business. The Hebrew, by "cutting" prices, has reversed the nature of the competition. Today, the low value of the goods produced is the principal object of commercial rivalry of the world. Whoever can manage to offer goods at an exceedingly low price—without any consideration for the quality, or, at any rate, only with the appearance of quality—is assured of success. And whoever makes use of deception, in addition, can rely upon brilliant results. Unclean competition has usurped the position once occupied by sound and straightforward commercial rivalry.

There is no doubt whatever that the ancient guilds possessed their good features. They not only required proof of the capability of each craftsman, but they tested also the quality of what was produced. Each master had to answer for the genuineness of the goods that he produced, and the guild- or hall-mark furnished the article produced with evidence of its soundness.

At that time, there still existed a morality in business; today, that has dwindled away to such an extent that only some pitiful traces are still to be found, here and there. That mutual "hunting-down" of customers that was formerly regarded as dishonorable is today the special boast of the Hebrew. In those days there was a maxim: "No one must force his way into the business of another, or push his own business to such an extent that another citizen is ruined." This morality, this regard for one's neighbor, this social sense—these are all unknown in business life of today. The announcement that one would accept lower prices than one's competitors was regarded, in olden times, as the lowest degree of commercial impropriety. The Hebrew, with mental machinery of an entirely different kind, has no sympathy with such dignity and propriety. These appear to him merely as irksome restrictions that make it more difficult to earn money; for this reason, he rejects them. An inevitable sequel to these modern business maxims is the relaxation of all morality, and of all social ties throughout the community. One looks around and asks oneself if humanity indeed has made any moral or social advance since those olden days.

Whilst the merchant of former times knew how to preserve the dignity of the independent man, and in the course of trading, never sacrificed his self-respect in order to obtain business, the Hebrew, on the contrary, has degraded the entire domain of commerce. He has cast honor and shame to the winds, simply to create business. He has introduced into economic life a degrading hurry-and-scurry that wears the soles off one's boots in order to one-up a competitor, and sacrifices self-respect and decency sooner than allow any business to go elsewhere.

Only the grossest form of self-deception could enable anyone to imagine that this kind of mutual "hunting-down" is of any economic value. In reality, this excessive activity is accompanied by an insane waste of energy. Formerly, as now, the merchant found his customers, but the whole process was carried on in a peaceful and dignified fashion. The merchant could wait until the customer came; and the customer came, surely enough. Thus all business traffic pursued the even tenor of its way, without haste and without excitement, and a man could obtain a decent subsistence without infringement of his self-respect. Today, businessmen harry one another to death; each has the feeling that a potential robber is lurking in ambush, in his preserve, ready to waylay his customers and to take their money if he does not come up quickly to prevent it.

This hurry and nervousness, peculiar to present-day business, first made their appearance when the Jewish traders assumed the ascendency. Sombart says:

> The world, well-arranged as it used to be, with all its ancient soundness and solidity, was simply taken by storm by the Jews. We now behold this people, stride by stride, thrusting back the former economic order and economic mode of thinking.

Actually, this assault by the Hebrews on our Aryan world is not only an attack on our economic arrangements, but is simultaneously an attempt to undermine the very foundations of our moral system. Sombart certainly offers his opinion that transgressions against the standards of rectitude and morality are "part and parcel of human nature." I protest against such a conception. Certainly there have always been individuals who have not known how to remain within the limits appointed by rectitude and morality, but they were invariably denounced as bunglers and disturbers, and regarded accordingly. Respect for the restraints of law and sound morality must be set down as a fundamental and marked feature of the Aryan or Nordic mode of living and thought; and if, at present, we are scarcely aware of this quality, we at any rate know that it was abandoned only through poor examples and dire necessity. *He who wishes to compete on equal terms with the Hebrew must descend to their moral level.*

This dire necessity has forced itself upon the German merchant sooner than upon his brother traders in other countries, as Germany, on account of its political disruption, has fallen an easier prey to the Jew than any other of the ancient cultural nations. Two hundred years ago, the German name already labored under the misfortune of being used as a cloak by the Jews. When Jewish businessmen began to come into prominence, an English writer (1745) expressed his indignation that there were certain people who publicly announced their readiness to sell their goods at lower prices than their fellow traders. He stigmatized this unseemly "cutting" of prices as shameless. In England, "Dutchmen"—which is to say, taken literally, Germans—were regarded as being the instigators of this practice. It was really the inhabitants of Holland, however, who were meant, and who, up to the year 1648, belonged politically to the German Empire, and were then, as now, called "Dutchmen." It is the Dutch Jews whom we Germans have to thank for the unpleasant fact that, even now, the English and Americans refer contemptuously to the Germans as "Dutchmen".[1] The Dutch Hebrews who arrived in England at that time were the real originators of under-bidding, and of the traffic in shoddy merchandise.

The Jews were also hunted out of Spain, and fled primarily to Holland, thus making their sinister influence felt upon the destinies of we Germans. Soon after 1700, they had already begun a system of predatory culture in a recovering Germany. The book trade is an example. There, they conferred the questionable benefit of sales, on a gigantic scale, at book auctions—a practice that they had introduced in Holland because the profit by the old-fashioned method of selling individual volumes was too slow for their taste.

In modern times also, it is highly regrettable that the German merchant has accustomed himself to, and definitely accepted, all kinds of unseemly practices that were formerly a monopoly of the Hebrews. Sombart admits that Jewish ethics differ from those of mankind in general, and that those offenses on the part of Jews against public morality cannot be laid to the account of any individual in particular, but arise rather from those general ideas regarding life and business morality that are implanted in the Jewish nature. He asks:

> What then was specifically Jewish? And is one entitled to assume, in general, a peculiar idiosyncrasy in the Jewish attitude towards all enduring arrangements? I believe so, yes. And I believe that this specific Jewish characteristic of infringing the law, expresses above all the idea that the Jews regard their offenses against right and morality as not being the particular concern of any individual among them, but rather as being the discharge of a code of commercial morality that is accepted by the Jews. They regard their business habits are only those that are sanctioned by the majority of Jewish businessmen. We are bound to conclude, from the general and continued practice of fixed customs, that the Jews do not at all regard their irregular mode of trading as immoral, and consequently as impermissible; rather, they are convinced that they are acting in a perfectly moral manner—the "correct"

---

[1] Ed.: This is further confused by the word *Deutsch* ('German'), which, to English speakers, sounds like 'Dutch.'

right as opposed to a ridiculous [non-Jewish] conception of right and morality.

As a matter of fact, our moral perception of things is "senseless" as far as the Hebrew is concerned; it is too lofty for him. If there is any pronounced feature of Jewry whereby it can at once be distinguished from the rest of humanity, it is precisely this absence of moral sensitiveness. *In reality, the Hebrew is a lower type of being*, in whom all those qualities are lacking that confer a real dignity upon mankind—honor, a sense of shame, a conscience, and moral consciousness. As our entire existence is confined within these barriers, we are naturally not so free to carry on a competitive struggle, whether it be of a spiritual or economic nature, as effectively as he who declines to recognize any such restraints. Just as a conscientious person steps aside to avoid the foul mess that a swine gladly plunges into, so does a man with clean instincts revolt against following the Hebrew into the swamp of moral degradation. If he tries to do so, either he or his better nature is ruined.

And this is the peculiar difficulty of the present time: that we have allowed ourselves to be overcome by the swinish predilection of the Hebrew, that we have descended from our moral altitude in order to scuffle in the mud and mire for our daily bread. It is vain to hope that we will ever be able to elevate the Hebrew to the plane of nobler manhood; for at least 3,000 years, he has shown himself to be incapable of improvement, and he will always remain so.[2] It is a false hope to believe that this moral deficiency became so glaringly conspicuous in the Jew simply because of his confinement in the ghettos, and thus that it would leave him as soon as he was permitted to move freely in a moral community. This fond expectation has been bitterly disappointed by the actual facts: the Hebrew, with his insensibility for higher moral values, will invariably drag down the rest of the community to his own low level whenever he is permitted full scope for his baneful activity. The same presumption has shown itself to be false in countries where the Jews have enjoyed unrestricted freedom for centuries, such as England, the Netherlands, and the United States. In these lands—as well as in France, where they have had full civil rights since the end of the 18th century, and are now the undisputed masters—their nature has not changed one bit.[3]

---

[2] Ed.: See again the book *Eternal Strangers* (T. Dalton, ed. 2020).
[3] The second-most common name in the French business world is Levy (second only to Martin)—a fact that the well-known Dr. Bertillon has established by reference to the various address-books.

Sombart speaks in the highest terms of a certain Jewess, the so-called "Glückel von Hameln," who lived from 1645 to 1724, and wrote her own biography. But despite his praise, he added a significant remark: "All the aspirations and endeavors, all the thoughts and feelings of this woman centered themselves on money. For the whole 300 pages of her memoirs, she speaks of nothing else but money, and of acquiring riches." And it is this trait especially that proclaims the lower nature, and which predominates in the Hebrew. We are entitled to maintain with confidence that man is more spiritual and moral, the less he is influenced by material goods. The noblest spirits have seldom been good managers. Interests of money did not occupy their minds to any considerable extent, and was regarded as a secondary consideration. It was the noble Nazarene, who announced: "You cannot serve both God and Mammon." The more idealism one has, the more spiritual purity and dignity, and the less regard for money.

The Hebrew tries to substitute cunning in the place of idealism, and to compensate for his deficiency in moral feeling and deep instincts by a more subtle understanding. The intellect—the cool power of calculation—in no sense belongs to the higher spiritual functions; it is invariably a poor substitute for the lack of deeper spiritual forces, and for perceiving connections between things. Just as the Hebrew tries in economic life to substitute the mere possession of money for the ability to work and create, so does he try to conceal his lack of a deeper, spiritual capacity by a veneer of sham culture. It is, for this reason, very questionable praise when Sombart refers again and again to the "preeminent intellectuality" of the Jews. In reality, all that he means is mental cunning, the subtle process of calculation that is peculiar to a low order of intellect.

Deviation in the Trend of Jewish Life

The Hebrew desires to possess riches in order to obtain mastery over others, and to oppress them; and it is in this particular, where there is a great difference between the acquisition of money by Jews, and the acquisition of money by other races. Certainly there are plenty of businessmen among Aryans and Christians whose inclination is predominantly towards making money, and people who do not pay much attention to the moral side of the question, and regard all means and methods as equally good, provided that they can profit. But in one respect, they impose a restriction on themselves. They content themselves with guarding and enjoying their wealth. They do not begrudge others, besides themselves, the opportunity to acquire wealth and to enjoy it. It is quite different where the Hebrew is concerned. It is as if he is consumed by an *insatiable hatred* towards all who happen to possess something; as if he felt himself alone entitled to claim all material possessions in this world for himself and for his people; as if he could not rest so long as goods and money still remained in the hands of those who are not Jews. This frame of mind is openly expressed in the Talmudic-Rabbinical writings. One finds there, for instance: "God created the world solely for the Jews, and accordingly all property in the world belongs to the Jews." The Talmud therefore declares: "The possessions of those who are not Jews are equivalent to possessions without an owner, and the first Jew who seizes them is entitled to them."

This is no theoretical interpretation; the Jews take it and act on it in deadly earnest. They regard it as their special mission in life to travel all over the Earth in order to acquire all the possessions of the Goyim. They do not consider that they have fulfilled their duty to their God, Yahweh, until all the riches in the world are in their hands, so that they can lay them at the feet of their idol. It is for this reason that the real Jew is animated by a feverish restlessness to dispossess the Goy of his property. It is as if he suffered mental distress as long as there remained any property in his vicinity that he had not yet acquired. It is precisely this behavior that draws such a sharp dividing line between Jewish and "Christian" business practices. The Hebrew does not only desire to gain, but to ruin and enslave others as well. The young deputy Otto von Bismarck, speaking in the Landtag of 1847, furnished a classical proof of this contention:

> I will give an example that contains the whole history of the relations existing between Jew and Christian. I know a rural district where the Jewish population is numerous, where there are peasants who cannot call a single object on their farms their own property, where the entire furniture, from the bed to the stove, belongs to the Jew. Here too, the peasant pays a rent for each separate piece of furniture. The growing corn and the corn in the barn belong to the Jew, and the Jew sells the corn for bread, seed, and feeding purposes back to the peasant again, by the peck. I, at any rate, in the course of my professional duties, have never come across nor even heard of a Christian practicing usury comparable with this.

Anyone who is acquainted with the activity of the Jews in Bavarian Franconia, in Hesse, in the north of Württemberg and other places, can provide more than enough instances of a similar kind.

When doing business, the Jew is always impelled by a *double motive*: not only does he desire advantage for himself, but he wishes, at the same time, to cause damage to the other side. It is for this reason that he will not reject a piece of business that brings him in nothing, so long as it serves his purpose of weakening others. His aim is to sweep all competitors away. "He does not ask," says Sombart, "if a profit can be made or not, or if it will be necessary to work for a time without making a profit, simply in order that, later on, he may make all the more profit." This is the "great," startling innovation that the Jew has introduced into business life, and which celebrates its economic triumph in the form of the great department stores. At the back of the Jewish fighting tactic is always lurking the idea of monopoly—of sole domination—and the desire to annihilate all competitors.

A dark instinct for disturbance and destruction, for confusion and dissolution, all of which facilitate the plundering of others, is the most marked feature in the Hebrew. Amid universal ruin, the richest booty falls to his share. In this respect he resembles the vulture that, scenting its prey, hovers over the battlefield. The ruin of others brings him his surest spoil.

While the merchant of former days willingly restricted his activities to dealing in one specialty and in one particular district, the Hebrew, by preference, deals everywhere with everybody. The former division of trade, according to specialties, had the great advantage of enabling the merchant to acquire a far more thorough knowledge of his goods, and at the same time, to provide the greatest variety of choice. The Hebrew, on the contrary, whose original business occupation was always in the old clothes shop, in which secondhand articles of all kinds were to be found, has not been able to free himself of his preference for a medley of secondhand rubbish. He preserves the atmosphere of the old clothes shop, even in his emporiums of trash and his great department stores; yes, and even into his great industrial undertakings. Even Sombart perceives in all this what he describes as a characteristically Jewish touch, and acknowledges that the great department stores are almost exclusively in Jewish hands.

Sombart mentions with pride that the Hebrews are the fathers of the "hire-purchase" business; and this may well be the case. One must not believe the notion that such practice originated in a sympathy for the common man. A far different tendency is at the root of the movement. Just as the Hebrew buys up the harvest for a mere song from a peasant who is short of money, or is in other difficulties, while the grain is still on the stalk and even before it is ripe—in this way, he secures for himself, by means of the "hire-purchase" system, all the wages of the poor man for weeks and months in advance. In Goethe's *Faust*, the Jew is spoken of as follows:

> *He creates anticipations…*
> *The swine are never left to fatten,*
> *Pawned is the pillow in the bed,*
> *And the very bread that is placed on the table,*
>   *has been eaten in advance.*

The Jew knows how to prevent the unfortunate people from taking their money elsewhere, by binding them over in a legal agreement in order to acquire the proceeds of their labor for a long time in advance. The "hire-purchase" system is therefore a particular and valuable link in the chain of business operations by which the Jews suck up the money in circulation. It prevents the saving of money by those who are not Jews, and quickens the return flow, even of the smallest stream of money, into the reservoir of Judah. Certainly, all these Jewish practices have introduced a novel and peculiar atmosphere into modern business life, but it is certainly not a healthy and beneficial one.

The final injurious effects of this kind of commercial activity upon economic life are not immediately apparent, for the excessive stimulation produces, with its color, variety, and movement, a positively dazzling effect. But it is no less certain that this Jewish tendency is continually driving public morality to a lower and lower level, and is destroying all regard for the general welfare of the community. The principle of ruthless selfishness has obtained mastery. The right of the individual to enrich himself, by any and all means, has established itself firmly—even if the rest of the community suffers grievously, and both state and morality are sacrificed. Social harmony has been replaced by mutual enmity, everyone fights everyone, and this can only end in universal destruction. It is no longer a cause for wonder when active business people break down prematurely from nervous exhaustion in their best years, and when all manner of insidious diseases and social disorders arise out of this mad state of affairs. We are being continually and insistently informed that all this "must be so"—that all this is inseparable from progress. We perceive, at any rate, that the physical and mental powers of mankind are giving way under these malign influences, to the verge of complete extinction.

This method of destruction must be opposed by wise and sensible discipline, whereby all the material requirements of life can be satisfied without impairing the constitutive powers of mankind. This disciplinary system must adopt, as its standard, the principle that the preservation and elevation of mankind are more important than the mere increase of business and the accumulation of worldly riches.

CHAPTER 12
HEBREWS AS SUPPORTERS OF CAPITALISM

Sombart advances the question as to whether the Jew possesses a special capacity for capitalism. It appears most extraordinary to me that such a question should ever have been propounded. Capitalism is not an activity that calls for a special kind of *capacity*, but rather a *condition*—the cultivation or administration of which calls for certain qualifications. Even in the case of the Hebrew, capitalism, for its own sake, is not regarded as the main object, but rather as a means for increasing his own power and for enslaving those who are not Jews. Thus, the question will take the following shape: Does the Hebrew possess a special talent for amassing capital, and for giving a capitalistic formation to economic life? No one has ever been in doubt concerning this fact.

Sombart claims for the Hebrews the merit of being the founders and upholders of modern worldwide commerce, of modern finance, of the Stock Exchange—and in fact, of the commercialization of the entire economic life. Furthermore, of being the parents of free trade, and of free competition, of being the exponents of the modern spirit in the realm of business. I will cheerfully concede all this, but, at the same time it is perfectly clear to me that this modern spirit is by no means a good spirit, for it is the spirit of the disintegration of political economy, of the destruction of productive nations. The explanation of the idea of capitalism that, according to Sombart, is as follows, seems strange indeed:

> Capitalism is the name we give to that organization of economic intercourse by which two different groups of the population—the owners of the means of production, who, at the same time, carry on the work of directing, and the ordinary work-people who own nothing—cooperate. Indeed, the representatives of capital (i.e. of the requisite store of the necessary goods) are the real economic subjects, that is to say, hold the power of deciding the nature and direction of economic management, and bear the responsibility for the issue, whatever it may be.

According to this, capitalism characterizes itself as the economic method of a proletarian state that is ruled and guided unresistingly by a few financial magnates, as a new version of slavery in its most acute form. In actuality, this is the Hebrew ideal, to whom it has been promised in the Talmud that a time will come when every Jew will possess 2,800 slaves. The only question is whether the other nations regard such a state of things as desirable, and are willing to help to bring it about.[1]

This might be expressed in a somewhat more general fashion as follows: *The capitalistic economic system regards the formation of capital as the principal aim of economic activity.* According to this system, capital, and not man, is of most importance. This system places man and his spiritual needs on a lower plane than the accumulation of capital. Money-making is regarded as the first principle of life. And the object of this creation of capital? The domination and exploitation of mankind by means of loan-servitude.

Formerly the earning of money was a side issue in the economic life. The more important objective was the satisfaction of human needs by the production of the requisite goods, and the guaranteeing of the possibility of an existence for the producer, as well as for the business or middleman. The man, and the possibility of his existence, were always the chief consideration. According to the Hebrew capitalistic system, the matter was regarded in a very different light. Sombart is of the opinion that:

> Out of a systematic direction of economic affairs—for the purpose of making profit that thereby provides the incentive for the effort to expand continuously all kinds of business activity—arises, as a natural consequence, a conscious guiding or directing of all trading activity towards the supreme reasonable method of establishing and maintaining economic relations.

---

[1] Ed.: The Old Testament (Lev 25:44-46) indeed endorses slavery by Jews, of non-Jews: "As for your male and female slaves whom you may have: you may buy male and female slaves from among the nations that are round about you. You may also buy from among the strangers who sojourn with you and their families that are with you, who have been born in your land; and they may be your property. You may bequeath them to your sons after you, to inherit as a possession for ever; you may make slaves of them, but over your brethren the people of Israel you shall not rule, one over another, with harshness."

It is certainly true that economic life receives a very marked distortion in one particular direction, if one asks at every moment what profit can be made. But we certainly cannot recognize the method so described as "supremely rational"; it is rather supremely *irrational*, because it is so busily engaged in the mad accumulation of capital that it entirely disregards the aim of all culture: namely, the preservation and elevation of mankind.

In olden times, economic method was grounded firmly on the principle of organic growth and building up, but the modern Jewish economic method aims at a ruthless extermination—at the so-called 'predatory culture.' It pulls riches together from all directions at the cost of human welfare; it produces wares that, to a considerable extent, serve but one purpose, which is simply to entice and trick money out of the peoples' pockets; it creates a rich few by the indebtedness and impoverishment of the masses. But above all, it uses up human energy to such an extent that it must soon end in the exhaustion and decline of the nation.

It is characteristic of this capitalistic system that it is unable to realize the effects of its own action—that it is actually killing the goose that lays the golden eggs. Impelled by the shortsighted greed for amassing money, it wrecks the organic foundations of national life. Is there perhaps an intention behind all this? In this Jewish-capitalistic economic method, perhaps one sees the means to the end of fulfilling the ancient commandment: "You shall eat the wealth of nations".[2]

Sombart asks the question:

> What is the meaning, in the capitalistic sense, of a successful stroke of business? Naturally that this activity, with its terms and conditions, should be followed by a good result. In what way, however, is this successful result to be gauged? Certainly not by the quality of the performance. Just as little by the quantity. All the more, simply and solely, if...

The reader expects now to hear: "...if, under the operation of this beneficial capitalistic system, culture and humanity are to be conducted to a still higher plane," or perhaps: "...if morality and social arrangement are to show a gratifying advance." Oh, dear no; completely wrong! According to

---

[2] Ed.: Cf. Isaiah (61:6): "you shall be called the priests of the Lord, men shall speak of you as the ministers of our God; you shall eat the wealth of nations, and in their riches you shall glory."

Sombart, the beneficial result of this economic method is to be gauged solely as follows:

> ...if, at the end of an economic period, the advanced money is back in hand, and has brought with it something additional that we call 'profit.'

The sublime blessings of this economic system could not be stated in a more pertinent manner. One must infer that Sombart is a man with a very keen sense of sarcastic humor, who, under the pretext of recognition, wants to expose the utter barrenness of capitalism. He doesn't even ask whether an improvement in the production of goods is the result of this economic method. No: "the sole consideration is that, at the conclusion of the transaction, the gain in money or property remains in the hands of the capitalist who initiated it."

Mankind, you have no need to be alarmed; capitalistic Jewry is leading you towards a splendid goal:

> ...so that the debit and credit of the ledger shall be closed with a balance in favor of the enterprising capitalist. All the successes and all the transactions undertaken by the capitalistic organization are thus included in this effect.

What is then an 'entrepreneur' or 'contractor' in the capitalistic sense? "He is a man," says Sombart, "who has a task to fulfil, and sacrifices his life in fulfilling it".[3] Certainly there are entrepreneurs or contractors of this kind but, for the most part, they are not of Jewish origin. Certainly there are men who devote themselves to some great work and who can be described as actually sacrificing their lives for these objects. Great industrialists, such as Krupp, Borsig, Schichau, Hartmann, and many others were men of this stamp, but we certainly do not find Hebrews among them. The Rothschilds, Bleichröders, Guttmanns, and Hirschs have accumulated hundreds of millions in a few decades, but we search in vain for any great and astounding work that they have accomplished. At best, we see that they have known how to exploit, in the most cunning fashion, other men who have been the real producers, in order to amass enormous riches for them-

---

[3] A strange formulation! As if the official, the officer, the doctor, and the worker didn't also have tasks to fulfil, and thus might not be said to equally sacrifice their lives!

selves. We are unable to perceive that they have in any way risked their lives while engaged in this kind of business. They were the money lenders and speculators who finally pocketed the entire benefit accruing from the work of others, without themselves accomplishing anything worth mentioning. If Sombart means that the real promoter of undertakings must be a combination of producer and dealer, it does not say much for the Hebrew capitalists as far as the promotion or origination of undertakings is concerned because, as a rule, we find nothing of the productive element in them, only the dealer. Sombart defines the dealer in the following manner:

> The dealer is a man who desires lucrative business; all of his ideas and feelings are concentrated upon the value in money of conditions and negotiations, and who therefore consistently regards all phenomena in terms of money. For him, the world is a great market of supply and demand, of crises and occasions, of possibilities of gains and losses. He is always asking: How much does it cost and what does it yield? And his incessant questions in this respect resolve themselves into the final momentous one: *What does the world cost?*

Truly, the character and behavior of the Hebrew as dealer could not be better portrayed. We have a strong suspicion that Herr Sombart is, in reality, a cleverly disguised opponent of the Jews. With still more exquisite irony, he characterizes the Hebrew actually as a "discoverer"—namely as the discoverer of fresh possibilities of "doing business," who knows full well how and where to discharge his goods. And who, in order to excite new needs, provides Eskimos with bathing-suits and African negroes with hot-water bottles. And Sombart also knows full well how to portray the tenacious importunity of the Hebrew, when he characterizes the specifically Jewish talent for dealing as:

> [the art of] acquiring a pair of old trousers by cunningly wearing out the patience of an elderly aristocrat, to whose apartments he may already have been five times without accomplishing his purpose, in order, later on, to talk some peasant into buying the garment, by exercising all his powers of persuasion.

According to Sombart, among the other requirements of the dealer must be included a power "to see with a thousand eyes, and to hear with a thousand ears," and this accomplishment has been brought to perfection by Jewry by means of the organization and consistent cooperation of all Jews. The German businessman can only see with his own two eyes, and only in exceptional cases has other eyes at his disposal, to help him to extend his vision. Jewry, however, has been organized into a hydra with a thousand heads that are all attached to the same body, and which all follow the same instinct. This Jewish "dealing" organization, with its thousand senses, spies upon the artless nations, never lets an opportunity slip of "doing business," and knows how to arrange matters so that the profit always falls its way.

According to the sound, old, time-honored ideas, trading or dealing was an honorable exchange in which one gave either goods for goods, or goods for money. A sense of fairness regulated the proceeding to mutual satisfaction. In the case of an honestly conducted transaction, both sides might well derive advantage and profit therefrom, because the object purchased might be worth more to the purchaser than the price paid, and, at the same time, the seller might secure a profit. It is quite different according to the Jewish perception. Sombart's opinion is that trading or bargaining means "a struggle with mental weapons." In reality, all Jewish trading and bargaining is made up of persuasion, overreaching, false representation, and imposition. The Jew is not desirous merely of satisfying a want but, in addition to endeavoring to secure an excessive profit for himself, he attempts to do the other side as much harm as possible.

The Hebrews, as a nation that, for thousands of years, has practiced nothing but haggling, usury, and overreaching, have developed the art of persuasion to the highest possible point. How often does one hear simple-natured people who have been talked into buying the goods of some Jewish peddler, excuse themselves by saying: "I had to buy something from the man because I could not otherwise get rid of him." Yes, it is impossible to ignore the fact that many Jews—at least, when they come into contact with artless and ingenuous people—possess an almost demoniacal power of suggestion, such that the latter follow unresistingly the intentions of those who are fooling them:

> One of the most effective inward means of coercion that the Hebrew uses, consists in arousing the idea that an immediate conclusion of the business at hand will prove advantageous.

Thus writes Sombart. The Hebrew knows full well how to utilize this means to the utmost. It is actually a fact that some Jewish peddlers are in the habit of suggesting to possible customers that the goods they offer are stolen properly, or are taken from a bankrupt stock, and must, on that account, be disposed of as quickly as possible, and at almost any price.

* * * * *

Sombart rightly refers to the peculiar fact of Hebrew isolation amidst other national communities as a circumstance that gives him exceptional advantages. He emphasizes that the advantages enjoyed by the Hebrew are rooted in the following four circumstances: (1) in their extensive dispersion, (2) in their foreignness, (3) in their half-citizenship, and (4) in their wealth. I examine each of these below. Unfortunately, Sombart has omitted the most important items, namely, (a) the open and the secret connection amongst themselves, and (b) the Jewish morality that is especially adapted for trading and deceit.

1. The Extensive Dispersion

Thanks to their extensive dispersion over all lands, the Hebrews are enabled to maintain an accurate survey of all economic events in distant lands. By this means, they secure, at all limes, the easiest and most reliable information concerning, for example: the prospect of crops, the production and sale of goods, stocks of goods in hand, the transport of goods, and the circulation (and possible deficiency) of money. It is also known for certain that they mutually exchange most valuable information and tips with respect to these matters, primarily via market reports that they control, but also by means of private letters and dispatches. Important facts like these are far too little known and appreciated today. Anyone who has an inkling of these matters cannot be in the least surprised at the success of the Jews. At least, he will not gaze upwards with amazement and admiration at the supposed eminent and unusual faculties for trade possessed by the Jews. There have always been men with keen insight who have seen through these inner workings. But unfortunately the wisdom of olden times seems lost to the present generation; it often appears to us as if our teachers and spiritual pastors, as well as our political leaders of today, are wearing blinders so as not to see what is happening before their eyes.

Even in the year 1698, a report from the French Ambassador at the Hague is devoted to a description of the activities of the Dutch Jews, and of their machinations on the Amsterdam Exchange. Among other things, mention is made therein of the secret brotherhoods (*congrégations*) that the Jews maintain, and which stand in the most intimate connection with one another. Mention is also made that these brotherhoods are only tolerated in England, and have to be kept secret in France. The result of the intercourse between these brotherhoods is that the Jews are the first and the best-informed concerning anything connected with trade, or of a novel nature. Out of this liaison, they build up their system and meet weekly on Sundays for consultation, while the Christians are occupied with their religious duties. Sombart explains:

> These speculative schemes that are of a most subtle nature, and have been prepared in accordance with the intelligence that has come in during the preceding week, are sifted and refined by their Rabbis and learned men. They are then, on the following Sunday, handed over to their Jewish brokers and agents, who are selected for their exceptional craftiness. After the latter have consulted with one another, each of them circulates, on the same day, the news that is specially adapted to serve their purposes. The next day, they at once set to work buying, selling, and exchanging shares. As they always have large sums of money and stocks of goods at their disposal, they are always in a position to judge correctly when the right moment has arrived to carry out their "coups," whether at the top or at the bottom of the market, or simultaneously in both directions.

This has been, in truth, the secret of the Jewish brokers for centuries. It is nothing less than astounding how neither our merchants, nor our learned political economists, nor our politicians, nor our statesmen can see through these secret machinations, and still cling to their naïve belief that "supply and demand" determine the price. In reality, the Hebrews, combined internationally, form a clique for exploring all opportunities, and for systematically influencing all market conditions. Even in the present day, similar conspirators and instigators of the same unsavory plotting and scheming are to be found amongst the Rabbis and in the Synagogues.

This Jewish system of espionage, and the secret machinations in the synagogues and on the Stock Exchange, place the Hebrew in a position to obtain quicker and more reliable information concerning all matters than anyone else in the country—governments included. And thus it comes to pass that the latter, in their naiveté and artlessness, frequently imagine that they must *make use of* the Hebrew, not only for the purpose of obtaining important news from abroad, but also in order to exert diplomatic influence in all directions. They forget that by doing this, they are putting the cart before the horse, and that it is Jewry and the money market that derive all the benefit from any new political move.

Anyone who wants to gain a correct idea of the methods and extent of Jewish interference with the higher political circles should read what Emil Witte—formerly commercial counsellor under von Holleben at the German Embassy in the United States—has to say in his book *From a German Embassy: Ten years of German-American Diplomacy*. This work is rich in disclosures concerning the nature of two major telegraphic news agencies: Reuter (London) and Wolff (Berlin). These two have acquired the chief role of broadcasting important political news to the public by means of the press.

In dealing with this subject, the following remarks will be of interest, as they afford glimpses into the career of a Jewish adventurer. The founder of the "Reuter Bureau" was Paul Reuter (1816-1899), born in Cassel of poverty-stricken Jewish parents; his birth name was Israel Beer Josaphat. After an obscure and apparently turbulent youth, Reuter became partner in a bookseller's business in Berlin; he left this position on account of certain "irregularities," and soon afterwards founded the Reuter Bureau in London, in company with a fellow tribesman, Dr. Sigmund Englaender (1823-1902). Englaender was one of those numerous men of honor, who, by their assumed German names, bring everything connected with that country into disrepute abroad, and who was, at the same time, a declared anarchist. With the help of the well-known Guelphic author and political agent Oscar Meding, Reuter was successful in inducing the blind King George V of Hannover to grant the concession of a telegraph-cable from Lowestoft to Norderney—something that he later sold, in 1869, to the British government for a profit of more than £200,000. Raised to the grade of Baron by Duke Ernst of Coburg-Gotha, he earned large sums of money by acting as impresario to the Shah Nasr-el-Din of Persia, and paid the latter's traveling expenses all over Europe. By so doing, he secured from the Shah every possible concession that Persia had to impart.

In order to put a stop to the mutual competition engendered by the founding, in Berlin in 1865, of the telegraphic bureau of Dr. Bernhard Wolff—also a Jew—Reuter purchased a part-share in the business; thus, the same genius ruled over two bureaus. Later, we will be able to ascertain the nature of this genius. Here, it will suffice to say that the owner of the Reuter Bureau—Baron Paul de Reuter—is portrayed as a man possessed by a demonical ambition, who is enabled, by his position and his enormous wealth, to play a pernicious part on the political stage, even though it takes place behind the scenes. A man, moreover, utterly unscrupulous as to the means he employs to enrich and advance himself—one can read a great deal more about him in Witte's book—and who was rejected by Bismarck on account of the hostile tone that his news service always displayed towards Germany. The German Baron took his revenge for this by securing a dominating influence in Wolff's Bureau that is supported by Prussia and Germany. Since then, he has taken his part in shaping politics in both of these countries by his peculiar method. How and when this takes place, the public has never been allowed to learn, although it is common knowledge that Reuters Bureau is the heart and soul of all the foreign animosity towards the German Empire.[4] Thus, this institution that exists to feed half the world with news—in other words, to influence vast masses of people—is connected by "the most intimate ties" with the Wolff Telegraphic Bureau in Berlin.

Witte explains what this means in a quotation from an article in *Black and White* by a former *Times* correspondent, Charles Lowe, concerning the bills of exchange transactions between Reuter and Wolff, as well as the inner organization of the Wolff Telegraphic Bureau (WTB):

> "Wolff" is a joint-stock company, composed of some of the first Jewish bankers in Berlin, and naturally enough, the members of this association claim the privilege for themselves of having the first look at all important telegrams—a privilege, the prodigious significance of which, for the twin worlds of international politics and international finance, is immediately apparent.

The WTB is a semi-official arrangement, the recognized organ of the German and Prussian government. *Do ut des* ('I give in order that you may give') or, *Quid pro quo* ('this for that') is the principle that regulates its relations to both governments, of which it is both henchman and mouthpiece. Many contemptuous expressions have been used concerning the "reptile" Bureau in Berlin, but as a matter of fact, such a Bureau does not exist, or at any rate, only in the shape of the above-mentioned telegraphic bureau. This is not to say that Wolff receives a cash subsidy out of the "reptile" fund of the government. In the case of a newspaper or similar

---

[4] Anyone who would like to know the instigators of the World War cannot overlook Reuter.

undertaking, however, payment in the form of important news is just as valuable, if not more valuable, than payment in hard cash.

What does the payment to Wolff consist of? First of all, there is the precedence that the government accords to all messages received by or emanating from Wolff's Bureau; they do this in order to assure to that office, whenever possible, of priority in the publication of its announcements—a consideration that is naturally of the utmost importance to a telegraphic bureau. Moreover, the government makes use of Wolff's Bureau as its channel of information and mouthpiece, when it wishes to publish a statement to influence public opinion, or to communicate certain information in a certain form to the world—especially internationally. This last item can be very comfortably accomplished, thanks to Wolff's international connection.

The WTB is an institution founded by Gerson von Bleichröder, and for which Louis Schneider, formerly non-commissioned officer and later courtier, was successful in obtaining the favorable notice of his august master. In his letter to Dr. Wolff, in which he praises the Doctor's intention, the King, in 1865, announced his expectation that "patriotic financiers like Messrs. Oppenfeld, Magnus, and Bleichröder" would support Wolff's undertaking. What the shareholders in Wolff's Telegraphic Bureau understand by "patriotism" is disclosed by the activity of this institution that Bismarck distinctly referred to in his famous aphorism "to lie like a telegram." The principal shareholders, according to Witte, are the chief of Bleichröder's Bank, Dr. Paul von Schwabach, English Consul-General, and Herbert von Reuter, chief of the English telegraphic bureau, whose enmity towards Germany is an established fact. Amongst other shareholders are the banking-houses of Mendelsohn and of Warschauer.

Similar agreements to that between the Bureaus of Wolff and Reuter exist also between these two institutions and official or semi-official telegraphic agencies in other European countries, of which the best known are the French "Agence Havas" and the Italian "Agencia Stefania." *All these are in the hands of Jews.* We should pause to reflect what it really means: One learns that, by means of contracts in which high penalties have been mutually agreed upon, each of the above mentioned "bureaus" engages to communicate to the press in unaltered form—that is to say, without any regard for the truth—any message, received from any other agency belonging to the Union or ring of telegraphic news agencies! Of the two competing American telegraphic news agencies, Associated Press and Laffan Bureau, the former enjoys, thanks to the "smartness" of its representative, and without any reciprocation on its side, official priority for the quickest dispatch of its news from Berlin. This occurs because one believes here in Germany that, by this complaisance, "good press" is manufactured in America. One must read Witte's book in order to learn from the actual facts of the World War, what astounding success has resulted from this policy. Witte continues:

> The men who are interested in the telegraphic bureaus, know no Fatherland, think and feel internationally. War, and danger of war, provide, as far as they are concerned, the most favorable opportunities for fishing in troubled waters. It has already repeatedly come to light in the Law Courts, and there is documentary evidence to confirm the statement, that Wolff's Bureau suppressed important news in the interests of its shareholders, so that the "patriotic financiers" (to whom King William I addressed himself) might be enabled, thanks to the exclusive information, to transact profitable business on the Stock Exchange. It was established, moreover, that the Foreign Office communicates the speech from the Throne of the Kaiser, at the opening and closing of the Reichstag, to Wolff's Bureau several hours before it is made known to the Reichstag and to the Press.

This "national" Telegraphic Bureau was not ashamed to receive subscriptions from private individuals for the quickest possible telegraphic information of the death of the Emperor William II. One asks oneself: Are the representatives of the German Empire unable to discover any means of protecting themselves against this "patriotic" Telegraphic Bureau and its dark machinations—such as by instituting for themselves a self-supporting independent news service that would protect us from the insidious peril that threatens the whole German Empire by the prejudicing of its outlook and opinions for the sake of Jewish monetary interests?[5]

Sombart also tells us something about similar secret methods of the Jews. He says:

> Their method in high finance has frequently been the following: They first of all made themselves useful to the prince or ruler, as interpreters, by means of their knowledge of languages; they

---

[5] Even during the World War, the WTB was allowed to have a monopoly of the news service! Who can wonder now at the way that the war ended.

were then sent as negotiators and agents to foreign courts; then the prince or ruler entrusted them with the management of his property—which opportunity, it may be remarked by the way, was skillfully taken advantage of to lead the prince or ruler into debt, and to become his creditor. By these means, they became masters of finance, and in more recent years, of the Exchanges.

The Jews work always according to the same old receipt. It is already sketched out in fullest detail in the history of Joseph of Egypt's behavior towards Potiphar and Pharaoh; and thus it is unnecessary for the Hebrew to develop any particular intelligence in order to repeat the same old artifice daily—especially as the Christian nations are brought up in complete ignorance of such tricks, and repeat, in good faith, the Jewish lie that the Egyptian Joseph was a pious, virtuous man, and a national benefactor.[6] Even in the earliest times, the Jews played a leading part at the courts of the German princes; thus, for example, Isaac at the court of Charlemagne, and Kalonymos at the court of Otto II. Frederick Barbarossa was surrounded by an entire stall of Jews, just like Rudolph I. Maximilian I, being an unbusinesslike man, was heavily in debt to the Jews. During the extensive German wars in the 17th and 18th centuries, espionage was carried on by the Jews, in all directions, to an enormous extent. Even during the Prussian-German wars of liberation in 1813 and later, more than half the traitors who served the French as spies, were Jews.[7] Jews could be found in swarms at the various Courts until the monarchs fell. The latter were blind enough to take the most dangerous enemies of the monarchy to their bosom, and to place implicit trust in them. The collapse of the monarchs is not undeserved; stupidity is a crime in rulers; there was no lack of warning.

In modern times, the notorious Bernhard Maimon provides a typical example of the Jewish intriguer behind the scenes on the political stage. On account of frequent thefts of documents from the Foreign Office in Paris in 1911, various arrests were made; Maimon, who was eventually unmasked as the leader of an extensive system of espionage, was included amongst

---

[6] Ed.: For the biblical story of Joseph, see Genesis 41 to 47.

[7] This much is certain: the Jewish boast, on the contrary, concerning the participation of Jews in the battles of liberation was proven to be false already in 1819. The same lie flourishes today, and even to a greater extent than formerly, so that one Jewish journalist even goes so far as to claim Eleonore Prochaska—the Potsdam heroine—as a Jewess. This is only in accordance with the usual Jewish falsification of history.

the thieves. Concerning this talented political adventurer, one could read the following in a Jewish paper:

> Bernard Maimon, who is perhaps 60 years of age, is, without doubt, one of the most interesting adventurers of the present time—truly a modern Casanova, who, just like his famous (Jewish) predecessor, is constantly and universally engaged in politics, works simultaneously for and against all parties, brings the greatest financial operations to successful issue, negotiates the most difficult state loans, and still has time and inclination to engage in most daring love-adventures.

Bernhard—or properly Baruch—Maimon is a Gallician Jew; this has not prevented him from playing, sometimes the Christian, sometimes the Muslim. He was well versed not only in the Talmud but also in the Koran and in the Bible, and understood, to a remarkable degree, how to make the most of this knowledge. The Hebrew paper is full of admiration:

> His extensive public, and still more extensive secret, relations with the British Embassy were in constant rivalry with his mysterious connections with other Embassies, and especially with the palace of Abdul Hamid. Taschin, the first secretary at Yildiz Kiosk, was literally a mere tool in the hands of Maimon. Whenever Maimon stayed away from the palace in his own hotel, there was an uninterrupted exchange of letters and messages between Yildiz and Maimom, night and day.

Apparently Maimon gave first consideration to British interests, but it is quite certain that he had other irons in the fire. He was a spy for the whole world, and it flattered his vanity to play with the top diplomatists of the day like a cat plays with a mouse, and to converse with monarchs, in their private apartments, concerning matters that their ministers only learned about for the first time much later on in the day. The Winter Palace on the Neva was open to him, and Abdul Hamid had the greatest personal regard for, placing the blindest confidence in him, in spite of, or just because, Maimon was on very friendly terms with the Young Turks. Whenever Maimon was staying in Constantinople, Abdul Hamid took counsel with him daily concerning all international questions, and when he was far from the Bosporus, his advice was often sought and given by telegraph. And at one and the same time, Bernard Maimon was the counsellor and friend of

King George of Greece, and served as his adviser during the Greco-Turkish War (1919-1922). He put in an appearance at Crete, accompanied by an entire staff of the leading French and English war correspondents. Even the renowned American photographer, Underwood, was not lacking; pictures of the most memorable episodes had to be provided for the great illustrated papers of both hemispheres—and Bernard Maimon was naturally the central figure in every case! This political adventurer traveled only by special train from one residence to the other, and lived only in the best hotels.

So much for the wisdom of the old governments, and so much for the wisdom of their diplomacy! No wonder that they suffered shipwreck!

The distribution of the Hebrews over all lands is particularly advantageous for their system of spying, and one can take it for granted that the distribution represents a carefully spread net, so that every important center has its appointed spy or scout. When governments frequently gave preference to Jews in the case of military contracts and similar business deals, it was always justified by the argument that the Jews, thanks to their far-flung network of agents, were in a far better position than other merchants to rapidly "assemble" provisions and other materials in large quantities. In a book with the title *Concerning Jewry and the Jews* (1795) the author, Ernst von Kortum says: "The Jewish contractor has no need to be scared by difficulties. He has only to electrify the Jewish community at the right place, and in a moment he has as many helpers and helpers' helpers as he requires." Then again, he emphasizes the fact: "formerly the Jew never traded alone as an isolated individual, but always as a member of the most extensive trading company in the world." And there is also a noteworthy petition of the Parisian merchants in the latter half of the 18th century that states: "they (the Jews) resemble drops of mercury that disperse themselves and run about in all directions, but which, on the slightest shock, reunite themselves into one mass."

The fact that the government gives the Jews still further support for their business espionage by entrusting them with the consular representations, is simply one more example of those incomprehensibilities provided by our wise administrators.

2. The "Foreignness" of the Hebrews

The fact that the Hebrew is a foreigner in all countries is of great use to him. The Jew never identifies himself with the interests of the country in which he lives. He has his own peculiar nationality, and constitutes, with those of his kind, an 'international nation' as it were. And the interests of this nation are supreme with him; they form, literally, the base of his religious faith. He would never break away from a community that is not only united by the double tie of blood and religion, but represents as well a gigantic business association that, simply owing to this adherence to one another, is able not only to maintain its own existence but can guarantee an existence to each individual Jew as well! An alien business association of this kind, with an alien religion, will see to it that its interests are sharply separated from those of other nations, and must accordingly confront the latter both as foreigner and enemy. The leaders of the Hebrew nation recognized this fact thousands of years ago; and for this reason, they drew up the rule: "remain a stranger in the land, for you go there to take possession of it".[8]

And as Professor Adolf Wahrmund very appropriately remarks, the Jews, even in the present day, regard their journey through the world as a warlike expedition, undertaken for the purpose of conquest. It is certainly not by displaying courage, sword in hand, but by the weapons of financial and mental enslavement, with which they overreach and infatuate the different nations, imposing usurious spoliation and moral degradation on them. Just as Jacob, the ancestor of Jewry, defrauded the honest peasant Esau of his rights as firstborn, and by trickery, sneaked into possession of what should have been another's inheritance, Jewry today remains the professional "sneaker" of inheritance among the other nations. Talmudic doctrine announces: "The possessions of those who are not Jews are to be regarded as property without an owner, and whoever is the first to seize it is entitled to it."

One must certainly concede that the Hebrews have acquired an uncommon mental agility, business circumspection, and a penetrating judgement as regards relations and persons. These capabilities are the inheritance of a race that, for thousands of years, has not practiced anything but trading, usury, espionage, and overreaching of honest people. It was by no means the external pressure of his environment that converted the Hebrew into a usurer and a deceiver; he has never been anything else. This can be seen from his fundamental laws and doctrines that scarcely touch upon anything except how to exploit and befool that part of humanity which is not Jewish. It must also be taken into consideration that a Jewry that is forever on the move, impelled by the lust for roving, and which represents nomadism of modern times, is enabled by constant change of relations and surroundings to develop a keener insight into affairs than those who never

---

[8] Ed.: This is a paraphrase of Deut 23:20.

Chapter 12 – Hebrews as Supporters of Capitalism

move from the spot where they were born. The Hebrews are intruders everywhere; they were obliged to capture a place for themselves by means of cunning, and who, for that reason, have always practiced, in a masterly fashion, the requisite techniques. "New settlers," as Sombart politely calls them,

> must keep their eyes open, in order to make themselves quickly at home in their new quarters, must be careful how they proceed, in order that they may, at any rate, make a livelihood under the new conditions. While the long-established inhabitants are resting comfortably in their warm beds, they (the Jews) are standing outside in the chilly morning air, and must first of all endeavor to build themselves a nest! There they stand—regarded by all settled inhabitants as intruders.

And the foreignness of the people of Juda, as even Sombart allows, is not only of an external but of an internal nature as well. He says:

> Israel, however, was alien among the other peoples since time immemorial in quite another—one might almost say, psychological—social sense, in the sense, of an internal contrariety to the population surrounding them, in the sense of an almost partitioned-off seclusion from the economic nations. The Jews were conscious that they were something out of the ordinary, and were, in turn, regarded as such by the economic nations.

That, in the last analysis, is the secret that stigmatizes Hebrewdom: this foreignness and contrariety that they, as guests in foreign countries, feel and display towards their hosts. And it is the chief defect of our education, that not only are these peculiar relations *not* made clear to us, but we are actually *deceived* concerning them! While the Jew never allows himself to forget for one moment that he must regard us as strangers and enemies, whom it is business to exploit and overreach, we are brought up under the false impression that the Hebrew is a harmless member of the human community, just like the members of any other nation. And even more, we actually befriend and favor the most dangerous enemy of our economic and national existence, thanks to the unlucky associations that Church doctrine has most erroneously derived from the traditions of Jewry.

The Church ascribes a moral and religious importance to the Jew that he simply does not possess. Out of this fundamental error on our part,

Hebrewdom draws its main strength; our blindness and foolish trust provide him with the most favorable opportunities. While he—with the demeanor of an innocent friend of humanity—lies in wait for each opportunity to overreach us, we advance towards him with open arms, open heart, and open pocket, and make his task of exploiting and harming us a very easy one. Viewing the situation as described above, one may well ask if the Hebrew really is in need of a special intelligence department, and of superior business ability, in order to gain an economic advantage over us, when the secret alliance of his racial companions and our unlimited trustfulness have already made the game so ridiculously easy for him.

We have already seen how the Hebrew, in his compartment-like seclusion, recognizes no moral obligations of any kind toward us; and how he considers himself entitled to abuse our trustfulness in any and every way.

One must realize that the whole culture of civilized humanity rests on a foundation of mutual trust. The cooperation of a great, civilized community is only rendered possible by each man honestly fulfilling his duty, and thereby justifying the reliance and confidence of others in him. The Hebrew knows nothing of fidelity and trust—at least as far as "strangers" are concerned. He knows only of a compact with his own clique that is more of the nature of a conspiracy, and which is indispensable for the successful issue of his plans for overreaching others. Regarding Gentiles, however, he considers himself freed from any moral responsibility whatever. And this is the position taken up by the Hebrew, even at the present day: all of us are strangers in his eyes, fit material for exploitation, whom it is his duty to injure, for the greater honor of Israel and of his idol Yahweh. These relations of the Hebrew with the stranger are the antithesis to the attitude and behavior of the German under like conditions. Overstrained conceptions of humanity prompt us to display special consideration and thoughtfulness towards those who are not Germans. We have had to pay dearly for this unpatriotic indulgence in the past; and to no one more than to the Jews.

3. Semi-Citizenship of the Jews

The semi-citizenship of the Jews has already been mentioned; it proceeds from their alien nature. They are semi-citizens among us because their allegiance to our national community is only feigned and superficial; secretly they retain their separate Jewish civil community, and their separate nationality. This causes them, however, to become double-citizens in another sense. According to the law, they belong simultaneously to two nationalities and states; among us they are, at one and the same time, German and Hebrew; they are amenable to two systems of law, and can claim protection from both. They have the option of invoking, at one time, the German, and at another, the Jewish code, selecting whichever system appears to be most advantageous. They thereby acquire privileges over all other citizens of the state. It is only a trait of their ancient mendacity and presumption, when they behave as if they were not treated with full justice in our country. As a matter of fact, as double citizens they enjoy *double rights*—and are actually privileged. Johann Fichte has already called attention to this:

> Through almost every country in Europe, a mighty, hostile state is extending itself, and is engaged in constant warfare with all the other states: its oppressive tyranny causes grievous suffering to the citizens of all the other countries. It is called Jewry. I do not believe that this fearful state of affairs has come about because Jewry forms a separate and exceedingly compact community, but because it is founded upon hatred of the whole human race.[9]

It has gone so far, in Fichte's opinion, that:

> In a country where even the King may not, of his own free will, deprive me of the cottage that I inherited from my father, and where I have my legal rights against the all-powerful minister, the first Jew, nevertheless, who takes it into his head, can plunder me with impunity.

and he then continues:

> You are all aware of this and cannot deny it, and utter sugary words about tolerance, the rights of man, and civic rights, and the whole time you are inflicting injury on our chief rights as men... Can you not recall in this case the instance of the state within the State? Does not the intelligible thought ever occur to you that the Jews, who, apart from you, are citizens of a state that is more firmly founded and more powerful than all of yours, will, if you once give them citizenship

---

[9] *Opinions Concerning the French Revolution* (1793).

in your own countries, trample you, the original citizens, under their feet?

The assertion that, in olden times, the Jews were denied entry into the honorable industries and consequently were forced to resort to usury, is emphatically contradicted by Sombart. He cites, among other proofs, an order of the Cabinet, dated 1790, that permitted the protected Jews of Breslau to carry on all kinds of mechanical crafts. It also mentions that, among these Jews, besides those who were tolerated, there were privileged and universally-privileged ones who were allowed full exercise of all Christian rights in the ordinary course of life. It is quite certain that some Jews enjoyed special privileges that were hereditary in their families.[10] Sombart also lays stress on the fact, that if the Jews neither obtained nor sought for admittance into the corporations and guilds, this was to be attributed mainly to the Christian character of these organizations; the crucifix repelled them.

The Jews, moreover, already in the 12th and 13th centuries, were not only on a completely equal footing with the great merchants, the shopkeepers, and the leading people as regards freedom of the markets, but they actually had the privilege over their competitors of being protected, together with clergymen, women, and pilgrims, against all action under feudal law. In olden times, the religiousness of the Christian, and the foreignness of the Jew himself, operated to the latter's advantage, just as German cowardliness and 'culture' do at the present day. Owing to their foreignness, the Jews possessed one peculiar advantage, namely, that there was no need for them to take part in the quarrels of other nations, and could, on that account, all the more easily benefit from political complications—at the expense of the two conflicting powers. Sombart says: "national conflicts became actually the principal source of Jewish acquisition." Espionage might also be included.

Besides this, one must not forget the farming-out of the privilege to mint money that the German emperors, since the 13th century, had passed over to the towns and large landowners, and who, in their turn, had handed it on to single tenants—among them many Jews. Up to the mid-18th century, these people secured enormous profits for themselves from debasement

---

[10] Richard Schröder writes: "The Jews lived among themselves (during the 10th to 12th centuries and later) according to the Mosaic-Talmudic Law, from which, later on, many legal ideas have crept into the common law of the community. In each town, the Jews formed a special community by themselves"—that is to say the Ghetto—"under a Jewish bishop, who was appointed by the King at their suggestion, and who exercised judicial powers among them in all cases of dispute."

of the coinage alone. "Outwardly good and inwardly bad, outwardly Frederick but inwardly Ephraim"[11]—this was the derisive comment of the people of Brandenburg concerning the badly silvered-over groschen, issued during the Seven Years War.

4. Jewish Wealth

The ancient complaint about the oppression of the Jews in olden times contradicts itself alone by the fact of their indulgent mode of living, and their display of luxury. We have already mentioned how they inhabited the most magnificent mansions, not only in Holland and London, but also in Paris and Hamburg. Glückel of Hameln discourses in the same strain concerning the princely splendor displayed at a rich Jewish wedding in Amsterdam. Sombart furnishes long lists of the names of rich Jews in England, Hamburg, and Frankfurt, during the 17th and 18th centuries; their fortunes are a sufficient refutation of the ancient fable about the "poor, oppressed Jew." He says:

> The peculiar and interesting fact—that the Jews were always the richest people—has continued unaltered for centuries, and remains as true today as it was two or three hundred years ago. If anything, it is still more pronounced and universal at the present time than formerly.[12]

We can explain this mystery by becoming acquainted with the means by which Jewry acquires its riches. But we must again reject the erroneous idea that Jewish riches are part and parcel of the national wealth. The Hebrews, of their own accord, place themselves outside the pale of the nation; their riches, therefore, are not to be included in our national wealth. On the contrary, Jewish riches are the sum of what is lost to us in prosperity. These riches, at the present moment, are in the possession of a foreign and hostile nation that is using them in order to oppress us. All the mighty banking foundations and gigantic Stock Exchange speculations of the He-

---

[11] The Jew Ephraim was the head of the mintage-farmers, of whose services Frederick the Great was compelled to avail himself when surrounded with difficulties.
[12] Sombart's book is especially recommended for Social Democrats, in order that they may learn who are the originators of the capitalistic system that they pretend to hate so much, and who are the real oppressors of the people. Perhaps then they will begin to reflect whether they are justified in selecting their leaders and advisers out of this particular circle.

brews are, in reality, consummated mainly with our money. In the case of all Jewish activity, there is no suggestion of the creation of sound economic values, but only of a crafty shifting of ownership.

An honest Hebrew, one Conrad Alberti (Sittenfeld), acknowledged as much when he wrote as follows:

> No one can dispute that Jewry takes a leading part in polluting and corrupting all relations. A characteristic of the Jew is the stubborn endeavor to produce values without work. This being a matter of impossibility, it simply means that these values are artificially produced by swindling and corruption, by maneuvers on the Stock Exchange in conjunction with the press in order to spread false rumors, and by other and similar methods. These artificial and fictitious values are then acquired, unloaded, and exchanged for genuine values, produced by real work, only to melt away and vanish in the hands of their new owners like Helen in the arms of Faust. The representatives of corruption on the Exchange, in the press, representatives of that class who strive to enrich themselves without working, are therefore Jews.

When Sombart says "Capitalism is born from loan-capital," I add this: Capitalism actually exists only in debt. Under the expression "capital" in the narrower sense, I understand only loan-capital, that is to say, the kind of capital that is utilized, not to generate productive activity, but solely to win interest. It cannot be disputed that the dangerous capitalism of the present day arises solely from the loaning of money, for the productive fortunes of our great industrialists must not be compared in this respect with the usury-capital of the Rothschilds and their associates. The productive capital of industry consists, like that of the large land-owners, preponderatingly of landed property, buildings, and industrial investments, and only gives a return through inventive intelligence, organizing power, and hard work. The distinguishing feature, however, of loan-capital—"speculative capital"—is to bring in a return without doing any work for it. Productive capital gives opportunity for work and wages simultaneously to hundreds and thousands, but loan-capital is only a steady drain on the return earned by others, taking often the lion's share; it makes sure of its percentage whatever happens, even when adverse circumstances or the failure of a harvest wipe out all profit.

Chapter 12 – Hebrews as Supporters of Capitalism

When certain people make the simple masses believe that the farmer and the large landowner—the hated "agrarian"—are the real oppressors and plunderers of the people, they omit to mention that very frequently this "agrarian" himself is grievously oppressed, and is on the rack from year's end to year's end, to raise the money to pay the interest on the mortgages. The workman in industrial service, or in possession of a handicraft, always remains a free man; he receives an honest wage for honest work, and can, if he chooses, give notice and change his employer. But whoever finds himself in the bondage of loan-capital and doomed to pay interest is seldom, if ever, able to shake off the fetters. The landowner, burdened with mortgages, is far less free and far less of a master than the youngest proletarian from the factory. All his life long, he, and often his children and grandchildren as well, are chained to the same piece of soil that claims all their labor in order to raise interest for loan-capital. How crazy it is then, to direct the envy and hatred of the town-bred proletariat against these supposed tyrants! In reality, many of these so-called owners—even the large landed proprietors—are themselves "owned" by the loan-capitalists.

A new kind of secret serfdom has come into being that is invisible to the ordinary public, and which consists in allowing the slave to retain the outward appearance of lord and master, whilst it condemns the much-envied owner to a kind of bondage. This bondage is rooted finally in our wrong arrangement of our interest system. It is opposed to common sense, in the case of a sum of money lent on interest once only, to make not only the recipient of the loan, but his children and children's children liable to pay interest for all time. This "eternal interest" is, on the one side, the curse of the productive classes, and on the other, the fertile soil in which are rooted the power and dominancy of that oppressor of the nations—Judah. The interest system invests the money lender with a relative might which, in reality, is more oppressive than the dominance and despotism of olden times. The despot of easier times invariably took the part of his bondmen, and protected them against dangers from without, because their preservation and his own economic interest were inseparable. Today, the lender of money does not recognize this personal concern for the welfare of those who pay him interest; he chases them ruthlessly from hearth and home when they are no longer able to pay him tribute.

He also enjoys the advantage that the unpledged portion of his debtor's property falls, in this manner, into his clutches as well. Sometimes he acquires, under a forced sale, the entire possessions of his debtor in satisfaction of his claim, and thereby gains that part of the property that had not yet been pledged. He then introduces a fresh "interest-slave" into the property, and proceeds to treat the same, who perhaps has increased the value of the property by his personal energy, in precisely the same manner should he fall into arrears.

Between the "interest-master" and the "interest-slave," all human relations have ceased; the connection between the two has become purely mechanical; it has become unhuman and soulless. On the other hand, the activity of the receiver of interest does not call for the slightest intellectual or physical exertion. The knight of olden times protected his bondmen with spear and shield against their foes; the lord of capital has divested himself of all such responsibilities. The accumulation of capital also has become a purely mechanical process. Interest and capital accumulate in accordance with the purely mechanical law of mass-attraction—an absolutely idiotic proceeding, devoid of any organic sense. Sombart says, "With regard to the lending of money, economic activity as such has lost all meaning; the occupation of lending money has ceased to be a sensible activity of either mind or body." There is one, and only one object: the material result, i.e. the acquisition of fresh capital, and thus the extension of the power of the lender of the money.

In this manner, loan-capital gains power over other men, and has forced itself into a dominating position that is founded neither on physical, nor on intellectual, nor on moral superiority. This position depends entirely upon a fictitious power, one that is devoid of any human element, namely the conception or notion of capital. It is enabled by means of eternal interest, extending into immeasurable time, to make foreign labor subject to itself, and to overpower and crush all spiritual and moral effort. The formation of capital out of interest is something automatic and spiritless, for it can be consummated just as well in the hands of an idiot as in the hands of a being destitute of all morality—simply by a fiction, by a false economic view.

> The possibility of earning money without any personal exertion by an economic transaction, makes its first distinct appearance in the lending of money. The possibility also, of getting strangers to work for one without physical compulsion, is immediately apparent.

Thus writes Sombart; it seems to us, however, that the "scooping-in" of interest is scarcely worthy of the name of "economic transaction."

After such illuminating reflections, it seems very extraordinary to me that it is precisely in the capitalistic Jewish press, where a bitter hatred is unceasingly fomented against the domination of olden times. Feudal-domination, knighthood, nobility are medieval ideas, and as such are exposed to incessant attacks from the so-called "liberal" press. With what right and for what purpose? Simply with the object of not allowing the infatuated population, who are ignorant of history, to wake up to the fact that they are languishing and wasting away under new tyrants, the interest-despots, who set to work in a far more selfish and brutal manner than was ever the case even with the most ruthless feudal-lord of the Middle Ages.

CHAPTER 13
BUSINESS AND RELIGION

Sombart speaks mockingly of the "fearful maxims" that Pfefferkorn, Eisenmenger, Rohling, Dr. Justus, and others have culled from the religious books of the Jews. It would have been a good thing if he had submitted a sample of these "horrors" to his readers, for, often as these sayings have been examined by other conscientious scholars, the maxims have invariably retained the same aspects. And when the explanatory artifices of the Jews are brought into play, one is in a position to understand that the Hebrew can interpret entirely different, and far worse meanings, out of those doctrines than can the conscientious Christian translator. The same Sombart, who reported to us some time back how, owing to the Talmud, the entire Jewish spiritual world had declined into impotence, and how every minute point, every letter, every word had its own important meaning, goes so far as to say lightheartedly a few pages later: "naturally in the course of so many centuries these particular doctrines have altered entirely in meaning."

This is untrue. The only thing that is correct is that, in the Talmud with its commentaries, one finds the most divergent Rabbinic opinions, and that its doctrines and expositions frequently contradict one another. This, however, is only equivalent to saying that it is open to every faithful Jew to accept as authentic whatever doctrine and exposition may best suit his purpose for the time being. Thus, when one passage reads: "you must not lie to, deceive, or rob the Goy," and another Rabbi says: "under certain circumstances, you may do so," more latitude is allowed to the conscience of the Jew who believes in his Talmud. He can act either in this way or that, and will still find himself in agreement with the law, and will still remain a pious and orthodox Jew.

Out of the mass of inconsistencies and contradictions contained in the Rabbinical writings arises a cheap form of diversion, one that the Rabbis have always carried on at the expense of those who do not happen to be Jews. If anyone calls attention to a passage in the Talmud that states: "You may injure the Goy," the Rabbi can at once turn up another place where it says: "You must not do this." The morality of the Talmud is like a conjurer's box with a false bottom, from which the moral and the immoral can be produced according to wish. It is therefore a trifling on the part of Sombart when, referring to the serious scientific study that Christian scholars have made of the Talmud, to speak of the "downright silly game that the anti-Semites and their Christian or Jewish opponents have been playing." The only question is, which side is playing a silly game. Sombart himself is engaged in a game of harassing and mystifying when he says:

> So far as the religious writings are read by the laity themselves, it seems to me essential that, generally speaking, a settled opinion should be expressed with regard to any particular question. It is a matter of indifference if, at the same time, the contrary opinion is also represented; for the devout man, who has been edified by these writings, is content to accept the view that coincides with his own interests, so that he is thereby in a better position to defend them.

According to this logic, one might well believe that Sombart had also attended the Talmudic School, for this is a genuine specimen of the Rabbinical expression of opinion: 'one particular view or manner of understanding suffices, if it suits the reader'! But if there happen to be two entirely opposite opinions, the devout man has the opportunity of selecting whichever one pleases him best. And one must admit that this is a very empty kind of morality. Sombart adds: "Since everything, in this case, is divine revelation, one passage is just as valuable as another." Quite correct! Here we have the morality with the double bottom—openly defended by a scholar who does not desire to be a Jew!

The most intellectual Rabbinical writings actually prove that, amongst the Jews, the feeling for true morality, and for the ethical consciousness, is entirely lacking. There is no good and evil for them; everything is gauged by momentary advantage. Sombart is more honest when he confesses: "I find in the Jewish religion the same leading ideas as those that characterize capitalism; I see that the former is filled with the same spirit as the latter." In reality, the conscienceless predatory spirit that distinguishes modern capitalism in its worst form—Mammonism—also fulfills the Talmudic Rabbinical doctrine. One must be grateful to Sombart for this admission. He proceeds to say that this religion

> has not arisen from an irresistible impulse, nor from deep fervor of the heart of those, whose souls have been mutilated, nor from the religious ecstasy of adoring spirits, but from a premeditated plan, like a carefully-considered proposition, resembling a diplomatic problem.

He designates it as a work of the understanding, calculated to break up and enslave the whole natural world. How strangely does this opinion correspond with the perception of the derided anti-Semites, who have been saying the same for decades!

Undoubtedly the Jewish doctrine arises from a kind of thinking warped with vanity, one that has lost all touch with the fundamental laws of natural growth or development, and which would like to convert life into a sum of arithmetic. The word 'rationalism' that one would like to apply to this particular frame of mind and this mode of regarding life, is not appropriate here. 'Ratio' always means 'reason,' i.e. thought that is in harmony with natural laws; reason is not merely understanding, but is, at all events, understanding united to instinct or feeling. It is being endowed with a keen sensibility as to the essential nature of things. Mere understanding is simply arithmetic, without instinct, without feeling. And the Jewish mode of thinking must be placed in this category.

When Sombart says: "Rationalism is the principal trait of Judaism, just as it is of capitalism," he means the mere mechanism of the understanding—soulless calculation. And when he goes on to say: "the Jewish religion does not recognize anything of a mystic nature," he might have said still more correctly that it did not recognize idealism, nor true morality, nor anything ethical. When he further maintains that the ancient religions were always ready to attribute any deed that aroused a sense of shame or remorse to the Divinity, it is the Jewish doctrine alone that entirely justifies the accusation.

Already, in the time referred to by the Old Testament, all kinds of disgraceful deeds, perpetrated by the people of Judah against other nations, were undertaken, always ostensibly at the bidding of their God Yahweh or Jehovah. The same diversion is continued in the Talmud. Yahweh not only approves of all manner of evil things, but he himself, as personification of the Jewish entity, tells lies and deceives. The philosopher Ludwig Feuerbach has already designated the so-called Jewish religion as nothing more than a business contract between Judah and its God. Nothing is to be found in these laws and doctrines which does not hint at some material benefit for the children of Israel. Yahweh demands obedience from his people, and promises them, in return, riches and long life. "Utilitarianism—profit—is the predominant principle of Jewry" says Feuerbach. "The Jews have retained their peculiarity up to the present day: their deity is the most practical principle in the world: egoism, and egoism in the form of religion."

Sombart is no different with reference to Jewish doctrine: "There is no kind of compact or partnership between God and man which is not consummated in the form that man performs something that is agreeable to God, and is rewarded by God correspondingly." But even Yahweh does not do anything for his chosen people except for cash down. He is no God of self-sacrificing love, but is an out-and-out businessman like the Jew himself; and thus, throughout the whole Jewish religion, there is no higher moral guiding star. There is nothing to raise man above himself, no unselfish sacrifice, no inspiration for ideals. Always only

> a constant weighing-up and comparison of the advantage or disadvantage that any action or omission to act may entail— a most complicated kind of book-keeping in order to keep the debit side of each individual's account in order.

Such is Jewish piety, according to Sombart. And just as according to the Jewish mode of thinking, everything resolves itself into action and reaction, into payment and acquisition, so in the so-called Jewish religion, the acquisition of money is regarded as the supreme and sole object of life. The Jew introduces the huckster's spirit even into his divine services, and Sombart reports that these ceremonies have, in many cases, developed into nothing less than formal auctions. Thus, for example, the official posts of the Torah in the synagogue are sold by auction to the highest bidders. He also confirms that the Rabbis were, for the most part, prominent business people, and therefore we are bound to acquiesce when he hints that the Jewish religious system has greatly assisted the capitalistic career of Jewry. In other words, the so-called Jewish religion is nothing else than the wrapping-up of sharp business practices in a religious garment.

A nation certainly has nothing to be proud of in having invented and retained, even to the present day, a code of morals that is devoid of all morality. But why shouldn't the Hebrew cling tenaciously to this traditional doctrine? Thanks to its help, success is on his side! Why shouldn't he cherish his Yahweh, who has been such an excellent adviser to him in all business matters? It is a fatal weakness of the other nations that, until now, they have been unable to perceive their real relations to the Jews. They have been unable to discover the ways and means by which the Jews enrich themselves. Thus, the Jew still retains the fantasy that not only is his intelligence of a higher quality than that of other men, but that his religion is also superior to theirs. He will only become sober-minded when the other nations finally settle accounts with him, and when he discovers that the accountant, Yahweh, unmasked and hurled from his throne, is no longer in a position to help him.

Judaism versus Christianity

Indeed, there cannot be any more striking contrast than that presented by the intense, unearthly idealism of Christ that disregards the material world, and the rabbinical spirit, which is directed entirely towards material advantage and earthly enjoyment. Sombart says:

> In this respect, the Jews stand in the most striking contrast to the Christians, whose religion has endeavored to its utmost to sour all joy in this world. As often as riches are praised in the Old Testament, are they cursed, and poverty extolled, in the New Testament.

It is therefore illuminating, why the devout Christian and the pious Jew play such very unequal parts in the acquisitive life. The Christian seeks to acquire in order to gain his living; the Jew is desirous of heaping up riches in order to control and to enjoy. At this juncture, the question arises: *Has the unworldly religion of the Christians perhaps been the unconscious agent, to fasten the golden chains of Jewry on the Aryan nations?*

Over the course of time, Aryan moral obligations and views of life have changed, becoming freer and more humane; but the same cannot be said of Jewry. Its law remains rigid and unchangeable up to the present day. In the course of 3,000 years, Jewry cannot record any moral advance. What stands written, stands written, and is just as valid today as on the first day, when, according to the legend, it was dictated directly by Yahweh to Moses on the summit of Mount Sinai. Jewish law is built up on a faith of sheer and literal acceptation, with exclusion of all common sense and of all unfettered judgement. It reduces its adherents to dumb slaves. Jewry is, in reality, a religion of servility.

Whenever the fable is repeated that the Jews were our instructors in moral and religious matters, and presented us, as it were, with a religion [Christianity], the repetition discloses either complete ignorance of the subject or a deliberate perversion of facts. The people of Judah were never moral and pious; they do not possess any faculty of perception in this respect. And whoever regards the blind subservience of the Hebrew to literalness as the highest degree of piety, is incapable of recognizing the spiritual and moral nature of the genuine man. The really religious man is he who untiringly searches for the deepest and most intimate associations between natural and moral occurrences, who is constantly extending his knowledge, who surveys and judges of his own actions according to their effect, and who does not cling blindly and incapable of judgment to mere literal forms. Lagarde says, appropriately: "A religion only lives as long as it is cultivated." In reality, it is only the constant striving for moral perfection and the constant seeking for and deepening of moral insight that form the essence of true religiousness. Where these are lacking, there is no religion; and they are lacking in Jewry. The slave to literalness, who conforms to the timeworn doctrine without passing any criticism, and who, at best, endeavors to pave a way by means of cowardly subtlety between the various precepts of these doctrines, is totally lacking in religious consciousness. And thus, from this standpoint, the Jewish doctrine cannot lay any claim to the name of religion.

With respect to the Torah of Israel, Sombart says:

> The commands and prohibitions of God contained therein must be observed most strictly by the pious man, whether great or small. Whether they appear sensible or senseless to him, they are to be fulfilled in the strictest sense of the word, just as they stand, for the simple reason that they are the command of God.

Thus, common sense and individual reflection, individual moral feeling and conscience are excluded—of necessity—in order to equip Jewry for the particular task that has been assigned to it as its world mission: namely, to ruin the other nations morally and physically, and to seize their possessions. The Jewish nation is the soulless tool of an abstract idea that has been exalted even to Divinity, and whose ultimate aim is the plundering and annihilation of honest mankind. The driving force in this struggle is the hatred of mankind, a disposition hostile to life, and an evil spirit.

From a superficial viewpoint—that is to say, the viewpoint of all those to whom the essence of true religion is unknown—the Jewish doctrine may certainly appear as a model religion because it concerns itself with the lowest functions of life and represents all such precepts as direct commands from God. Moreover, the Jewish language possesses a peculiar pathos, a fact to which Goethe has already called attention, and readily avails itself of extravagant expressions. But we must not be led astray by the high-sounding words. It is frequently the case in ordinary life that the person who has the richest vocabulary and the most touching phrases at his disposal has a cold heart, whilst another, whose soul is almost choked with overpowering emotion, is unable to utter a word. Both the written and the spoken language of the Jews use occasionally extravagant expressions for what is actually base, worldly, and even immoral; by this means, a semblance of religiousness is aroused, where, in reality, nothing of that nature exists. On the other side, blind obedience constitutes the might of the business managers of this "religion," namely the Rabbis. And thus it is intelligible if the apparent piety of the Jews appears exemplary to priests, who are greedy for power.

In reality, the Hebrews have borrowed many devout words from the religions of older and more deeply-feeling nations, in order to act as a cloak to their selfish and worldly aspirations. When a comparatively honest Hebrew, like Dr. Jacob Fromer, maintains that in Jewry everything is ethical, all that he means to say is: everything therein is regarded from a practical point of view.[1] The conception of morality is foreign to this man as well. I am inclined to believe that the Hebrew meant 'art' when he said 'ethics,' so as to give to all bargains and transactions, even of the lowest description, a decent appearance. He also sought to invest them with a mantle of piety, although the pretense could not be extended beyond claiming that the transaction in question lay within the province of God.

For instance, a Hebrew who was about to rob a man actually went so far as to clothe his intention in the following words: "My Lord God, thou hast given thy servant power over the goods of the stranger; and see, I hasten to execute thy divine Will." In this manner, the Hebrew has introduced an element of untruthfulness and hypocrisy into the life of mankind, one that is devoid of all naturalness and morality, and which is intended to detach the rest of humanity from any dependence on Nature and common sense. And this hostile principle works with amazing results, and is, at this moment, steadily and irresistibly dragging mankind down that stairway of degeneration prepared for it by the Jew.

One may say: Jewry is an attempt to tear the existence of mankind apart from Nature, and to mold it into a kind of calculating and exact comprehension. This is what is understood by the much-praised "intellectuality" of Hebrewdom. However, a life without dependence upon Nature cannot continue for any length of time; and just as the Hebrew with his disintegrating intellect has never succeeded in maintaining a state of his own, and has never succeeded in creating an independent, self-contained, and self-supporting society, so does he convey the spirit of disintegration into the midst of those nations who believe in culture.

---

[1] Dr. Jacob Fromer, *Das Wesen des Judentums* (The Essence of Jewry). The author has been fiercely attacked by many of his co-religionists on account of his frank and frequent criticisms.

From whatever point he is regarded, the Hebrew displays the features of a parasite. He does not derive his means of existence directly from Nature—from the soil—but only by means of an intermediary system of living. He then sucks dry the essential members of this system. But it is the custom of the parasite, if unchecked, to entirely consume the juices and energy of its host; and then, if it is unable to migrate to a fresh source of sustenance, it perishes together with the host. Accordingly, there is little that can be regarded as rational in the nature of the parasite. But there is, on the contrary, a blind and greedy stupidity that finally destroys the foundation of the parasite's own existence. The Jews, therefore, are not, as Sombart believes, "rationalists," but rather short-sighted beings, lacking in sensibility, and nothing better than spongers. His aversion to everything natural does not allow the Hebrew to feel any unfeigned pleasure in the simple expressions of Nature. A lovely flower, the song of a bird, are meaningless to him; he is scarcely aware of them.[2] Human emotions, such as affection, and sympathy with other beings that would impede his cold and calculated pursuit of advantage, appear to him mere folly. The Talmudic doctrine has no room for this. Rabbinism is a stern schooling for the Jewish soul that finds its counterpart, perhaps, only in the arts, principles, and practices of the Jesuits. Everything is calculated and adapted toward making the pupil the hard tool of another's will. A good heart and a gentle disposition must not be tolerated, because these would prejudice the objective and purpose of trade. Sombart calls the Jewish doctrine a "mechanism of means to carry out a purpose."

Certainly a great deal of what is contained in the Rabbinical writings sounds very fine and virtuous; especially the unceasing zeal manifested towards unchastity, something that even goes so far as to spurn womankind and all natural pleasure derived from the senses. "Let not thine eyes lust after women, turn a deaf ear to their voice, avert thy gaze from their form. Thou shalt not even look upon the garment of a woman with approval!" And so it continues in the same strain. But how does all this agree with what is actually practiced? From time immemorial up to the present day, the Hebrews are known as the most shameless pursuers of women. And anyone who undertook to write a history of Jewish unchastity would have to extend it into countless volumes.[3]

---

[2] Heinrich Heine's classification of plants, as those which one eats, and those which one cannot eat, is an excellent instance of the Jewish perception of nature.

[3] Ed.: This has echoes in the modern day, where so many prominent and influential Jews have been accused or convicted of sex crimes.

If the Talmudic Rabbis are so zealous in warning their people against unchastity, the main cause for this would appear to be fear regarding their own peculiar weakness. Even Sombart admits that, in the case of the Jews, we have to deal with a people strongly disposed towards sexual excesses— a people whom Tacitus has already described as a *"projectissima ad libidinem gens."* Just as the Hebrew is unnatural in everything else, so is he unnatural in this respect; his sexual inclinations and desires exceed all usual bounds and are unrestrained.

The Separation or Shutting-off of the Jews

I will now return to the affinity between the Jewish religion and capitalism. Sombart also allows that the object of the Jewish doctrine is to conduct a life contrary to Nature, or apart from it, in order to develop an economic system that likewise builds itself up alongside Nature and in defiance of it. And he is of the opinion that the Jewish religion must be the means of accomplishing this:

> In order that capitalism could develop, it was first of all necessary that all the bones in the body of the industrious and forceful, but neutral, man should be broken; that a specific psychology or mechanism of the soul, equipped solely from the intellect, should be substituted in the place of the original and natural life; and that a subversion, as it were, of all the values of life should be introduced. The *homo capitalisticus* is the artificial and artful creation that finally emerges from this subversion.

One is now entitled to ask: What was then the motive for such an extraordinary object? What normal human being could entertain the desire to renounce and subvert all his natural inclinations?

Here it is not the case, as Sombart thinks, and is generally believed, of the Hebrew being the product of a cunningly thought-out doctrine of life; but rather as follows: The strange doctrine arises from, or is the product of, the Hebrew himself, and his attitude towards honorable society. The conjecture holds good that Jewry originated amongst the expelled elements of the ancient, civilized, oriental nations.[4] One must also bear in mind the

---

[4] See Fritsch, *Handbuch der Judenfrage* (Handbook of the Jewish Question) and *Der falsche Gott* (The Wrong God).

'chandala' of the Indians, composed of the degenerates and criminals excluded from the honorable castes, in order to find an enlightening explanation of the peculiarity of Hebrew mentality. Those who had been expelled and despised by all the other castes, revenged themselves by deriding and reversing all moral conceptions. What was sacred to others, they made a mockery of; they praised, on the contrary, those attributes and dispositions that other people despised. "Among these people, everything is profane that is sacred in our eyes; and, on the other hand, what appears abominable to us is permissible to them," says Tacitus of the Jews.[5] In reality, the very essence of Jewishness is a subversion of all the views of moral humanity. Whether it happens unconsciously or is undertaken deliberately, it still remains a fact that the Hebrews, in their nomenclature, reverse the names of many things; thus, for example, those who have been expelled, they call "the chosen." Out of this compulsory segregation—the chandala were not allowed to dwell among the honorable castes—they established, in the course of time, a voluntary separation. And finally, they raised their segregation to the status of law, and in their turn—like the Gypsies and the wandering people of the Middle Ages—looked down with contempt upon all who stood outside their circle, which is to say, upon all honest people.

The exclusion of the Jews from the rest of humanity, which is commonly seen as some kind of cruel despotism, has always been *voluntary*; they were not driven into the ghetto, but united of their own free will to form it in order to practice their own peculiar customs without interruption, and also because their law forbids contact with the rest of mankind. It was therefore an *advance* on the part of the public authorities, when they allowed the Hebrews to erect separate quarters for the Jews. Many Jewish historians admit this frankly, and they also admit the proven fact that it is precisely the ghetto life that is mainly responsible for preserving Jewish national existence. Sombart says:

> The Jews themselves created the ghetto that originally, from the non-Jewish viewpoint, was to be regarded as a concession or privilege, and not the consequence of a hostile attitude. They wished to live apart because they regarded themselves as superior to the common people surrounding them; because they felt themselves 'the chosen'—the priestly people... Their disposition that is hostile to every foreign element, their tendency towards seclusion, extend far back into the ages.

---

[5] Ed.: See Tacitus, *Histories* 5.2.

Already, at a very remote period, they were forbidden to contract mixed marriages with other nations; and the Old Testament is full of outbursts of contempt for the surrounding nations—Edom and the Canaanites. The reproach, so often raised by people prone to sentimentality, that the Jews have become what they are, in consequence of the scorn and exclusion that they have experienced from other nations, is thus quite beside the mark. It was far more a case of the Jews *excluding themselves* from other nations; they regarded themselves as a peculiarity, high above all other peoples, upon whom they looked down disdainfully. "The Jews desired and were obliged to live thus, in accordance with their destiny that was their religion," says Sombart.

The economic nations have often approached the Jews with goodwill and trust. The Jews enjoyed, during the Middle Ages, not only all rights, but often actual privileges. A bishop named Hausmann built a well-fortified town, especially for the Jews, at Speyer in the 11th century, from which they used to undertake veritable pillaging excursions into the surrounding country, without anyone being able to intercept them. They were not obliged to restore any stolen property that might be found among them—and they could, at any rate, charge any price they liked to return it.

> The important consequence of this segregation and concentration of the Jewish population was just that foreignness of which we have already recognized the importance: namely, that all traffic of the Jews, as soon as they emerged from the ghetto, was a traffic with foreigners.

Thus writes Sombart. Foreigners or strangers are, as we have learned from our examination of the Talmudic writings, outlaws, beasts, fit material for exploitation. In the case of such strangers, usury was not only allowed, but ordered to take precedence over everything else. If there are perhaps passages in the Talmudic writings that seem to teach the contrary, these are only variegations customary in Rabbinical Jewry that are intended to obscure the real sense. Even Sombart concedes this much: "I am inclined to think that a great part of these discussions serve the exclusive purpose of obscuring, by all kinds of sophistry, the extraordinarily clearly-defined situation that has been created by the Torah."

Thus, according to the Jewish doctrine, you may practice usury at the expense of the foreigner (Deut 23:20); and plainly stated, the larger the amount of undeserved wealth that the Hebrew amasses during his life, the greater the complacency with which he looks back on that past life. By so doing, he has rendered a supreme service to his God—that God, Yahweh, who so ardently desires the spoliation and extirpation of all the other nations of the world. "While the pious Christian," continues Sombart,

> who has practiced usury, is seized with agonies of remorse on his deathbed, and is ready, before the end comes, to divest himself of all his property because he, at this moment, regards it as unjustly acquired, and it weighs upon his soul; the pious Jew, on the contrary, in the evening of his life, surveys with gratification the well-filled trunks and chests, filled with cash that he has succeeded, throughout his long life, in squeezing out of the wretched Christians. This is a spectacle upon which his pious heart can regale itself with the utmost satisfaction, for every dollar that lies there is, as it were, an offering lain before his God.

Sombart believes that only ignorance or malice could deny that the foreigner's standing, as far as Jewish justice is concerned, is an exceptional position, and that Jewish obligations and responsibilities refer always and only to the "neighbor" i.e. to the Jewish racial companion. And he adds this: "But the fundamental idea, that you should have *less* consideration for the stranger than for the racial companion, has not altered from the time of the Torah until the present day." This is a most important admission. It can always be brought forward as a challenge to those who believe that this Jewish doctrine is, at the present day, no longer efficacious, and that the Talmud contains views that have been overcome. By these very words, Sombart at the same time contradicts his opinion expressed above, namely, that the Talmud doctrine has altered in the course of the centuries:

> This completely vague perception: that you are not committing any sin, and that it is permissible in the course of business with a stranger to tell him that 'odd is even,' became firmly established wherever that formal Rabbinism developed out of a study of the Talmud that existed in many districts of Eastern Europe.

Even the Jewish historian, Graetz, who otherwise certainly cannot be regarded as impartial, confesses that:

Chapter 13 – Business and Religion

> Distortion and perversion, the trickiness of the lawyer, affectation of wit and precipitate rejection of whatever might not be included in his range of vision, are the essential features of the Polish Jew. Honesty and a sound mode of thinking have deserted him, as well as simplicity, and a desire for and an appreciation of truth.

I believe that, so far as moral negligence in the case of the Jew is concerned, it is not a question of the loss and disappearance of moral qualities, but is, on the contrary, to be attributed to a *primitive* and *hereditary* defect. We discover this trait, not merely since the origin of the Talmud, but already even in the Old Testament. One need only call attention to the treacherous behavior of the sons of Jacob, who persuaded the honest Levites to undergo circumcision, and then attacked and slew them while suffering from the effects of the operation (Gen 34).

It is worthy of note how the Rabbis, in their Talmudic writings, concern themselves in a most intimate manner with all kinds of business practices. Again, it is fully in accordance with the principles of the Talmud that warnings should be issued ostensibly against immoral business practices, whilst later on, the prohibitions are withdrawn and the same practices are declared permissible. Rabbi Yehuda speaks thus in one and the same breath:

> The grocer shall not present the children with cakes and nuts, for, by so doing, he attracts them to his shop; the Sages, however, allow it. Further, one must not cut the price; the Sages, however, are of the opinion that the precept is worthy of remembrance [i.e. it would be a praise-worthy habit]. Abba Saul has decided that the split beans are not to be picked out; the Sages, on the contrary, allow it.

Here we find the contradictory and discordant morality of the Talmud expressed in the sleekest manner—apparently while unaware that it is a doctrine of nonsense and immorality. That is to say: *Everything is forbidden and everything is allowed; see which suits you best.* However, the compilers of the *Shulchan aruch*, without any attempt at concealment, have made this question perfectly clear; they say in Choshen Mishpat 228,18:

> A storekeeper is permitted to distribute toasted grain and nuts to children to get them to buy from him frequently. Similarly,

he may sell below market rate to get people to buy from him, and the others in the market cannot stop him.[6]

Unrestricted license in underbidding and competition form the very life-breath of the Jewish existence; everything is permitted that makes business easy; everything is allowed that puts the Jew in a position to overreach and fleece others. For this reason, Sombart says at the conclusion of this chapter: "God desires free-trade, God desires freedom of industry! What a motive to make the same ideas effective in economic life."

Sombart's references to the accordance of English Puritanism with Judaism are interesting, and Heine, in his time, made fun of this association by calling the Puritans "pork-eating Jews." Sombart emphasizes the fact that Jews in England, especially among the Puritans, enjoyed during the 17th century a respect and reverence that are only to be described as fanatical, and many writers of the period vied with one another to prove that the English were direct descendants of the Jews. At all events, certain pietistic circles in England were at great pains to copy the Jews in their mode of living, nomenclature, and other externals. This symbolism was carried so far that the Christian clergy and even the Christian laity studied the Rabbinical literature for preference. Sombart refers to a "droll little book," which appeared in 1608, under the title of the *Calvinistic Mirror of the Jews*, and which, amongst other things, examined the relations between Puritanism (Calvinism) and Judaism. The following quotation from this book is worthy of note: "the Jews penetrate into every country to cheat the inhabitants."

In Dutch and German pietistic circles also (Wupperthal, Swabia etc.), one encounters reminders of English Puritanism in the form of nomenclature, intense veneration of the Sabbath, and so forth. These form, without doubt, the strongest props of that fateful validity that the Old Testament possesses in the German Protestant Church. There are even Protestant clergy who are ready to represent the Jews as the pattern of religiousness, and—perhaps unconsciously—to work more for the cause of Jewry than for that of Christianity.

---

[6] Ed.: Translation from Wikisource.

Chapter 14
The Race Problem

In General

Sombart gives himself great airs in his 12th chapter, where he examines Jewish peculiarity when regarded from a racial point of view. He is of opinion—obviously with a dig at the 'wicked anti-Semites'—that the racial problem and national psychology have become a plaything of caprice and dilettantism, and that in particular, the portrayal of the Jewish entity is "undertaken as a kind of political sport by coarse individuals with gross instincts." It certainly cannot be denied that, in the course of the anti-Semitic movement, many people and tendencies have started up, whose origins and pretensions will not defeat investigation; but, at the present day, even these people who can never inflict enough derisive pain that they cast upon the opinions of others, refuse, in a superior manner, to listen to anything anti-Semitic.

And yet, a very considerable number of leading minds and estimable characters have belonged, and still belong, to the spokesmen of this movement. I do not wish here to dwell upon the fact that great men in all times—that philosophers from Giodarno Bruno and Voltaire to Fichte, Herder, Schopenhauer, and Feuerbach, that statesmen like Frederick the Great, Napoleon I, and Bismarck, that artists like Richard Wagner and Franz Liszt—must be included amongst the opponents of the Jews.[1] The more modern anti-Semitic movement also includes in its ranks individuals like Paul de Lagarde, Eugen Dühring, and Adolf Wahrmund, whose profound erudition cannot even be approached by any of their opponents, however much it may be belittled or ignored by the public press, itself completely under Jewish domination.

However, before everything, it must not be forgotten that it was the 'wicked anti-Semites' who first tackled the race problem and aroused a racial consciousness again among the nations. If, at the start, it was only

---

[1] A collection of extracts from the writings of these men can be found in the *Handbuch der Judenfrage*. The racial question is dealt with exhaustively by the well-known geographer Richard Andree in *Zur Volkskunde der Juden* ("Popular Information on the Jews," 1881). [Ed.: A current, thorough, and well-documented history of anti-Jewish sentiments by famous individuals can be found in T. Dalton, *Eternal Strangers* (2020).]

the difference between Aryan and Semite that engaged their attention, it is nevertheless due to their initiative that the whole of the modern racial movement has come into being, and has built itself up upon the fundamental views of the anti-Semites.

If, now and again, objectionable behavior puts in an appearance in the course of the anti-Jewish movement, and epithets are applied to the Hebrews that are not exactly flattering, there is no cause whatever for undue sensitiveness in this respect on the Jewish side. One has only to recall how low-class Jewish wits, in the so-called comic papers that are founded, almost without exception, by Hebrews, let themselves go concerning other nations, classes, privileges, and political opponents. Scarcely anything is too low or too foul for the Hebrew to give full vent to his hatred against those who differ from him in their opinions; for this reason, there is little or no justification on his side for moral indignation and extreme sensitiveness on hearing an expression of opinion concerning himself that is often remarkably appropriate. This assumption of indignation collapses in a ridiculous fashion if the fact is disputed, from a purely Jewish point of view—like a certain Friedrich Hertz and others attempt to do—that there even are such people as Jews at the present day. This is more than droll. So long as the so-called Jewish religion continues, so long will Judaism, as a compact hostile force, live and operate amongst other nations. But even if it were possible to extirpate this religion, the racial peculiarity of the Jew that has acquired an extraordinary tenacity by incessant inbreeding, would long continue to function.

Sombart then takes pains to put an end to those chatterers who wish to deny the existence of a Jewish race and a Jewish peculiarity. But he himself is certainly not clear in his own mind concerning the racial entity, when he says:

> On the other hand, it is senseless to give the name of 'Jew' to an Israelite of unmistakable origin who has succeeded in throwing off the fetters of Ezra and Nehemiah, in whose mind there is no longer any thought for the law of Moses, and whose heart no longer feels contempt for other races.

In the next place, it is doubtful if a Jew can ever completely free himself of the views derived from his racial peculiarity—views that were being prepared and established from the time of Moses to that of Ezra and Nehemiah, and which, later on, under the influence of Talmudic Rabbinism, were extended and expanded until they became a gross exaggeration. But even if he is capable of emancipating himself, Jewish instincts will survive and function in his offspring. So long as we have no experience of a Jewish businessman causing his son to become a farmer, a conductor, a carpenter, or a sailor, it is certain that no one will seriously believe in the transformation of the people of Judah into genuine human beings. I am in agreement on this point with our own most excellent Fichte, who also did not believe that the Hebrews were capable of being converted, unless "all their heads were cut off in one night, and other heads were substituted in which there was not a single Jewish idea." These words aptly describe the indestructibility of the Jewish racial entity.

The study of the racial problem has taught us that an indissoluble bond exists between the blood and the mental disposition of mankind. It is said in the Old Testament that "the life of the flesh is in the blood" (Lev 17:11), and that means that man's mental nature is inseparably united with his blood. We must ultimately learn to accept this fact in all its seriousness. We have long been accustomed to attach value to the blood and stock amongst animals; we do not desire that a poodle should become a sporting dog, or that a horse from Brabant should develop into a racer. We know that advantages, just like disadvantages and defects, are transmitted with the blood. Further, I have no intention of conveying the impression that all good and bad characteristics must be transmitted with unchanging fidelity from generation to generation, that the children of a clever father must be, without exception, geniuses, and that the offspring of a criminal is invariably criminal. But I perceive a certain constancy in the transmissibility of average qualities, whereby only those deviations and variations crop up that Nature allows herself everywhere as a diversion.

If the constancy in the transmissibility of qualities is comparatively insignificant as regards the present-day generation, this must be attributed to the excessive intermingling of tribes and races that has been taking place for centuries—even for thousands of years. The pure races certainly have almost completely disappeared, and only mongrel descendants surround us. In spite of this, one must not straightway deny that the racial entity has ceased to operate. The frivolous doctrine that "all men are equal" has caused unspeakable disaster and has actually introduced degeneration into the human race. We Germans of today have certainly no reason to boast of our race, for its worth is seriously depreciated—both blood and intellect having been dulled. But this should not restrain us from appreciating to the utmost the importance of the racial entity, and from attempting, by means of racial culture, to restore what has been sacrificed by an irresponsible racial lottery.

It is a fact, and it is about the only reputable thing which one can say about Judaism, that racial consciousness is fostered to a greater extent among the Hebrews than among any other nation, whether consciously or unconsciously, by the rigid law that enjoins that everyone who does not belong to the Jewish race must be regarded with hostility and contempt. Thus the irrefutable fact remains, that the racial entity amongst the Jews is today of greater validity, both physically and mentally, than amongst all the other races. The Hebrew, almost everywhere, can be recognized amongst other races both by his external appearance and, if anything, still more by his mental cast. And this racial constancy asserts itself, even when mingled with other strains.

The Jewish Professor Eduard Gans (1797-1839) expresses himself as follows:

> Baptism and interbreeding are of no avail; we remain, even in the hundredth generation Jews, as we were 3,000 years ago. We never lose the odor of our race—not even by tenfold crossing. And in every case of cohabitation with every woman, our race dominates: young Jews result.

Whoever, in face of facts like these, still persists in denying the existence of a Jewish race, cannot have much regard for truth. But we can very well understand why it is so distasteful to the Hebrews to see racial recognition and racial consciousness awakening among other nations. In the moment when this comes to pass, the Jewish alienation will, for the first time, make itself apparent to all, and this will, in every respect, make the Hebrew's business more difficult. Until now, the Jew has been able, in an inimitable manner, to mingle with other nations, and to delude them into believing that he really belonged to them—a circumstance that rendered his overreaching operations extremely easy to carry out. As soon, however, as the other nations become aware of their own particularity, and of the value of their own especial gifts, both moral and intellectual, they will soon recognize the Hebrew as a disturber of their domestic peace and of their harmonious development, and will endeavor to keep him at a distance.

The Psychology of the Jews

The Hebrew certainly possesses a great adaptability, but it would be erroneous to expect, from his external adjustment to the habits and customs of other nations, that the Jew is absorbed and disappears. The Jewish peculiarity differs far too much from the nature of all other nations to allow a complete fusion to appear even probable. In the last analysis, it is the Jewish view of life and the Jewish moral law that do not admit of any permanent association with other nations.

Sombart makes a vain attempt to sum up the Hebrew entity in precise ideas. He sees, amongst these, only a few of a disagreeable nature, and is unable to connect them with fixed characteristics. The distinguishing features of the Jew that he enumerates appear to me to be insufficient. I believe that I shall meet with but little opposition when I characterize the average Jew as follows:

- sharp at business and glib of tongue,
- greedy for money and of a saving disposition,
- cunning and addicted to dishonesty,
- averse to bodily labor,
- sensual and shameless,
- vain,
- cowardly, and
- impudent.

There are but few Jews in whom the majority of these characteristics cannot be detected. When Sombart speaks incessantly of their "prominence in intellectuality," it is clear that he means only the calm, calculating intelligence of the Jew—generally speaking, the mere operation of the cold understanding as opposed to the sensibility of deeper and more emotional natures. This much-praised intellectuality of the Hebrew is, in reality, only the outcome of necessity.[2] How could a people devoid of all capacity for production otherwise maintain their existence unless they unceasingly made use of cunning and deception, and knew how to fool others into furthering their own secret plans? It cannot be denied that Hebrews have occasionally distinguished themselves as clever physicians, scholars, and lawyers, but only so far, in these professions, as the possession of a coldly calculating and subtle understanding permitted them to advance.

---

[2] The well-known oriental traveler H. Vámbéry (originally Bamberger) confirms this fact, amongst others, in his report concerning *The Jews of the Orient* (1879), in which he states that it is a delusion to assume that European Jews possessed higher intelligence than the nations who acted as their hosts—for, to take Central Asia as an example, the Jew, when confronted by the Hindu and the Armenian, invariably came off second best.

And in this respect, they have frequently been actually favored by their own low standard of morality. Moral laxity frequently gives the Hebrew an advantage over other people. Whoever is not particularly scrupulous concerning his moral duty towards mankind has a much freer hand on many occasions than those who are restrained by their conscience and consideration.

Just as the Jewish businessman, thanks to his moral laxity, outstrips competitors in commerce, so is it in many other departments of life. A sense of duty, conscience, and honor have but little value in the eyes of the Hebrews when compared with intellectual capacity. The Jew is desirous, at all costs, of passing as clever; everything else is a matter of comparative indifference to him. There are a number of Jewish proverbs that regard stupidity as being far worse than any other mental or moral defect. All of these are centered on the idea: it's ok to be a rascal as long as you only show yourself to be sly. Whilst the civilized and honor-loving nations attach the highest value to moral character, and to the emotional side of human nature, the Hebrew appraises a man merely according to his mental adroitness. Whoever is clever is therefore worthy of admiration, even if he uses his cleverness to the detriment of others—perhaps, for that reason, all the more to be admired! It can often be observed in the Jewish press the attempt to make excuses for grave crimes on the grounds that considerable intellectual capacity has been displayed in committing them. This confusing and disordering of moral ideas by the introduction of intellectual standards is among the most dangerous means by which Jewry seeks to destroy the other nations.

Unfortunately, moral sensitivity in many classes has already been considerably weakened because peoples' power of discrimination has been injured by the fact that—thanks to Jewish example—admiration is frequently accorded to the criminal. It thus happens, that when a crime is being discussed, one can often hear good-natured men mitigating their abhorrence somewhat as follows: "But, after all, he showed himself a very sharp fellow!" — Indeed, a sign of the Judaization of our mode of thinking.

Sombart characterizes the Jewish—and probably at the same time his own—perception with the words: "the highest humanism is supreme intellectualism." I am compelled to object to this appraisement. For, measured by this standard, the most accomplished rogue and swindler could, under certain circumstances, represent humanity's supreme ideal. Heroic nations have an assured conviction of another ideal. They seek it in the direction of self-sacrifice of the individual for the general welfare, or, for an idea—for freedom or for honor—but, above all, in the complete subjugation of selfishness. The hero of our dramas, whose fate rivets our attention and affects us deeply, is not a sly customer, one who, thanks to his crafty alertness, knows how to dodge all dangers; on the contrary, he is an upright, inflexible character, who accepts his recognized duty courageously, and who does not turn aside from the path of truth and justice, whatever menace may stand in his way. He thinks little of his own advantage, but all the more of duty and honor. A real hero of this type will appear to the eyes of the Jew as no better than a fool; "better a live dog than a dead lion," is a Semitic proverb. This indicates the deep chasm that exists between the Jewish and the genuinely human mode of thinking.

However, an intellect that merely calculates is generally inadequate for dealing with all serious matters in life. There is something higher than the intellect. A man of high character allows himself to be swayed more by innate and instinctive feelings than by cold calculation. And these instinctive feelings that, in reality, indicate an intimate spiritual and emotional insight into the connection between things, are a far surer guide to mankind than all the speculations of the intellect. Where the guiding instinct is wanting, we see the intellect straying into all manner of blind alleys, clambering too high on its own artificial structures that have lost all touch with reason and nature, and at last, for this reason, failing completely.

The Hebrew—a being who is not of immediate natural origin, and who, for that reason, makes his journey through life without any intimate connection with nature—is devoid of instinctive feelings. He endeavors to replace them by conscious intellect. This may confer a certain apparent superiority on him, so long as he moves in artificial surroundings that depend, more or less, upon intellectual foundations. He is, however, completely at a loss, and feels immediately helpless, when he finds himself in a situation where the relations are entirely natural. A Robinson Crusoe, alone on a desert island, can contrive, with scant resources, to keep body and soul together; a Hebrew is incapable of doing so. The Jew is a second-rate man, whose existence depends upon all kinds of artificial assumptions. He is Nature's stepchild, and cannot get along with this mother. He is always in need of some man, a real man, who has grown up in touch with Nature and who is full of natural impulse, to carry him—the Jew—through life.

And when Sombart believes that he can perceive the acme of genius in 'freedom from all natural law,' and in 'tearing oneself loose from all natural instincts,' he betrays, in spite of himself, his own Jewishness. The opposite is correct; genius stands—unconsciously in most cases—in closest relationship, in inmost feeing, with the natural laws of being and becoming! It draws from a source whose deepest spring is scarcely known to itself. It is only because of the internal and external obedience to law resides also in the creations of genius, that they are eternal and inextinguishable. And it is also for this reason that they stir the emotions of mankind, so long as men do not close their ears to the voice of nature.

The Jew's conspicuous intellectualism is direct evidence of his weakness and of his inferiority from a human point of view. It is only when the natural feeling fails, when instinct is no longer a safe guide, that the calculating intellect begins, in its distress, to strain after artificial remedies, and seeks to create artificial conditions that are agreeable to it. The Jew can only flourish in an artificial world. In reality, the mental speculations of the Hebrew are confined to comparatively narrow fields of activity, where it is a matter of obtaining an advantage and of misleading and confusing the opponent. Only there is he a master. Everywhere else, where it is a case of penetrating more deeply into artistic, technical, and exact scientific knowledge, the intellect of the Jew does not suffice. And therefore, the Hebrew is never inventor and artist in the grand style.

Whoever follows up the refined subtleties of the Rabbis in the Talmud, can often observe how their petty, shortsighted, calculating spirit leads them into incredible imbecilities. According to popular opinion, the devil is a professor of slyness. But also according to popular tradition, there are all kinds of legends showing how the peasant gets the better of the devil; and from this popular notion emerges a deep meaning. The peasant may appear to be awkward and helpless in the external affairs of life, especially when he is brought face to face with the artificial conditions of town life. He possesses, however, and for the most part, although it may be only by means of his feelings, a deeper insight into natural things than many a learned townsman. And the devil, for all his arithmetic, always miscalculates when he encounters natural cleverness, and when the inalterable laws of nature break through his web of deceit. Yes, after all, the devil is stupid, and so is his cousin, the Jew. Place him face to face with Nature, with no creative men to assist him, and all his lordly intellectualism will suffer a miserable shipwreck—it will not save him from starvation.

On the other hand, the Jew knows how to confer an extraordinary power of attraction on the modern towns with their artificial and refined methods of traffic and intercourse; he entices the simple villagers away from nature into these modern paradises of vice, where everything is cast in an unnatural and artificial mold. Jews and Jewish mentality reign supreme in the large cities, and the natural man feels that he is a stranger there, more like a child, straying helplessly into the Jewish traps that are laid for him on every side. Therefore, whoever wishes to escape from the Jewish illusion must fly from these places and seek refuge again on the maternal breast of Nature. And just as surely is he doomed to certain ruin, who imagines that he can continue to live as a child of Nature in the deceptive and false world of the Jew.

Even Sombart admits as much: "We frequently find in the case of the Jew that all instinctive feeling is stunted, just as if all sensibility and sensitive relations to the rest of the world were foreign to his disposition." Here, however, he concedes that the Hebrew himself stands forth as both foreign and contrary to Nature. He moves in the midst of Nature as a dull and insensible being. He certainly sees things separately, but he passes over the causal connection of the natural phenomenon and the inward obedience to law of all life, without paying the slightest attention. For this reason, he is unable to judge the final effects of his scheming and plotting; he is always directed merely by the advantage of the moment. He hankers after the goods and chattels of the peasant; he knows how to get hold of them, and to drive the peasant from hearth and home; but he neither stops to reflect, nor does he care, what will become of the village when all the peasants have been plundered in this fashion and driven away. He sucks the last drop of blood out of the workman and the small employer of labor, and dispatches them to ruin, without asking: What will become of the world if we weaken the productive classes in this manner? He entangles the various countries in debts and loans, and hands them over to ruin, without taking the trouble to think that these operations will eventually cause human society itself to collapse—that very society that nourishes him with its flesh, and out of whose body he derives his parasitic existence.

We see here the same fool who saws off the branch he is sitting upon, and who kills the hen that lays golden eggs for him. Accustomed to the constant provision of new hunting grounds and fresh objects of usury by an inexhaustible Nature, and by the indefatigable industry of the nations, he is unable to conceive that the world dominion for which he is striving would mean simultaneous world ruin. The vain nature of his understanding does not look beyond today and tomorrow, but operates destructively and suicidally in all directions.

Only powers that stand in organic relation to Nature can work constructively, and the profoundest essence of natural things can only be comprehended by means of sensitivity. The intellect alone is insufficient to sound the well of life. The Jewish mode of thinking is inorganic, and is, for that reason, incapable of creative operation. For that reason also, the Hebrews are incapable of forming a state of their own—for, in the last analysis, the state is of an organic nature, and endures only through organic laws. Society, in a well-ordered state, requires organization of the classes, a rational constructive policy, and internal connections—i.e. sound relations and ties with one another that enable the whole to prosper.

The Hebrew has no understanding of all this. He regards individual men merely as objects to be turned to profitable account; he is incapable of comprehending why these same men are desirous of retaining a scale in their social order, why they band together in organic associations the better to fulfill their duties as men and citizens. All this appears to him as foolish prejudice and antiquated institution. He would like to alter, loosen, and dissolve everything in order to find an easy and convenient field for his profiteering operations. The Jew is, therefore, hostile to all organic social creations: the guilds, the trade associations, the nobility, the army. These are like a thorn in his eye. He would like to disrupt and atomize them, and to isolate the members. He is guided in this policy by the calculation that he can deal better with the individual, with whom he can more easily bring to subservience than with the whole. He calls this disruption of all organic structures "bringing freedom" and "liberalizing." He knows how to delude men into believing that their organic connection is a barrier that must be broken down, a fetter that must be shaken off, in order to attain true liberty—the liberty of the wolf amongst sheep.

Sombart remarks very appropriately:

> The Jew is very sharp-sighted, but he does not see much. In the first place, he does not perceive that his environment is a living one. And for this reason, any feeling for what is singular in life, for its entirety, for its indivisibility, for what has organically developed, and for what has grown naturally, is lost to him. Consequently, all conditions and relations of dependence that are built upon *personality*—such as personal rule, personal service, personal sacrifice—are foreign to him. The Jew, from his very disposition, is averse to all chivalry, to all sentiment, to all nobility, to all feudalism, to all patriarchism. He is also incapable of understanding a community that is built upon these relations. Everything to do with class or rank, everything incorporative, is hateful to him. He is a political individualist.[3]

---

[3] I am justified in supposing that this train of thought on the part of Sombart was set in motion by the journal *Hammer*, which, ever since it was founded in 1902, has often thrown light upon the "Jewish Question" from this same viewpoint.

Chapter 14 – The Race Problem

And yet he is individualist only in a restricted sense; he is himself the slave of a rigid principle, of a law of compulsion that, in place of a natural tie, binds him together with his kind. The Jew himself possesses no individuality; he is invariably only the more or less successful repetition of the *Jewish pattern*. The Jews, amongst themselves, resemble one another in their national characteristics to a much greater extent than the men of other nations; and the extraordinary limitation of their disposition is rooted in the above fact. The Hebrew is, as it were, an automaton, trained and adjusted to carry on definite social activities; he fulfills exactly the same functions in all grades of society. For this reason, a Hebrew is easily replaced by another Hebrew, whilst the same cannot be said of men of other nations.

The Hebrew is now wishes to transfer this systematic constitution of the Jewish league—i.e. this mechanical placing together of elements, all equal in value and devoid of individuality—to other social creations, and even to the state. He is unable to understand why organized society is on the defensive against this subjugation to one pattern, and he denounces this opposition to his endeavors to break up and dissolve as "reactionary." In reality, this reaction is the natural and healthy resistance that an organized society evolves against the efforts of the Hebrew to introduce decay and dissolution; in other words, it is the instinct of self-preservation.

The actual and harmful reactionary is, on the contrary, the Hebrew who checks the natural growth of national life by his plan to reduce all to one emasculated pattern, and who desires to force this life back into its primordial state—this struggle for existence of all against all. It is he who hinders natural development, and thereby disturbs the steady progress of life.

This fact, to our unspeakable misfortune, is only recognized by a few. The enormous liberation of energy caused by the speculative principle of the Hebrew, and the enormous development of the external life caused thereby, deceive everyone as to the true state of affairs. The glitter and gleam all around us appear to many as the veritable light of life, but it is, in reality, only the phosphorescence of corruption. The Hebrew, by inciting to that wild struggle for existence, has forced into action the last reserves of national energy, and thus the national life itself seems to have experienced a tremendous stimulus; and yet it is only the waging of a desperate battle for mutual destruction that must end suddenly from exhaustion.

But what does the Hebrew care about that! As a man who depends upon the momentary fluctuation of affairs, he derives his chief benefit from such conditions, and that is enough for him. Sombart says:

> The Jew brings everything into relation with his ego. The questions that have first claim on his interest, are: Why? To what purpose? Where do I come in? What do I get out of it? His real living interest is the interest for success. It is un-Jewish to regard an activity as an end in itself, to live life itself for its own sake, without purpose and in accordance with destiny; it is un-Jewish to harmlessly rejoice in Nature.

And just as he is himself, so has the Jew devised his God. The Jewish God stands outside the pale of Nature as a despot, who alters the course of affairs arbitrarily to suit his purposes. He allows all kinds of miracles to take place that are contrary to Nature, and arranges everything so that it turns out to the advantage of his favored people.

Apparent Jewish Superiority

When Sombart expresses the opinion:

> In the present day, the Jew of Western Europe no longer desires to retain his faith and his national peculiarity. He wishes, on the contrary, so far as national consciousness has not again been aroused in him, to allow his peculiarity to disappear as completely and quickly as possible, and to adopt the culture of the nations who act as host to him.

we must ask circumspectly: Where is the proof of this suggested effort? Who authorizes Sombart to assure us of this? For my part, I defend just the contrary.

It may well be conceded that, in the present day, the Hebrew is occasionally uncomfortable under his skin, since observant men have begun to make a practice of watching his activity, and are now revealing his tricks; it may well be the case in the present day that many a Jew no longer wishes to be recognized as such, and would prefer to change his appearance. But the fact remains that it is simply impossible for the Jew to be absorbed by other nations, even if it were his wish. His distinctive nature is far too different from that of other nations, and moreover his self-esteem is too great. He has no intention of resigning his privilege of being regarded as a "chosen people." But also the aversion of the other nations, so far as a healthy instinct is still alive in them, will protest against any such fusion. Certain sections of society that have already completed their resemblance to the Hebrew represent types of degeneration doomed to disappear. It is only the degenerate who shows inclination towards the Hebrew; the degenerate, by the loss of the finer instincts, has sacrificed his real manhood, has been discarded by nature, and sinks into that swamp of corruption represented by Jewry—the dregs of culture.

The following judgement concerning the Jews testifies that Sombart, in his scientific positiveness, is gradually coming around to my perspective, even though it may be in a circuitous manner:

> [The Jew's] intuition has not grown out of his innermost being, but is a product of the head. His standpoint is not the level earth, but an artificial building in the air. He is not organic-original but mechanical-rational. He is not rooted in the mother-soil of sensibility: instinct.

All this is covered by the perception expressed a long time ago by the anti-Semites. Only, at the same time, it must not be forgotten: the Jewish entity, and its inward perception of life, is certainly an artificial creation of the intellect. But in the course of thousands of years, it has become so ingrained in the Hebrew, has entered so thoroughly into his flesh and blood, that he is actually less capable of changing his skin than the representative of any other race. He certainly possesses adroitness enough to adopt superficially the manners, and even the mode of thinking, of others; he has sufficient powers of dissimulation and of acting, to make us believe that he is a being very similar to ourselves; but in the end, the unadulterated Hebrew always comes to the surface again. This pliancy, this outward adaptability, this talent for representing oneself as something different than what one really is, might appear admirable to us, if it was not at the same time so dangerous. All these Hebrew talents are only means to mislead us, and to make us subservient to the designs of this stranger. It is correct that the Hebrew, regarded from a purely intellectual point of view, appears to display great superiority in a number of respects. We may admire the Jew from an intellectual point of view, but our feelings reject him.

Sombart speaks appropriately concerning the "moral mobility" of the Jew; in the pursuit of his purposes, "no irksome restrictions of a moral or aesthetic nature are allowed to intervene." His morality is lax and elastic; he is ready, at any minute, to proclaim that odd is even, if he sees any advantage in doing so.

> In this respect, his poorly developed sense for what one can call 'personal dignity' is of assistance to him. It is very little exertion to him to deny what he himself has said, when it is a question of accomplishing his purpose.

Thus writes Sombart. In reality, the Hebrew possesses so little of what we call 'character' that he is ready at all times to barter his honor and self-respect for material advantage. An old proverb says: "The Jew will wade through seven puddles in order to possess one dollar more."

With the help of Talmudic schooling, the Hebrews are educated to become cunning dilettantes, for, from youth onwards, the practice of dishonesty is enjoined upon them, practically as a command. There is, accordingly, little cause for surprise when they distinguish themselves later on in life as lawyers, journalists, and actors. The art of being able to transpose oneself quickly into a strange world of ideas is absolutely essential to speculative dealing; if the Jew did not possess it, how else would he gain respite for himself, entirely dependent as he is on the exploitation of other men, and on the misuse of law and thought?

The advantages possessed by the Jew mirror his weaknesses; these are shiftiness, evasion, and adroitness in escaping from embarrassing situations, all of which he requires in order to conceal his failings from us. There is a well-known contradictory principle in Nature, whereby she endeavors to conceal and compensate for prominent defects by other qualities. She provides weak, defenseless creatures with properties or qualities that serve as a means of protection against the pursuing enemy. Thus Nature protects young birds in their nests by their ugliness, other animals by an obnoxious smell or by a disagreeable secretion—the snail, for instance, by a nasty slime. And in the same way, Nature dispenses properties to a section of mankind burdened with hereditary weakness, that must serve as a protection. Even the evasive intelligence, craft and cunning are protective qualities of this order, and they are to be found amongst the weak and the criminal.

Men of great bodily strength are, for the most part, open and upright, good-natured, patient, and obliging. They can put up with a good deal without losing their tempers because they know that when the decisive moment arrives, they can rely upon their good, natural strength that, if required, will sweep every obstacle out of the way. This good nature and this indulgence that are sometimes taken for weakness—but which are, in reality, only an expression of self-confidence or assurance—are occasionally displayed also by men of mind and character. On the other hand, it is a matter of common knowledge that weakly and deformed beings display a sharp mental activity that can even become caustic, and which represents, in their case, a means of defense to protect them against unexpected attacks.

When he finds himself in the presence of honest men, the Hebrew's situation is analogous. He, the weakling who is incapable anywhere of shaping a life for himself by his own exertions, whom political incapacity has condemned to lead a parasitic existence amongst other nations; he, who is lacking in all the higher mental powers necessary to produce an imaginative and creative culture; he, it is, who has been equipped with a cunning intellect, and with boundless impudence and slyness as a means of defense. *In reality, the Hebrew is the mental cripple amongst mankind, a type of intellectual deformity.* The Jew represents the lower side of human nature. Let those wonder at him who will; we would only feel sorry for him if he did not happen to be, at the same time, a poisonous snake that endangers the peace and safety of honest people everywhere.

But the slyness of mind and the threadbare morality are still not sufficient to assure him of prosperity. He requires yet another weapon for defense and attack, in order to outwit and overcome honest people. As a substitute for the natural ability that he does not possess, he has created for himself a principle in which an almost demonical force resides, namely, *finance-capital*. Money plays so great a part in the existence of the Jew that the individual sinks into insignificance when compared with material possession. "Whoever does not pay me my money, deprives me of my honor," wrote old Amschel Mayer Rothschild to the Elector William II. And the socialist leader, Karl Marx, who was himself of Jewish origin, admitted that "money is the real secular God of Jewry".[4] From an allegorical point of view, it is worthy of note that the Hebrews erected a Golden Calf on Mount Sinai, and arranged a dance around it.[5] This is also recognized by Sombart:

> Money, and the increase of money, must always be the center of interest for Jews, just as it is for capitalism. Not merely because its abstract nature is congenial to the equally abstract nature of the Jew, but above all, because the appreciation of money is in conformity with another leading trait in the Jewish character, namely, teleology. Money is the absolute means; it has but one meaning with regard to the purpose to be realized.

---

[4] Ed.: See Marx's "Essay on the Jewish Question" (1843).
[5] Ed.: See Exodus 32:1, 32:6, 32:22; Nehemiah 9:20; and 1 Kings 12:28.

Sombart expresses himself as above in his scientific German, and thereby recognizes money as the highest potential in all Jewish endeavor.

Money is, however, an imaginary value, an artificial creation of human speculation. It has nothing to do with nature, nothing to do with organic things; it has no inner relation to the being of mankind. Money does not make a man stronger, wiser, or nobler. The capability conferred on it by the human imagination—of possessing not only buying power but, in the form of loan capital, power to produce interest—has invested it with an almost supernatural might. And this imaginary might has been recognized by the Hebrew as the correct means to provide him with a substitute for his deficient powers. Money places the subhuman in a position to pose almost as a superman, and to force all human affairs under his yoke.

In what then does the renowned 'Jewish superiority' consist? In reality, in a kind of mental provocation and harassing. It is precisely because the Hebrew's essence is averse to Nature that he is destined to deceive and overreach the man who thinks naturally. It is because the Jew does not think organically, and consequently does not think naturally, that the unspoiled and unaffected man is unable to keep pace with his speculations. While we are accustomed to think straightforwardly, the Jew thinks, as it were, "around the corner;" his mental process is perverse, warped, subverted. Consequently, his conclusions confound all natural logic.

It frequently happens that a man who has been overreached by a Jew is unable to restrain a feeling, akin to admiration, for the cunning deceiver. The unnatural sequence of Jewish thoughts confuse a natural brain, so that it loses the power of thinking logically while under the influence of the Hebrew's seductive language, and falls into a kind of stupor—a condition in which a weak-willed man, or a man who is unable to think quickly, is inclined to succumb to the influence of an external will.

This power of suggestion that operates by imposing one's own will upon another is one of the most dangerous means employed by Jewry to infatuate not only individuals, but whole nations. There is scarcely any other way to explain this extraordinary state of infatuation in which the civilized nations of today find themselves, when confronted with Jewry, than by describing it as the result of a kind of suggestion or mesmerism. Indeed, both states and their populations scarcely know what is really happening to them; in addition to the demonical power of money, the Hebrew has also enlisted the gigantic power to deceive and mislead possessed by the press, in order to hypnotize everyone and to paralyze their mental activities. Perhaps, however, it only requires an unmasking of the hypnotic agent, and a thorough exposure of his dishonest expedients, to break the spell forever.

Chapter 15
Origin of the Jewish Entity

Descent of the Jews

Sombart searches around to discover the origin of the Jewish race, and hence raises a question: Whence does this race come, and whither is it proceeding? He does not hesitate to describe the Jews as a kind of freak, as a lower order of humanity, of entirely different blood to the nations amongst whom they live. I add to this: difference in blood means also difference in mind and spirit, for among the most important disclosures of the science of race must be included the fact that certain mental qualities are firmly and inseparably united with a certain kind of blood.

Additionally, in accordance with general acceptance, Sombart believes that the tribe of Israel, as well as that of Judah, originated from a mixture of various oriental peoples. This notion is contradicted by the fact that all Jews regard themselves as the descendants of a common tribal father (Abraham or Jacob), and that already at a very remote period, the Jews were prohibited by strict laws from mixing with other nations. Actually, one can only begin to speak of Jewry from the moment when a particular caste arrayed itself in conscious opposition to the rest of humanity, and declined either to mix with it or to entertain any feelings in common with it. It is precisely the exclusion of their stock from any mixing with the remainder of mankind that makes Jewry what it is.

That the Bedouin, that is to say, Semitic tribes, have provided the ground floor of the structure of Hebrewdom is universally accepted, and Adolf Wahrmund, in his frequently quoted work *The Law of Nomadism and the Present-Day Domination by the Jews*, has provided convincing proof of the spiritual affinity of Jewry with the Semitic desert tribes. Nomadism and changeableness are common to both; the conception of a firmly founded state is foreign to both, and both seek their salvation in continual wandering and traversing. They graze the pastures bare, and then move on to where fresh booty beckons to them. Both practice the sudden method of attack, allow no quarter, and exterminate; both are animated by the spirit of the desert that leaves a train of burnt-out settlements along its track.

Amongst the civilized nations, however, our Hebrews have altered the methods of their predatory expeditions. They no longer slay with the blade of the sword, but throttle their adversary with the golden noose of capitalism.[1] The surprise and slaughter of the opponent is accomplished, in its modernized form, on the Stock Exchange. There the die are cast that determine victory and dominion; there the economic fortunes and the economic freedom of the nations are gambled with; and as Judah plays with loaded dice, it is assured of victory. There the strangler of nations twines the golden snares in which he entangles not only the economic but also the spiritual and political life of the peoples.

But one must certainly not any longer speak of our Jews of today as pure Semites. They have also taken up all manner of foreign national elements; and it is truly remarkable to what a complete extent they have assimilated them. One is entitled to ask whether the Talmudic spirit alone has rendered this complete adaptation possible, or whether a few drops of Jewish blood have sufficed to give an unvarying stamp or impression—at least psychologically—to the entire mass. Externally the Jews of today present marked differences in their appearance; Negroid and Turanian (Mongolian) types can be discerned amongst them, as well as Semitic. Even amongst the Hebrews who hail from Russian Poland, one not infrequently comes across blond and blue-eyed examples. It is practically certain that the people who were formerly called the Khazars, who are regarded as belonging to a Finnish-Tartar stock, and who, about 800 years after Christ, formed a separate empire in the South of what is now Russia, went over to Jewry and were completely absorbed. The Jews themselves are conscious of this racial distinction, for the western Jews—who have come across Spain, call themselves "Sephardim" (if baptized: Marranos), and have North African blood in their veins—describe the Eastern Jews as "Ashkenazim," and look down on the latter with a certain amount of contempt. In spite of this, the Talmudic law embraces them all, and the Rabbinical despotism welds them into a close caste, absolutely united in its hostility to all non-Jewish peoples.

If, therefore, the Jews of today are not to be regarded as a united race from a physical point of view, all Jewry is inspired, nevertheless, with the uniform racial spirit of Hebrewdom. And—one must not forget this—the spiritual entity is of higher importance to the racial idea than the purely physical, and this fact may well play a part in all manner of chance externals without prejudicing the racial groundwork of blood and soul.

---

[1] We find here a parallel with the Indian Thugs (Robbers), who consider that they can best serve their God by strangling as many victims as possible. Perhaps these Thugs also stand in relation to the old rejected caste of the "chandala."

Chapter 15 – Origin of the Jewish Entity

If an explanation is required of what is understood by the expression 'race,' it can be formulated on the following lines: race denotes a community that, starting from a common ancestor, is based on blood relationship and exhibits, for that reason, a number of physical and mental characteristics. One must also reckon with the fact that, with the blood, the attributes of the mind and disposition, of the temperament and character, are inherited equally with the bodily properties. The purer and more united the race is, the more stable and constant is this inheritability. Through admixture with other race-elements, racial peculiarities are partly masked—the external ones more so than the internal—but they assert themselves again, often after generations, with astonishing distinctness. One is therefore entitled to say: A race characterizes itself by means of a complex of unvarying, transmissible qualities.

The German people of today represent a mixture of Germanic, Slavonic, and Romanic (Celtic)—or, according to modern methods of indication, of Nordic, Alpine, and Mediterranean elements—that have melted into a certain sort of homogeneity after the lapse of centuries, at least to the extent that scarcely any doubt can exist as to the uniformity of German thought and German feeling. It is only comparatively recently, after distinct signs of degeneration have become visible, that it appears as if these racial constants are about to be dissolved into their original elements, and, in the course of this process, to release a multitude of mongrel-products (degeneration-forms) that cannot be classified racially.

If the existence of a separate Jewish race is disputed, as Felix von Luschan,[2] amongst others, attempts to do, the contention may perhaps have a certain amount of justification, as there was not an original Jewish race; it appears to me much more likely that the Hebrews arose out of a mixture of the dregs of all kinds of races—a mixture, however that has been welded by thousands of years of inbreeding into a racial type.

In the meantime, whoever is searching for the anthropological peculiarity of the Jews will find this rather in the constitution of *mind* and *character* than in definite physical relations. It is quite correct that the Sephardim are preponderantly long-headed, that the Ashkenazi Jews are round-headed, and that the profile of the face passes through a great variety of gradations. Perhaps shortness of limb can be regarded as the most noticeable physical feature of the Jewish race. Nearly all Jews possess remarkably short arms and legs and a proportionately long trunk. Whereas the normal European, and especially the German, spans more than the entire length of

---

[2] Ed.: Von Luschan (1854-1924) was an Austrian scientist, researcher, and writer.

his body, in the case of the Hebrew it is the reverse. The inferior development of the arms might certainly be accounted for by the fact that the race in question has never occupied itself with honest manual labor, has employed neither weapon nor oar, and, for these reasons, has failed to develop the arms properly. Other unmistakable physical features include the relation and position of the ear to the nose: amongst the pure Aryans, the ear and the nose, on an average, are of equal length and are on the same level; in the case of the Jew, variations and startling irregularities in both of these respects are noticeable.

As a matter of fact, however, Jewish racial constancy is stronger in the present day than is the case in any other human strain, and this is also confirmed by the declaration of Professor Gans that has been already quoted. That the peculiar mental tenacity of the Jewish people was already in evidence in the remotest period is testified to by the excited references of the ancient prophets to this "stiff-necked and stubborn" people.

Jewish peculiarity may also acquire exceptional solidarity from the fact that this nation, more than any other, possesses a religion entirely suited to its nature, and which occupies itself at the same time, in the most painstaking fashion, with laying down the most detailed precepts for the conduct of ordinary life. Race, religion, nationality, mode of living, and business behavior are all cast in the same mold as far as the Hebrews are concerned. These are all a uniform expression of the same fundamental nature. The mentality and character of this people, owing to uniform schooling and tense discipline, and owing to the mode of living that has become strengthened by inbreeding and habitual by the practice of thousands of years, must have established and incorporated itself to an unusual degree, so that the Jews are less susceptible to outside influence than any other race of mankind that is capable of culture and development.

The voluntary segregation of this race and the consciously fostered aversion to all other peoples both contributed to maintain Jewry in its singularity. It must be repeated with emphasis: the segregation, so far as the Jews were concerned, was voluntary—just for the preservation of their singularity and their singular rites. Sombart insists that the Jews have not always been "half-citizens" in foreign states, but on the contrary, in olden times, were frequently actually endowed with peculiar rights and privileges. They held themselves aloof, however, of their own free will, from all participation in civic and state affairs. They did not accept their share of the spiritual and political destiny of the nation. They regarded themselves everywhere merely as visitors and foreigners, and were always ready to fasten up their bundle, so that—laden with gold and silver, after the manner of their forefathers—they could slip over the frontier.

Sombart also confirms the fact that Jewish peculiarity did not first develop out of the Diaspora, as biased Jewish historians try to make us believe, but that the Diaspora itself is a production of this peculiarity. Equally invalid is the contention that Jewish peculiarities are the fruit of religion and rabbinical doctrines; rather, the Jewish religion grown out of the fundamental nature of Jewry, and is the inevitable product of the Jewish mode of thinking. Indeed, it is an indispensable expedient for sustaining the Jewish mode of existence. Without this "immoral morality," the Hebrew could not continue. The rabbinical doctrines are merely the undisguised expression of the real thoughts and feelings of the Jew; if these doctrines had been artificially constructed, and had been forced upon the Jews against their inclination, the whole Jewish mass would have revolted against such views of life. But no one has ever heard of anything of the kind. Rather, the Hebrews have gladly adopted these senseless doctrines because the latter suit them perfectly. Sombart is therefore entitled to say that one may, without hesitation, infer the peculiarity of the Jewish religion from the national peculiarity of the Jews. Certainly, when he expresses doubt if one is justified in attributing the dishonest behavior of Isaac, Jacob, and Joseph to some fraudulent trait in the Jewish nature, we must leave it to the reader to form his own opinion on this point.

One legend that always crops up—that the Jews were originally an agricultural people—is to be accounted for by the excusable failure to distinguish between the two tribes, Israel and Judah. The widely-held opinion, especially amongst theologians, that Israelites and Jews are identical, is an assumption that must be challenged, for it is refuted by numerous passages in the Old Testament in which Israel and Judah are mentioned.[3] Ancient Israel was a people composed of honest farmers and graziers that eventually came under the yoke of the intruding Hebrews. The real Jew made his appearance in Palestine, just as in other countries, as the financial-political usurper; he came with the gold that he had abstracted from other countries—as in the case of the excursion from Egypt—into the land, and made the honest population tributary to him by money-lending and usury. And thus the honest agricultural Israelites were enslaved by this alien money-bourgeoisie, precisely as many other nations are in the present day. But the

---

[3] Among other matters, it is worthy of notice that in the apocryphal story of Susanna and Daniel, a sharp distinction is drawn between Canaan's stock and not Judah's on one hand, and the "daughters of Israel" and Susanna as "daughter of Judah," on the other [Ed: see Daniel 13].

detestation of the real Israelites for the new money-lords must have been very pronounced when the Israelitish captain, Abner, answered an unworthy imputation with the indignant words: "Am I then a scoundrel like a Jew?"[4]

Development of the Jews as a Commercial Nation

During the subsequent vicissitudes of the people of Judah, there was opportunity and spare time to devote themselves to agricultural occupations; the Hebrews, however, never availed themselves. They feel little inclination for this burdensome and upright occupation because it is impossible to make a fool of nature. And already, one wise Talmudic rabbi said as much in the following words: He who spends 100 shekels in trading can enjoy meat and wine every day; but on the other hand, he who spends 100 shekels on tilling the soil has to be satisfied with salt and cabbage, must sleep on the ground, and endure all manner of hardships. Thus, there is no lack of historians, even amongst the Jews themselves, who openly admit that the Jews are inclined by their very nature to trade, are devoted to it, and are a nation with a very pronounced commercial tendency. Their most ancient scriptures also bear testimony to this fact. The cuneiform documents from Nippur as well provide additional evidence that the Hebrews were already wholesale dealers and bankers in ancient Babylon. They cheerfully relegated dangerous maritime trade to the Phoenicians, for this branch of commerce called for personal courage, and was inseparable from peril to life.

Sombart must think us great simpletons when he tries to represent the notorious robbery of gold and silver by the Jews on their departure from Egypt as if these were loans. This discloses an astounding lack of any understanding for national psychology. Since the Hebrews, in olden times, scarcely ever conducted any other occupation than those of grain dealer, cattle dealer, usurer, and pawnbroker, it may be taken for granted that they carried on these occupations in Egypt also. I consider it likely that the gold and silver vessels and costly garments that the Hebrews took with them on the occasion of their Exodus from Egypt were pledges that the Egyptians handed over to the Jewish usurers, into whose clutches they had fallen. To what extent the Jewish usurer was in demand in olden times is testified to by the punitive sermon of Nehemiah, and especially by Amos (8:4-7).

It is only part and parcel of the Jewish doctrine and worldview that the Rabbis, all their lives, have never declined to participate most actively

---

[4] 2 Samuel 3:8. Katsch translates: "Am I then a Jewish scoundrel?" [Ed: Most English translations use the wording, "Am I a dog's head for Judah?"]

in all monetary transactions. Even Sombart admits that the Rabbis are, in many cases, the chief moneylenders; there are even passages that seem to suggest that the Rabbis have a monopoly on usury. Sombart cites an instance out of the Oxford Papyrus that actually describes a case of Jewish usury on a grand scale, for it is distinctly declared in this document that is a bond or obligation, that the debt shall be doubled each time that it is not repaid at the appointed term—a true Jewish mode of operation, one that we are continually coming across at all times and in all places.

Is it any wonder that the Hebrews have managed by such practices, throughout the ages, to draw the money of other nations quickly into their own hands? And thus Sombart remarks that already in the Hellenic period, and in the time of Imperial Rome, rich Jews were acting as moneylenders to the kings; and much was said in the Roman world concerning Jewish hagglers and usurers. Amongst the Arabs, the Hebrew has the reputation of being a born usurer and wheeler-dealer. The Jews were likewise the financiers and businessmen of the Merovingian kings. And in Spain, where they enjoyed the most freedom for their operations, they very soon had the nation in debt to them. Already at the time of the Crusades, they were engaged, to an excessive extent, in money transactions, and "bled" the Crusaders mercilessly. Sombart adds:

> It is really about time that the fairytale disappeared, that the Jews had first been driven into the money-lending business during the European Middle Ages because all other occupations were closed to them. The history of Jewish loan-traffic, extending over a period of two thousand years before the Middle Ages, ought really to be sufficient proof of the erroneousness of this historical fabrication.

And even when the path to other occupations lay open to the Jews, they still turned aside to devote themselves, with preference, to the loaning of money against pledges. Indeed, at certain times, authorities even offered premiums to induce the Jews to choose other vocations, but all attempts in this direction proved futile.

It is characteristic of the Jewish religion that the Jewish temples, in olden times, were the centers of the money traffic, and were, to a certain extent, banking houses. A large quantity of gold was accumulated in the Temple at Jerusalem. And this alliance between religion and money traffic is not to be excused on the grounds that other Semitic nations, like the Babylonians, are said to have done the same. At any rate, the same reproach cannot be leveled at the Christian Churches. And although a talent for usury can occasionally be found amongst the other nations, the non-Jewish usurer is, generally speaking, more or less an amateur; the Hebrews alone have brought usury to an art and a science—have exalted it even to a religion. Sombart also admits that the Jews have developed the technique of loan agreements to an uncanny perfection. He says:

> If one reads the fourth and fifth chapters of the Bava Metzia [in the Talmud], one gets the impression that one is taking part in a usury-inquisition in Hesse, some 20 or 30 years ago, so multitudinous are the tricks and devices that are introduced into these loan-contracts.

It is, therefore, not without full justification that both wealth and usury have come to epitomize Jewry.

While the priests of other nations have to be the guardians of what is ideal, the Hebrew priests are businessmen to their very fingertips, and even usurers. Sombart says:

> It is remarkable what a number of rich and very rich men there are amongst the Talmudists. It is not at all difficult to draw up a list of several dozen Rabbis, all of whom enjoy the reputation of being extremely wealthy.

But Sombart confesses that all his investigations into the faculty of Jewish acquisitiveness do not satisfactorily account for the phenomenon of Jewish wealth. He has actually forgotten the most important factor, namely, the confederation of the Jewish business demeanor, the "Chawrusse"—the secret networks of the Jews. The enormous gains of the Jewish capitalists are also only to be accounted for by the existence of the Chawrusse. The Chawrusse continues, at the present moment, on all sides; on the Stock Exchange, amongst the banks, in the press, in the "White slave" traffic, even amongst Jewish pickpockets and burglars; and it has ramifications over the whole world. There is only one satisfactory explanation for this phenomenal enrichment of the Jewish people; it is the organization in bands, of trade, of usury, of fraud, and of theft; and all these again are federated with one another—however vague and shadowy such connections may appear to be.[5]

It is exactly as Herder has already stated: "The Hebrews are a despicable race of cunning dealers, a race that has never desired honor, home, or country. That they ever were valiant warriors and honest peasants does not appear credible to us, for the disposition of a nation does not alter so quickly."

Sombart makes a last attempt to save the honor of the Jewish nation and to explain away its peculiarities by representing the Jews as an oriental people that became mixed up with or dispersed amongst Northern nations, and started a cultural system in conjunction with them. Certainly one has every right to acknowledge that the penetration of a nation with alien racial elements can impart a tremendous cultural impulse. Gobineau,[6] as is well known, has attempted to explain the origin of the ancient cultures as being the consequence of the penetration of Southern nations by elements of the Northern race, the blond Aryans. The Aryans assumed leadership amongst those who had been subjugated, and by means of their organizing power and heroic mode of thinking, they sowed the seeds of future great developments.

It is unlikely that anyone will attempt to compare the part that the Hebrew plays amongst us in the present day with the above example. Nowhere can the Hebrew be regarded as the bearer of culture and of a new social order; his entire method of working is too negative. When Sombart continuously talks about "capitalistic culture," he is only using a euphemism. We learned already at the beginning of our examination that although the capitalistic economic method can certainly effect a prodigious release of latent forces, the only result is a rapid wasting-away of the nations concerned; in no case is a constructive culture ever produced.

Justifiably apprehensive of the above fact, Sombart occasionally speaks of "the strange blossom of capitalistic culture." Even more remarkable is his expressed opinion that this oriental race wastes its best faculties in an environment that, racially and climatically, is unfavorable. On the contrary, it seems to me that it wastes the faculties of *others*. I can agree with him, however, when he calls the Bedouins "itinerant cattle breeders and nomads," and then continues:

---

[5] There is a particular association in Russia for the purpose of business and exploitation, called Qahal, that embraces the whole Jewish community. Important disclosures concerning this are to be found in Dr. Richard Andree's book *Zur Volkskunde der Juden* ("On Jewish Folklore"; 1881).
[6] Count Gobineau: *Essay on the Inequality of the Human Races* (1902).

> Such a restless and roving tribe of Bedouins were those Hebrews also, who, about the year 1200 BC, burst into the land of Canaan, pillaging and murdering, in order to compel the native population to work for them.[7]

He also admits that the land was subdued, less by martial valor than by financial subjugation, and that the Hebrews had known how to make the greater part of the territory pay tribute to themselves, and thus to achieve the same result by a loan relationship. He allows—as thoughtful anti-Semites have always held—that

> Considerable numbers of Hebrews resided in the towns, drawing rent and interest, whilst the enslaved population cultivated the soil as if it were a colony…

All the idle talk about the Hebrews having been formerly an agricultural people, can, as Sombart also admits, be dismissed as a myth; he says:

> But the spirit of nomadism must have remained active in all tribes, for if it had been otherwise—if Israel (that is, Judah) had been an agricultural people, even merely in an oriental sense—we would never be able to understand the origin and first formation of the Jewish system of religion.

As a matter of fact, an agricultural people is not inclined to invent a religion of usury and deceit, and to choose a God who ordains that the destruction of countries and their populations is a sacred duty. Whatever suggestion there might be of honest agriculture in the history of the ancient Jewish people must surely refer to the original and permanent population, the Israelites, and not to the tribe of usurers, called Hebrews, who migrated into the country at a later date.[8] That the Israelite history has become intermingled with the Jewish, and that, now and again in the Old Testament, glimpses of a loftier conception of divinity occur side by side with the

---

[7] These ideas of Sombart, however, are not original; they were already expressed my book of 1886, *Anti-Semitic Catechism*.

[8] Scheuermann, in referring to the book of Maurice Fishberg, an American Jew, traces the legend of agricultural Jews back to the fact that, in olden times just as in the present day, converts to Judaism by agricultural peoples were straightway designated Jews. [Ed: Fishberg's book is likely *Jews: A Study of Race and Environment* (1911)].

hate-breathing, vengeful destroyer of nations, Yahweh (Jehovah), can be ascribed to the influence of the non-Jewish Israelites.[9] Sombart seems to have some hazy notion that such is the case when he says that the Pentateuch has been composed to suit the mind of a nomadic people, and when he continues:

> The God who maintained his position victoriously against all other false gods is a god of the wilderness and of the shepherd. And, in the conscious establishment of the cult of Yahweh, all the ancient traditions of nomadism from Ezra and Nehemiah are quite distinctly adopted, without any notice having been taken of the intervening agricultural epoch that, in the case of the Jews themselves, perhaps never really occurred.

He then cites Julius Wellhausen, who corroborates as follows:

> The priestly records reject every reference to settled life in the land of Canaan; they confine themselves to an exposition of the desert migration, and claim to be, in every sense of the word, desert legislation. Sombart is of the opinion that if nomadic instincts and inclinations had not prevailed to a great extent amongst the broad masses of the Jewish people, this preponderantly nomadic religion could never have been permanently imposed upon them. And the destiny of the Jewish nation proves that it has remained a nomad and desert race throughout thousands of years.

This is my opinion as well. But all this again is nothing more than what discerning anti-Semites—who, so far as ethnological matters are concerned, are far in advance of their times—have been insisting upon for decades. But in order to avoid all points of contact with these intelligent racial-psychologists, Sombart finds it necessary to speak about "anti-Semitic pamphleteers" who have drawn upon these facts in a most odious fashion in order to obtain material to carry on their "campaign of abuse." He knows very little about those concerned when he includes Eugen Dühring and Adolf Wahrmund amongst writers of this class, for both of these, and more especially the latter, have only written in a most refined

---

[9] See my book: *Der falsche Gott* (The Wrong God).

and scholarly manner concerning the Jewish problem. Sombart regards all anti-Semitic utterances as "silly and odious"; but what he has to offer us, although presented in another form, does not differ essentially from the conclusions of those farsighted individuals who had comprehended the racial problem long before certain loquacious men had even formed an idea on the subject.

He is justified, however, in his derision of our incorporated professional wisdom that proceeds crablike, with logical considerations of the following kind: "In olden times, agriculture was carried on in Palestine; at that time, the Jews inhabited Palestine; consequently the Jews have been agriculturists." Really, one might just as well argue: In the present day, the Jews hold a dominating position in Germany, and since the German Nation that maintains itself for the greater part by agriculture, and has readied a high stage of culture, these Jews must be agriculturists, and the creators of German culture!

Dispersion of the Jews over the Earth

Sombart has only irony for the Diaspora—something that provides a most acceptable motive for evoking howls of lamentation from the children of Judah, and a whine of sympathy from many other sentimental people.[10] He is of opinion that, if we wish to be honest with ourselves, we are quite unable to form any correct impression of the Exile, whether of the departure or of the return. The Jewish account states: "And Nebuchadnezzar led away all the captains and all the soldiers; ten thousand were led away, and all smiths and metal-workers; no one was left except the common people of the country." And when it proceeds to state: "He led away all the nobility of the land from Jerusalem into captivity at Babel," the thought occurs to me that perhaps only the parasitic upper classes were transported, whilst the honest, agricultural population was allowed to remain undisturbed.[11]

There is, incidentally, obviously a mistake in Luther's translation of the latter passage. This reads: "But the rest of the people, who remained in the town, and who sided with the King of Babel, and that other poverty-stricken section of the populace, were led away by Nebuzaradan, the Governor." This must manifestly mean "not away," for, later on it reads: "and

---

[10] Amongst other things, it is interesting to know that Alexandre Dumas, in his play *La Femme de Claude*, which glorifies the Jews, makes his hero, Daniel, say: "the Diaspora has not scattered us; on the contrary, it has extended us in all directions. In consequence, we enmesh the whole world in a net, so to speak."

[11] 2 Kings 24:14-15 and 25:11-12.

the Governor called for peasants and vine-dressers from amongst the lowest in the land;" and again, later on, in verse 22, that the king had placed "the remainder of the people" under the order of Gedalja.

To the Governor, Nebuzaradan, Sombart gives the title "Chief of the executioners." What then is the point of this objectionable translation? Does it not disclose the ancient Jewish hatred for the enemies of Judah? But Sombart himself, referring to the exiles, speaks in confirmation of the above:

> The real country-people were not to be found amongst them. Thus the wisdom of the Assyrian kings obviously recognized the kind of plague that was afflicting the fruitful land of Canaan, and endeavored to purify the new province by deporting the parasitic class—the plutocracy—and leaving the honest peasant and working-class undisturbed in the country.

Excellent! This is exactly the reading that the anti-Semites adopted 30 years ago. And we are in agreement with Sombart, that these honest people were the remainder of the original native tribes. Thus our author, Sombart, has adopted the perception of the despised anti-Semites in its entirety when he characterizes the dominion of the Jewish nation in Palestine, and the conditions that they took along with them to Babylon, in the following words:

> Town-bred masters, who are, at the same time, money-lenders, have their land cultivated by non-Jews, who act as tenant-peasants; that, at any rate, is the typical picture that we obtain from the Babylonian Talmud.

Sombart allows it to appear that the Exile of the Hebrews in Babylon was by no means enforced by compulsion, and that the Hebrews, on the contrary, had gone there voluntarily so that they would be able to practice their usury to greater advantage in the centers of culture.

> For we never learn that those self-banished Jews ever returned to their native soil after they had acquired a small fortune, like emigrant Swiss, Hungarians, or Italians do in the present day. They remained, on the contrary, in the foreign cities, and maintained merely spiritual-religions relations with their native land. At the most—like genuine nomads—they undertook their annual pilgrimage to Jerusalem at the Feast of the Passover.

The diffusion of Jewry over all lands open to commercial intercourse must already, at that time, have been considerable, for, referring to Strabo, Josephus writes that it was not easy to find a single place on the inhabited earth that was not occupied and dominated by this race. Philo (ca. 20 AD) also reports that the Jews resided in numerous maritime and inland cities of Europe, Asia, and Libya. We do not hear, however, of any brutal act of violence that caused them to be dragged there against their will; for this reason, the dispersion of the Jews throughout all lands of culture has been manifestly voluntary. How closely packed they were, for example, in Rome during the early period of the Empire is testified by various authorities. An embassy from the Jewish King Herod to Augustus was accompanied by about 8,000 members of their faith who were domiciled in Rome, and in the year 19 AD, 4,000 men of military age, who had been released and were "infected with Egyptian and Jewish superstition," were sentenced to be deported to Sardinia.

Sombart goes on to speak about the very considerable immigration into the German Empire, and shows, by means of figures, how the Hebrews are streaming from the East to the West, and especially to Berlin. It certainly sounds more than strange when he speaks of "a people hunted from place to place." For my part, I am of the opinion that if the Jews move from Birnbaum and Meseritz to Berlin, they do so because they can do better business and procure more pleasure in the metropolis, and not because someone has chased them there. At the present moment, actually more than half of the Jews in Germany reside in the large cities, feeling more in their element there, because the brisker business life and the pleasures and noise of a large city are more in accordance with their taste. It is also pertinent when Sombart, in another passage, compares the great modern cities to the desert, indicating thereby that the spirit of the nomad and of the desert has a close affinity to that of the modern cities, and that the great modern city acts devastatingly on the national life. "Desert and Forest," says he, "are the great contrasts, around which the distinctive natures of countries and of mankind group themselves."

The forest is actually the real birthplace and home of the German, and it was on this account that *Germania* (or ancient Germany) appeared so gloomy and abhorrent to the Romans, who disliked forests. In the present day, the real German can prosper only in the field and in the forest; and, as forest and desert are contrasts, so also are the two extreme contrasts of mankind to be found in all that pertains, on the one hand, to the German, and on the other, to the Hebrew. It is a firmly-established fact that agriculture has, at all times, been the most important institution of the Germanic races, and was never entirely unknown at any epoch of early Indo-Germanic history. By living and working continually in the presence of Nature, as peasantry must of necessity do, the essential and true nature of the German is formed, as indeed is that of all truly constructive, cultural peoples. An estranged attitude towards Nature is the hallmark of the Semitic race—concerning whose tribal father, Cain, the murderer of the gentle and peaceful farmer Abel, it stands written: "A fugitive and vagabond shalt thou be upon earth! Let thy hand be against everyone, and everyone's hand against thee!" (Gen 4:12; 16:12).

Sombart betrays his predisposition for Jewry by commending what a 16th century Jewish physician in Spain thought, to account for the "high-spiritual" nature of the Jew. The physician was of opinion that the dry, pure air of the desert, the "clear water," and the "delicate food of Manna" have produced a marvelous spiritual refinement in the Jew. The ridiculousness of this perception is obvious. Must not correspondingly all Bedouins also have refined spiritual natures? And how will Sombart explain away the fact that the Arab, strangely enough, who must certainly be regarded as a true son of the desert, feels himself separated by a yawning chasm from the Jew? There is scarcely any other nation that fosters such abhorrence for the Jews as the Arab. Arabian authors have expressed their contempt for the Hebrew in the most biting terms. Already in the year 545 AD, Abd al Qâdir al-Jilani wrote as follows:

> The Jews, who live scattered throughout the entire world and, in spite of this, hold firmly together, are cunning, misanthropic, and dangerous beings, and must be treated just as one treats a poisonous snake—namely, by stamping on its head as soon as it approaches. For, if one allows it to raise the head for one moment, it will infallibly bite, and the bite is fatal.

And when Sombart makes a further attempt to account for the peculiar disposition of the Hebrews by ascribing it to their former life in the desert, one is entitled to ask: Why then haven't the Arabs become Jews? Why have they preserved a disposition that can be regarded as aristocratic and heroic in comparison with that of the Jew?

Sombart attempts to explain away the malevolent attitude assumed by the Jews towards the Northern nations by attributing it to the "wet-cold" manner of the natives of the North.[12] But this attempt at defense is also doomed to failure, for we see how the Hebrew, in southern countries such as Egypt and Morocco, behaves in exactly the same way and becomes usurer, just as he does in the North.

And when it is finally brought forward in excuse of the Jew, that his bad character must be attributed wholly to the circumstance that, for thousands of years, he has been the appointed custodian of the economies of the various nations, we then ask: Who appointed him? Did he not choose this role himself?

With regard to this particular aspect of the Jewish Question, there is a favorite perversion or distortion of facts that is repeated endlessly, and which is in conflict with all history, especially with the spirit of the Old Testament. It must be included amongst the clumsiest subterfuges employed by Jewry, but unfortunately belongs also to those adopted by the idealists amongst our fellow countrymen. The Jew is always represented as having had his particular role "forced upon him," against his will. In reality, he has chosen this role of his own free will in order to create conditions around him which are congenial to his nature. When Sombart says: "They became the lords of money, and by means of money, lords of the world," these words amount to a confession that the Hebrews made themselves masters of money in order to dominate.

To anyone who looks more deeply into the matter, the question certainly occurs as to whether the actual existence of money in fact introduces a dangerously deceptive and unnatural factor of power into human life, that the deceitful spirit of the Hebrew is thereby accorded the utmost license to develop its sinister activity. It is quite possible that the nations will not be freed from the Jewish plague until they can get rid of the bane of money—the kind of money, the value of which rests on a fiction, and which introduces a demonical element into culture. Or, until—according to Lagarde's plan—the State takes the entire money-business into its own hands.

The Hebrews did not invent money, nor have they dug the glittering gold out of the bowels of the earth; but they may well have devised that misuse of money that, in the shape of loan capital, loads the honest, productive nations with fetters of *interest*, to all eternity. The strange mystery connected with money lies not so much in the money itself as in the notion or conception of *capital that is derived from money*, and in the further

---

[12] In former times, the German attitude toward the Jews was by no means hostile. But the Jews have abused the great patience of the Germans, beyond endurance, and have thereby incurred the lasting hatred of their hosts.

notion or conception that is inseparably connected with the former, namely, "ever-lasting interest." It is unnatural to demand for a loan of money, so long as it is not repaid, a continuous, unchanging rate of interest for hundreds and thousands of years. It is here where the source of the distress of the honest, productive nations lies; here we find the cause of the unlimited growth of Jewish capital and Jewish dominion.[13] Sombart is therefore right when he says: "money places in the hands of the Jew the means to exercise power without being strong." In very truth, the feeblest and most cowardly nation in the world, by a misuse of the glittering gold, have arrogated to themselves the demeanor and position of lords and rulers.

It is amusing to read Sombart's account of how hateful the German-Polish Jews, the so-called Ashkenazi, are to the Sephardim, their western brethren-in-faith from Spain and Portugal. At Bordeaux, in the year 1761, the Portuguese Jews issued a drastic order: that all foreign Jews should leave Bordeaux within 14 days. They called the eastern Jews "vagabonds," and took the utmost pains to get rid of them as soon as possible. Now, if the more "aristocratic" Jews themselves harbored a detestation for the lower-class Hebrews, the Ashkenazi, how can anyone take it amiss when we feel this aversion in an enhanced degree? For the Sephardim and Ashkenazi are, to say the least, closely united by the ties of religion, morals, and their conjoined view of life; how then, shall these abhorrent beings not be doubly repulsive and hateful to us, to whom their feelings, mode of thinking, and entire nature are completely alien? The spiritual and spiritual-moral difference between these two sections of Jews cannot well be great; for they are both steeped in the atmosphere of the Talmud. And even Sombart admits that the habits of those of Jewish blood, however low on the social scale they may be, acquire a remarkable fixity; for instance, inclination for petty deception, obtrusiveness, lack of self-respect, lack of tact, etc.

These selections from Sombart's writings should suffice to convince anyone who regards the Hebrew in as favorable a light as possible—but who is, at the same time, unable to close his eyes to a number of serious faults and failings in the Jewish disposition, in themselves of sufficient warranty for regarding the Jews as a highly undesirable and entirely alien element—that the aversion and dislike felt by the moral nations for the Jews has been thoroughly deserved.

---

[13] I have already proposed in 1892 that it should be made obligatory and legal to include, in every loan contract, provisions for the reduction of the debt (so-called sinking fund) so that the debt could be paid off within a conceivable time—see my book *Land-usury and Stock Exchange*.

It is most valuable when a man who repudiates the slightest tendency to anti-Semitism, and who collects carefully every word said in praise of the Jews, makes such important admissions. It is for this reason that so many passages from Sombart have been quoted and criticized here, although they contain little that is new for anyone versed in the Jewish Question. It is evident that Sombart has learned much from the anti-Semites, but he employs a tactic that, though it may be ingenious, is certainly not noble: of repudiating the source of his instruction. I hope that our German countrymen will be ready to believe certain facts when stated by a person who refuses to be regarded as an anti-Semite, although they would flatly decline to accept these same statements when made by a declared anti-Semite.

CHAPTER 16
THE INFLUENCE OF THE JEW UPON WOMANKIND

Women exert an important influence upon the development of retail trade. It is they who oversee, for the most part, the purchase of necessities for the household; it is through their hands that the greater portion of the income earned by the man is returned into business life. And it is, for this reason, surely not a matter of indifference to whom women entrust their concern.

It is now a generally recognized fact that most women and girls give preference to Jewish shops. The apparent cheapness of Jewish goods might be offered as an explanation of this. Women—and even those women who are by no means entitled to include thrift amongst their other virtues—seem to find a peculiar pleasure in the mere idea that they have been successful in purchasing some article at a cheaper price than it is usually sold for—even when this supposed cheapness exists only in the imagination of the purchaser. Such women regard this result as being directly due to their own cleverness—in some cases, perhaps, even as a triumph of their own personal charm. For this reason, the shopkeeper—who, by exposing his wares in calculated disorder to be pulled about and hunted through, advances halfway to meet this landed feminine capacity for ferreting out and overreaching—will stand a far better chance of doing business than a rival tradesman who prefers a conventional and orderly method. Women often require "chance goods," and for that reason, visit by choice those shops or stores where everything lies jumbled up together, and where they imagine that they will be able to pick up something cheaply. They pass by the well-ordered shops—or so, at least, is the admission of a domesticated woman who knows her own sex.

By the cunning utilization of this feminine weakness, the salesman is enabled to kill two birds with one stone; he confers a special favor upon his female customers, and saves himself the trouble of sorting out and arranging his rubbish, of which task his customers obligingly relieve him.

If, in addition to this, the same salesman knows how to create the impression that—overcome, as it were, by her personal charm—he is prepared to part with some article below its proper price, he will infallibly secure her goodwill. And if, moreover, he is expert and nimble enough to flatter all of his customers in like manner, and to lead each individual one to believe that she has been especially favored over all other customers, he will have no cause to complain.

Our women are extraordinarily simple when confronted with any economic question, although they surpass men in many other matters where cleverness and intuition are required. They allow themselves to be perverted by the dazzling exterior of an object, and to be guided by the prospect of a momentary advantage without taking any account of the further consequences of their conduct or action. They do not stop to ask whether they are supporting, with their custom, principles that are unsound, and business practices that are harmful, and are thereby depriving genuine and deserving tradesmen of their custom—perhaps even forcing entire branches of industry into difficulties, promoting inferior manufacture, and, briefly put, imparting an ominous tendency to all business life. All such considerations are foreign to them.

Possessing these particular failings, they come face to face with the natural disposition of the Jew, who is likewise a man who believes in and upholds the dazzling exterior and the momentary advantage. The Hebrew, who takes more pains to study the psychology of his customers than the trader of Aryan descent—because he looks for his return less in the quality of his goods than in the exploitation of human vanities and weaknesses—has always been able to detect these peculiarities in the feminine disposition, and knows how to take the fullest advantage of the weak side of a woman.

As it is, his shop window acts confusingly and disturbingly on the feminine mind. It is difficult to define exactly what the particular art may be that the Jew uses in displaying his goods, so that the same items have a more attractive effect on the glances of the passersby than the wares in the window of a Gentile tradesman. There must be some kind of affinity or connection between the capricious and abstracted nature of the average feminine mind and the Jewish manner and touch when they exhibit or display anything. The Jews most certainly do not show superior taste in the arrangement of their wares, and it is rather a bewildering jumble or an obtrusive thrusting-in-the-face of certain articles that seem to excite and lure the female spectator.

The Jew also tries to puzzle and confuse by marking up unusual prices. An article in the shop of a Gentile tradesman that remains comparatively unnoticed at the price of 75 cents can be prominently displayed in a Jewish shop at the price of 97 cents—and here it seems, all of a sudden, to create the impression as if it were in reality several cents cheaper than elsewhere.

Chapter 16 – The Influence of the Jews upon Womankind

At any rate, it is a matter of fact that the Jewish show windows exert an almost mesmeric influence over the great masses of curious and inquisitive people. But for all that, the Hebrew embraces any other means whatever by which he may achieve the same result. Calculating upon the herd instinct of the public, many of the larger Jewish businesses engage and pay people solely for the purpose of walking to and fro on the pavement in front of their establishments at such times as the traffic is highest, and of occasionally stopping before the show windows as if curious and interested. Their example prompts others to imitate them, and businesses of this kind are always besieged by people. As soon as one of the hirelings separates himself from the throng and enters the shop, the movement seems to become contagious, and others follow.

An unceasing and striking series of advertisements in the newspapers by Jewish firms also serves to attract customers to their shops, and in this particular sphere of activity, the Jewish trader gives full rein to the obtrusiveness and heedlessness of his race. Doubtless such artifices ensure that Jewish shops are more extensively patronized than other establishments, but still they are insufficient to account for certain, almost unaccountable, phenomena. It is rather *the personality of the Jew himself* that acts upon so many women with absolutely forcible suggestiveness.

Without doubt, the well-known susceptibility of our women for everything "foreign" has prepared the soil for this astounding Jewish influence. It is an absolutely incomprehensible fact to people from other countries that representatives of our womanhood—from school girls up to women in their 40s—are to be found in large numbers, who act towards Negroes as if they were of their own race and standing. These same women behave in a downright shameless manner towards the various men of color. And yet other women, especially in the colonies, display an unbelievable intimacy toward the natives. This is a state of things that, quite apart from the unrestrained sensuality involved, is a miserable indication of a steady decline in national and racial self-respect. All this has reference to the relations that unfortunately exist between a large section of our women and the Jews.

And now I must step aside into a dark territory that the majority of our contemporaries pass unsuspectingly, but which must be explored and opened up in order to help to account for the unholy influence that the Jews have acquired amongst us. Certainly it is a region that a clean-living and conscientious man enters with reluctance, and it was a long time before I myself could make up my mind to lay it open to public view. But as this book runs but little risk of falling into the hands of the young, the idle, and the pruriently inclined, it will not be dangerous, in the presence of mature readers, to treat with candor a subject that, as a rule, normally shuns all publicity. As it is a question of the secret undermining of the moral and physical strength of our nation by the machinations of the Hebrews, undue sensitiveness in this respect may well be laid aside for once. Moreover, a discussion of this question cannot be avoided here because it is necessary to a proper characterization of the racial and ethical domain in which the Hebrew lives, and out of which sphere he molds his life and carries on his business. In order that the chief features may be recognized, it will be best to cite some instances selected from the experiences of daily life.

As an introduction, the following remarks are not out of place. The many thousands of single and married Jewish sensualists are causing such devastation amongst our young women that, from this quarter alone, the ruin of our nation is assured, even without considering all the other closely connected economic and social evils. Much can be learned from a thoughtful perusal of the following text. But, from my own personal observation, there are many experienced men who are ignorant of these facts, or, who are ignorant at any rate of the extent and depth of the injury that is being inflicted upon our nation. They simply proceed blindly on their way.

There is no doubt whatever that the real nature of the Jew is completely unknown and incomprehensible to the great majority of the most-educated people of today. They have had no opportunity to gain an insight into the more secret machinations of the Jew. Their acquaintanceship with Jews is confined, for the most part, to occasional and brief contact in social and business circles, and, since in this respect the Hebrew is inclined to show his most harmless and agreeable side, there is little cause for wonder when one repeatedly hears that the Jews are really nice, decent, amiable people. Others, again, only know the Jew from flattering literary presentations of him, like "Nathan the Wise" or Sir Walter Scott's *Ivanhoe*,[1] and yet others are inclined also to transfer their instilled and unquestioning reverence for the Biblical Patriarchs to the Jews of today. And has not our popular literature always been utilized in a most subtle manner by Jewish authors, to convey an entirely misleading portrait of the Jew? With a cunningly calculated appeal to German susceptibility, Jews and Jewesses have been portrayed invariably as high-minded, innocent beings—as patient creatures,

---

[1] Ed.: "Nathan the Wise" (*Nathan der Weise*) is a philosemitic play written by the German playwright Lessing in 1779. *Ivanhoe* is a philosemitic novel written by Scott in 1819.

bearing their burden of "eternal pain" because they have to suffer severely under the prejudice and unfounded hatred of the malicious Christians.

Moreover, as our daily press and our literature are completely under Jewish influence, all personalities who gain publicity are appraised and judged accordingly as they show themselves well-disposed, or the contrary, towards Jewry. This circumstance has always formed the standard of criticism for Jewish authors, and is more the case today than ever. The consequence is that from youth upwards, our dispositions are made susceptible to a false philanthropy, and become especially sympathetic to the "poor, innocent, persecuted Jews." And, in older years, "refinement" and "tolerance" both play a part in shielding the Hebrew of today from any unpleasantness that he might experience on account of medieval prejudice. Yes, we actually give ourselves trouble: not only to make all manner of excuses for the Jews, because of the illusory state of suffering in which they are supposed to live, but even to assist them, and to further their interests whenever we can—as if we had to make restitution for an ancient wrong that our ancestors are supposed to have inflicted on them.

Such a sentiment does credit to our hearts. But what about our intelligence? All people who are acquainted with history and with the actual facts of life know perfectly well that the Jews have never emerged guiltless from the occasional disasters that they have encountered, and that the tales of cruelties said to have been perpetrated against the Hebrews proceed, in many cases, from the imagination, and in others, from gross exaggeration. Thus, the so-called "Jew battles" of the Middle Ages were mostly confined to an expulsion of the Jews who had become far too numerous, from the towns and districts in which the economic pressure, directly due to their usurious practices and maneuvers, had become unbearable. Given that a tremendous clamor arises from the whole of Jewry in the present day whenever one of their race loses his life, or has even one hair of his head touched, one can easily understand how it is that all incidents in which Jews appear as the injured party have been so extravagantly described in history.

Assaults on Young Girls

The only person who really understands the Jew of today is one who has had the opportunity to associate with him on intimate terms for years; but an opportunity of this kind does not offer itself to many. For the Hebrew is just as cautious on his side in the selection of his intimate friends as any intelligent German might be; and the German knows instinctively, despite all conventional toleration, how to preserve a certain distance between himself and the Jew. Of all the greater importance, then, are the experiences of Jewish companionship that we will now let a correspondent relate in his own words.

> I came, as a guileless youth of 20, from a small provincial town to Berlin. Chance brought me into the company of Jews of the same age as myself. I was introduced by them into their family circles, and both saw and heard there much that came as a surprise to me. As the acquaintanceship with my Jewish friends became more intimate, opinions and sentiments were occasionally expressed in my presence that secretly horrified and angered me. But whenever I attempted to object, I was met with such universal laughter that I began to be ashamed of whatever delicacy of feeling I still possessed.
>
> In the circle of my more intimate Jewish friends, the conversation turned almost exclusively upon women and sexual matters. They preferred to boast about the various tricks and artifices that they had employed in order to seduce innocent girls; and in no case, did any one of them display the slightest trace of being conscience-smitten. It was regarded as a matter of course that the female servants must be at the disposal of the men in the Jewish household. "We have just got a new servant," announced one. "Is she pretty?" asked another. "Well, it is scarcely likely that my father would select anything bad for me," was the answer. One related with considerable ill temper that a servant girl, who had only been a short time in his family, had rejected his advances; his father, however, very quickly brought the girl to reason by saying: "Have I not engaged you as general servant? Very well, then! This is included in your duties!" And the universal assent of his listeners proved that they all regarded the incident from the speaker's point of view, and approved of the way it had been dealt with.
>
> Many years later, after other events combined to make me a convinced opponent of the Jews, these first and lasting impressions of my early manhood came vividly into my mind.
>
> I had, without success, repeatedly tried to convince a well-known educational reformer of the injuriousness of the Jews. He was too much of an idealist, and was too remote from practical, everyday life, to be susceptible to the influence

Chapter 16 – The Influence of the Jews upon Womankind   193

of commercial, economic, and political fads. According to his opinion, all hostility to the Jews arose from the incapability and envy of the "Christian" businessmen who did not feel able to compete with the "superior" Jew. In order to bring him down from his utopia into a sphere in which every man who had any regard for morality and decency would find it difficult to control his anger, I related to him some of my past and recent experiences as set down in a chapter on "Jews and Women." Still, even these made no impression upon him; he regarded them either as incredible, or at least, as grossly exaggerated.

After a considerable lapse time, he called on me again, and made the following admission:

I must confess that I have become convinced that the descriptions that you gave me of the relations between Jews and women are believable. At Munich recently, a passenger got into my train compartment, and I soon recognized, in the course of conversation, that my companion was an educated Jew in very comfortable circumstances. He might have been either a merchant or a banker. The conversation happened to turn upon the servant question, and he exclaimed: "At last, thank God, we have again found a nice and proper kind of servant girl." When I asked him if it was difficult to get servants in Munich, he replied: "There are servant girls enough to be had, but when I engage a girl I have my own particular conditions. I have a son who is 15 years of age, and one of my conditions is that he shall have free access to the girl."

The relater continued:

I could scarcely believe my ears; my heart almost choked me, but I managed, with effort, to assume an appearance of indifference, and asked: "What does your wife say to this?" The reply was: "What should she say? My wife is a sensible woman. Is it likely that she would wish the boy to have intercourse with unclean, street prostitutes? It can only be a source of satisfaction to her, that her son should have access to a clean and healthy girl in his own home!"

Our educational reformer was still more shocked at this answer than he had been at the first; but it had at last dawned upon him what a world-wide gulf lay between Jewish thought and Jewish perception, and ours.

But how few of those sentimentalists amongst us who are always disputing and denying everything of which they have not had any personal experience, have such a drastic opportunity of refuting their Nathan-like views of the Jewish character? We recognize one fact: The education of the Jewish youth is a very different process from that of the German. Is there any cause for wonder when boys, growing up into manhood, continue to extend the experiences that they have gained in the manner described above, so ruthlessly in every direction, that they become accustomed to regard every female—who, according to their view, is socially inferior, or who may be dependent upon them for a living—as an instrument for the gratification of their lust?

Anyone who does not shrink from the logical conclusions cannot but be astonished at the racial degeneration that is making itself only too visible by the countless thousands of illegitimate and falsely legitimate children that result from this Jewish-German sexual intercourse. And the easily recognizable mixed type, to be found amongst the populations of Berlin, Frankfurt, and other cities and districts that teem with Jews, will not come as a surprise and shock to the honest observer. And, keeping pace with this, is the appalling decay of national character that is the inevitable consequence of mongrelizing the race, and which invariably means national ruin. *A nation can save itself from moral lapses and decline, but never from racial decay.* Ancient Rome is a historical instance of the former case, France of the latter.

The lascivious impudence displayed by Jewish youth especially towards female employees in business houses, in dancing establishments, and in restaurants, and generally towards females of no social pretensions or devoid of all worldly experience, is only too well known. Neither married women nor girls scarcely emerged from childhood are safe from the demands of the most conscienceless of these fellows, and an unending succession of cases of this nature occupy the police courts; they would soon attract the attention, even of the most stupid, if the names, nationality, etc. of the criminals were not intentionally and systematically suppressed in all the newspapers.

It is a fact, confirmed by many police court cases, that Jews violate maidens who are so young that they are only to be regarded as girls, and even children. For these unnatural offenses, a kind of authority is actually to be found in Talmudic literature; for a Talmudist Rabbi tries to prove, by going into details, why a girl of *three years of age* is fit for sexual intercourse.[2]

Berlin, at the end of the 1770s, was the real field for conducting observations of a very convincing nature. The advance of Jewry was at that time extraordinarily in evidence. The fraudulent maneuvers on the Stock Exchange, during the so-called "promotion years," brought enormous wealth to the Hebrews, who forced themselves to the front in all directions in society as well as in public life. Even then, one could not avoid seeing what was a deeply humiliating sight for every honorable German, namely, splendid specimens of German womanhood hanging on the arms of Jews—and even then, not enjoying, at least, the respected position of a married woman. Dazzled by the flash appearance and behavior of Hebrews who have amassed wealth in every conceivable manner, and allured by the most cunning methods of seduction, countless women, well-qualified to be the mothers of the nation, fall victims, year after year, to the Jews, and descend to the level of purchasable commodities.

Prostitution always flourishes luxuriantly wherever the Jews have lived. It is a matter of common knowledge that a scandalous lawsuit scarcely ever runs its course without implicating one or more Jews, either as "friend," seducer, usurer, cheat, or receiver of stolen goods. The Leyden Papyrus that dates from Egyptian antiquity, as well as the Old Testament, refer frequently to Jewish sexual excesses. The Jew, as Oriental, is a supporter of polygamy—or, as the well-known Jewish author Max Nordau (Südfeld) expresses himself, "is not a monogamous animal." If he happens to live in countries where monogamy alone is legal, and conforms outwardly to this law, he can always find plenty of ways of evading it in order to indulge his oriental proclivities. Jewish married women place no obstacles in the way of their husbands in this respect, whether it is because the idea of polygamy is something innate in them, or because they derive a secret satisfaction from seeing the women of a foreign race—rivals in a double sense—in a state of complete subjection to their husbands.

With regard to the phenomenon, it is interesting to establish how occurrences of this kind are judged by Jewesses. In the *Literary Echo* (1912, no. 3), the Hebrew woman Anselma Heine deifies her racial companion, the author Jacobowski. In the course of her article, she treats of his love affairs, and expresses herself in connection therewith as follows: "Suddenly I discovered in him the ancient typical trait of pain, peculiar to his race.

---

[2] Ed.: This in fact is true. See the documented passages of the Talmud in *The Book of the Shulchan Aruch* by Erich Bischoff (2023).

He experienced a vindictive rapture in displaying his power over women, and never indicted the plebeian with more scorn than when he boasted how he had subjugated the elegant wives of the blonde nobility by brutal force." Try to imagine, if it were possible, that a Christian authoress would announce to the whole world, with such a voluptuous thrill of veneration, of the sexual triumphs of a fellow countryman over Jewesses.

And still one more instance of this kind. The publishing house Velhagen and Klasing has gradually built up a sound literary reputation by the loyal and strictly evangelical inclination of all their publications; they have been issuing, for about the last 25 years, the *Monatshefte* which form a periodical of interesting contents, edited by Zobeltitz and Höcker, and which of late has been giving preference to novels from the Jewish pen. The following noteworthy passage concerning the Jewish hero of a story is to be found in the novel *Der Tunnel*, by the Jewish author Bernard Kellermann (Fürth), published in the periodical:

> S. Woolf was a perfect specimen of a gentleman. He had only (!) one vice, and he concealed it carefully from the outside world. It was his extraordinary sensuality. The blood began to sing in his ears as soon as he caught sight of a young and pretty girl. He travelled at least once every year to Paris and London, and had his "friends" in both cities. From these expeditions he occasionally brought back "nieces," whom he transplanted to New York. The girls had to be young, pretty, and blonde. S. Woolf avenged (!) in this way, poor Samuel Woolfsohn (his father) who, years before, had been hopelessly driven out of the field, so far as all good-looking women were concerned, by the competition of stalwart tennis players and large monthly checks. He took his revenge on that blonde race, who had formerly spurned him with their feet. And above all, he recompensed himself for the privations of his youth.

Thus, the cynical debauchee, who deals with blonde girls as if they were nothing more than so much human flesh, captures them, enjoys them, and then flings them aside, is, according to Jewish notions, the "pattern of a gentleman!" And then this foolish idea of revenge: because old Woolfsohn could find no favor in the eyes of German women, is that any reason why his son should revenge himself on other women of the blonde race? Has the Jewish author here, by mistake, revealed too much? Accordingly, it is not inclination or mere sensual desire that attract the Hebrew to blonde women, but rather—*hate and revenge!* He desires to ruin and dishonor as many of these females as possible, whether they stand in any sort of relation to his scheme of revenge or not, and thus procure retribution—for what? For a wrong existing only in a Jewish imagination clouded with conceit and hatred.

Indeed, logic of this order can only flourish in the swampy carnal-mindedness of a people who celebrate today, just as they celebrated more than 2,000 years ago, with songs of triumph, the memory of the massacre of those 75,000 Persians who fell victims to the lust for revenge of the whore Esther and her cousin Mordecai.[3]

But without doubt, the real motive for the revenge lay, as far as the Jewish "gentleman" was concerned, in the concluding sentence: "he compensated himself for the deprivations of his youth." He did so by dishonoring, with the help of his money and all the tricks of the professional seducer, as many women of the blonde race as possible; and the incarnate hatred sweetened his triumphs.

And what about the "ancient, typical trait of pain in the Jewish race"—"the eternal pain of the Jews," of Heine, Jakobowski, and company? It is nothing but the mortification of Mephistopheles that the Jew is not left at liberty to do exactly as he likes; the mortification of Shylock when he is prohibited from mutilating his business rival in order to gratify his demonical hatred. This pain, born of hatred and insolent pride towards everything that is not Jewish, is certainly an ancient inheritance of the race, and one of its fundamental and lasting characteristics. The Jew disguises or conceals it under the appearance of melancholy, whereby he deceives simpleminded people, as long as he dares not exhibit his real nature; and it discloses itself as insolent sensuality or ruthless rapacity, when it feels that it is safe enough to step, unveiled, into broad daylight. Woe to those who allow themselves to be deluded by the harmless exterior. And may shame and disgrace descend on all who assist the Jew in deceiving the rest of humanity as to the true nature of his "pain" and "revenge."

What kind of spiritual offspring this "typical, ancient pain" of the People of God is, is disclosed in a poem published in the Jewish periodical *Die Aktion* (February 1913), from the pen of a certain Paul Meyer. Perhaps it may open the eyes of a few, here and there, to the thinly veiled ultimate aims of Jewry.

---

[3] Ed.: See above, Chapter One, note 2.

THE MERRY SONG OF THE VAGRANT AHASVER

Behold! I am a man rooted to no spot,
A man unwedded to any environment:
The narcosis of home-sickness
Does not drive my heart into my breeches,
For I am proof against grief.

If you drive me from your thresholds,
I still remain more sought-after than anyone else,
Your cries of envy resound,
For I drink at your fountains,
And I weigh up your values.

The sleek skin of my soul
Conceals what I have expiated as a beggar,
Still, my booty mounts up
And, your brides call joyfully to me
— me, the refuse of a foreign desert.

Yawningly you exhale your tobacco-smoke
As you honorably digest your meal,
But I am a clever juggler,
And I know how to excite your vices
So that they develop to the utmost.

Thus I continue to play the game
Of my mature insolence,
The strange, very subtle, final aims
Of my Asiatic blood.
Which are hidden from you!

It is a fact that the Rabbinical doctrines of the Talmud deny the right of the Jewish wife to raise any objection to her husband's intercourse with women who are not Jewish, even though the latter may be married. The circumstance that the marriage of those who are not Jews is, according to Rabbinical perception, not to be regarded as marriage but "as no better than the living together of beasts," confirms this. According to Talmudic doctrine, those who are not Jews are never to be regarded as human beings, but only as "animals in human shape".[4]

Such a perception accounts for a whole series of Jewish views that would otherwise remain enigmatic. An animal has no moral rights, and consequently Rabbinism does not recognize any moral duties towards those who are not Jews. A beautiful woman who is not Jewish is nothing more than a beautiful animal in the eyes of the Jews, and therefore the individual Jew is at liberty to do with her as he likes. In any case, there is no need for him to trouble his conscience with what becomes of her.

Now and again, one hears the voice of a superior type of Hebrew, frankly admitting and disapproving of this shameful behavior on the part of their racial companions towards Gentile women. Conrad Alberti (Sittenfeld), for instance, writes as follows in M. G. Conrad's *Society* (1889, no. 2), after he spoke of Jewish intolerance towards those who are not Jews:

> The only exception is sexual intercourse, and especially the behavior of rich, young Jews towards girls of the poorer class, seamstresses, etc. This reaches an incredibly low level of cynical brutality, and one to which I have never seen young Christian men sink. The latter, for the most part, still preserve some lingering traces of shame in the presence of the opposite sex. But in the case of our young "jobbers" of the Stock Exchange, not a spark is to be found.

The thousands of girls who, year in and year out, come to their ruin in Jewish firms and in Jewish families, could provide terrible evidence that this honest admission is founded upon fact. Certainly, the objection is justified that employers and people in positions of authority, who are not Jews, frequently abuse their position in the same shameful manner; but in all cases of this nature, a characteristic difference always distinguishes those instances where the culprit is a Jew from those where he is not. And this difference lies in the attitude that Jewish women take towards such conduct on the part of their menfolk. When confronted with a servant girl's complaint that the "master" or "young master" is annoying her with his attentions, a German married woman will, 99% of the time, severely reprimand the men of her household, and will replace the girl by one less dangerous. It is far otherwise with the Jewish wife or mother. She not only shows herself tolerant to her young son, but overlooks as well the weaknesses of her

---

[4] See Bischoff, *The Book of the Shulchan Aruch* (2023), pp. 69-70, 121.

husband, and actually assists him to attain his object—thus following the Biblical example of Sarah—by advising the girl that it is in her own interests to yield to the desire of her pursuer.

In one particular instance, I was told a story in which a rich married Jewish woman heard a complaint by her pretty housemaid that the master of the house was persecuting her with his attentions. Smiling almost sympathetically, and with a goodwill that had something motherly about it, the lady of the house said to the girl: "What a foolish child you are! You are young and pretty. If you leave and go to another house, there will be men there also, and they will also pursue you with the same object. And if you again leave your place and go to another, it will be the same there as well. Men are like that; a pretty girl is never free from pursuit. And at last you will yield. So, be sensible and remain here; my husband is rich and can pay you well!"[5]

In this case, the girl possessed enough character to leave at once; but how many others would be strong enough to resist such plausible argument and insidious temptation? They fall victims to the Jews, and preserve silence concerning their shame. Moreover, the Jew is astute enough to flatter the girl's vanity with timely presents and liberal treatment, so that those who have fallen, after they have lost the initial sense of disgrace, find little difficulty in speaking in glowing terms of their Jewish employers.

This story may surprise some readers on account of the peculiar attitude adopted by the Jewish married woman, but this fact is nothing new to anyone acquainted with the circumstances. And quite apart from the Talmudic perception, this behavior arises out of another and absolutely materialistic frame of mind. The Jewess knows only too well that her lascivious husband will not be satisfied with intercourse with only one woman. Accordingly, he will seek opportunities away from home. This, however, is generally expensive, and carries, moreover, dangers in its wake—not the least of which are those affecting health. The astute, frugal Jewess thus reasons with herself: *a healthy servant girl, who is paid a few dollars more than the usual wages, and who receives an occasional present as well, is the cheapest expedient for appeasing my husband's lewdness. And of course, danger of infection is much less.*

---

[5] It is well known to the inhabitants in Berlin that, in exchange for a special payment, many registry offices for servants send out all good-looking country girls exclusively to Jewish households.

Chapter 16 – The Influence of the Jews upon Womankind

The Enchanter

It has already been suggested above that the Jew's personality exercises a remarkable, even puzzling influence over many women, something that can be described as suggestive and will-destroying. When, in recent years, this subject was discussed publicly in the periodical *Deutsch-sozialen Blättern*, personal experiences and observations confirming this influence poured in from all sides. Powers seem to be at work that one is tempted to call demonical, and there is an unnatural sensual stimulation that apparently robs the victim of her reason. The role of "enchanter," which one otherwise assigns to the female, seems in this case, by some inexplicable means, to be transferred to the opposite sex. And this power must be described as unnatural and disquieting, because the woman who is susceptible to its influence appears to succumb literally without showing the slightest trace of resistance.

Amongst the communications already mentioned are the following that have been selected as particularly characteristic. A lady describes what was actually observed on several occasions:

> A somewhat shabby-looking Jew met a respectable middle-class woman. He glanced at her, she stopped, remained standing as if rooted to the spot, looked around at him, and finally followed him. Much the same thing happened in another street, where a red-haired Jewish clothes dealer was standing at the door of his shop. A respectable young female, in fact scarcely more than a school girl, passed by. The Jew catches her eye or whispers something to her; she stops suddenly as if shot, and remains before the next shop window, her gaze fixed on the Jew. It is not long before she follows him into his shop. And again: An old and ugly Jew called at the house of the young widow of a merchant who recently died. She admitted him again the same evening, and allowed him to spend the night with her. She came from a good family, and was educated and refined; he was a repulsive old fellow, devoid of refinement.

The lady continues:

> The question arises: Are there, perhaps, secret Talmudic arts at the bottom of all this? It is said that many Jews have

brought their art to such a pitch that they can, with one glance, cause a female to quiver and tremble just as if she had received an electric shock. A lady who allowed herself to be implicated with a Jew gave the following account to her family as soon as she regained her senses: The first time that the man spoke to her, and gazed at her with his penetrating dark eyes, she felt stricken to the core, and from that hour she was drawn by an irresistible force to him; that he had appeared to her in dreams, etc...

Who is going to solve this riddle? Is it the look, or is it, perhaps, the extraordinary Talmudic knowledge and experience of life acquainted with secret alterations in relations—with certain mysterious, sympathetic forces? Or must we, in these cases as well, take into consideration Jewish energy, whereby the Jews have perhaps learned how to dominate the female mind?

As a matter of fact, in such cases as these, one is confronted with something obscure and mysterious that must be made clear at all costs. The great majority of the countless girls and women who have fallen victims to Jewish seducers relate afterwards that they were driven towards them, as it were, by some unknown evil power.

Unquestionably, many Hebrews utilize hypnotic powers in order to render women submissive to their will. A correspondent, writing from Trieste on 16 July 1913, announced:

> The authorities here have just succeeded in arresting a certain Ziffer, who had abducted a 19-year-old girl of noble descent, and daughter of a great silk manufacturer, after he had previously hypnotized her. It is said that, years before, Ziffer had abducted the wife of a Breslau sugar refiner by employing similar methods.

Further, one read in the Berlin papers of 20 July 1913:

> The tragic fate of a young girl who had been robbed by a marriage swindler of all her savings, and who had committed suicide in her despair, was revealed yesterday in the course of a case that came up for hearing before the 2nd Vocational Criminal Chamber of the Provincial Court of Justice. As a

Chapter 16 – The Influence of the Jews upon Womankind

result of the enquiry, the fitter Frederick Ziffer was brought up on a charge of fraud.

In April of the same year, the accused had made the acquaintance of the single woman, Johanna Simon, who had arrived in Berlin from her home a few days before. Ziffer represented himself to the girl as an engineer and promised, after a short acquaintanceship, to take her to South America and to marry her there, describing to her at the same time in glowing colors, the delightful life that would be their lot. The girl, who was a strict Catholic, told him that she would not marry out of her faith, and so the accused, who was a Jew, pretended to be a Catholic also, and carried his hypocrisy so far that he raised his hat ostentatiously every time he passed a Catholic place of worship in the company of the girl. By all kinds of pretexts, he succeeded in inducing the inexperienced girl to part with her entire savings. When he had extorted the last dollar from her, and had, in addition, brought her to physical ruin, he let his mask fall and became brutal and callous. After the victim notified the police, it came out that the accused had already deceived and robbed another girl in a similar way. The Court sentenced him to ten months imprisonment.

The next day, the girl, who had gone to Hamburg, committed suicide in despair at her ruined life. On appealing his sentence, the accused had the incredible impudence to maintain that it was *grief at his punishment* that had driven the girl to take her life. Despite this, the Court actually reduced his sentence! The final judgment was six months and two weeks imprisonment.

This is one example of thousands. It was common in the "dark Middle-Ages" to safeguard the community against the repetition of such a crime by hanging the scoundrel at once. The occasional outbursts of outraged national feeling at Jewish misdeeds have been erroneously described in our falsified historical records as "Jew-baitings." For his "servitude" under German law, Ziffer knows full well how to satisfy his "typical, primitive Jewish pain" by taking further revenge on the female portion of the blonde race as soon as his mild punishment is completed.

And the men of the blonde race? Are they too "tolerant" and too "refined" to be any longer aware that the blonde women's honor is also their own honor?

Just as in the case of Ziffer, one is also inclined to assume the presence of some hypnotic power when one observes how even old and ugly Jews render young females docile and submissive to their desires. Many a story could be told, in this respect, about the small rooms behind the actual shops, into which Jewish dealers know how to entice pretty customers during slow business hours, usually under the pretext of showing them some exceptionally attractive patterns or garments. Feminine curiosity can seldom resist an invitation of this kind, and the Jew then has it in his power to create such compromising situations—for instance, by a further invitation to try the garments on—that the feminine nature proves too weak to resist.

The Berlin story continues:

> A respectable young woman, who had been enticed, in the way described above, into a small room leading out of the shop, became absorbed in the examination of some particularly beautiful patterns: hearing a peculiar rustling sound behind her, she turned sharply round and saw the Jewish shopkeeper standing completely naked before her. With a cry of horror, she rushed out of the shop.

But even if one is not willing to accept the theory of hypnotic influence, the weakness of women, when confronted with Jews, can be reasonably accounted for by other facts. Already in their own ancient writings, in The Old Testament and in The Talmud, the Israelites are described as a voluptuous and lewd people who were addicted to the grossest sensual excesses. Lust and desire stand written on the faces of the Hebrews, and this doubtlessly has an effect upon weak individuals of the opposite sex. But above all, it is the complete absence of a sense of shame that makes the Jew so dangerous to women, and which makes the game so much easier for him to play. The Rabbinical writings bear ample testimony to the complete absence of all sexual shame amongst the Hebrews by unabashedly relating the most intimate affairs, and always in a manner as if the most harmless and ordinary topics were being discussed.

A particularly significant example, taken from the Talmud, book of Berakhot 61b,2 relates as follows:

> Kahana [the student] entered and lay beneath [Rabbi] Rav's bed. He heard Rav chatting and laughing with his wife, and seeing to his needs, i.e., having [sexual] relations with her. Kahana said to Rav: "The mouth of Abba, Rav, is like one

whom has never eaten a cooked dish, i.e., his behavior was lustful." Rav said to him: "Kahana, you are here? Leave, as this is an undesirable mode of behavior." Rav Kahana said to him: "It is Torah, and I must learn".[6]

That the pious books of the Jews consider such filth as fit for narration, is sufficient comment on the Jewish perception of morality and decency.

Unhampered by ethical considerations, the Hebrew carries his lustfulness openly for all to see, and thus discovers and arouses latent, kindred feelings in the opposite sex. A woman's nature is adaptable; it acquiesces involuntarily and unconsciously in the actual feeling and way of thinking of the man with whom she comes into immediate contact, and for whom she feels sympathy. In proximity to a noble-natured man, a woman will also preserve and uphold all her innate dignity and distinction; but brought into close contact with a low voluptuary, she is just as much in danger of sinking to his level.

The Jew has a peculiar knack of speaking of sexual matters, as if these were perfectly harmless and ordinary topics of conversation. In this way, he contrives to lull, or even deaden a woman's natural sense of shame. In the vicinity of the Jew, feminine sensibility sinks to the lowest plane; one may even go so far as to say that each Jew transforms the women around him into prostitutes. He regards them merely as instruments for gratifying his lust, and they, for their part, accept his appraisement of them, and no longer feel acutely that this appeal to their animal instincts is a gross affront—or, at any rate, do not resent it to the same extent that they would if it were made by other men.

The late Professor of Natural Philosophy at Leipzig, J. K. F. Zöllner, has preserved for us, in a small brochure, the various tricks and frauds of the Jewish swindler Glattstern. Some of these are worth repeating:

> Glattstern, an indigent Polish-Jew student, who, in addition was half-blind, had somehow managed to gain a footing in the best Leipzig families, and to associate on the most intimate terms with the daughters of the same. He represented himself everywhere as a well-to-do man, and procured the means for playing the part—on the one hand, by patent-swindles, on the other by instituting collections at the best social functions, ostensibly for charitable purposes, but in

---

[6] Ed.: Text from www.sefaria.org.

reality, for his own pocket. He employed a trick, the main feature of which was to start a subscription by laying a large banknote on the collecting table, an example that prompted others to give lavishly; he then embezzled the proceeds. When he was sentenced by the General Court of Justice at Leipzig to six years imprisonment, he left the daughters of several wealthy families with excellent prospects of becoming mothers. Influential people must indeed have interceded on his behalf for, strange to say, he was pardoned after the passing of two and a half years.

Amongst the notable exploits of this dissolute rogue must be included the following: He had provided a poor woman, whose husband acted at the same time as his private secretary, with the means to fit up and stock a small shop, in order to carry on a business selling and repairing washing garments. The main responsibility of the woman, however, was the engaging and employing of a number of young seamstresses and female apprentices, who worked in a small room that was lighted by a skylight, and which led out of the shop. Glattstern was accustomed to come, whenever he liked, whether in the daytime or in the evening, to send away the owner of the business on some pretext, and then to lie down with one of the girls on the sofa—in the presence of the others. After this was witnessed several times through the glass roof by the neighbors, the police were notified, who then interfered.

This is not the only case of which I have been personally informed, where Jews have satisfied their lust in the presence of other women and girls. And, strange as it may sound, each of those present accepted the occurrence as inevitable, and kept silent about it, as long as particular circumstances did not lead to a discovery. Just as the mere glance of a snake is said to have the power of paralyzing a bird with horror, so too does the Jew's behavior appear to effect a complete paralysis of the senses in the case of weaker-minded females; it blasts them, as it were, with a curse, from which there is no escape.

Women of character and noble-mindedness, on the contrary, feel an insurmountable aversion towards the Jews and all that is Jewish; thanks to their fine instinct, they are conscious of the repulsiveness of the Jewish nature even when it escapes the eye of an observant man. On the other hand, weak and vain women succumb to the Jew's influence as if bereft of willpower. In this case, it looks as if the conditions governing the mixing of races is playing a part: Anyone who is racially clean and true to type is keenly alive to the alienism and enmity of the Jewish nature, and avoids the destroyer, either consciously or instinctively. In the case of the mongrel or mixed-breed person, however, all these fine instincts, as far as one can see, are extinguished; incapable of resistance, they become a victim of the enticer.

One can, if one chooses, discover a higher purpose behind these events: the Jew has been sent, as it were, amongst mankind, in order to help to destroy and obliterate all who are feeble in their vital instincts—that is to say, all who are degenerate and of little value. Such an explanation might afford some consolation, if it were not a fact that it is precisely the most pronounced Germanic type of woman who is most eagerly pursued by the Jew, and who eventually succumbs. As the Jew represents, in all respects, the exact opposite of the Germanic man or woman, he does so in this particular respect as well. It is the sexual contrast of both races that seems to operate most bafflingly and fatally.

At any rate, the above considerations lead to the firm conviction that, should the Germanic and Jewish races attempt to live together for any considerable period of time, this spells doom for the German race. Such mixing will inevitably lead to the decay and disappearance of Germanic ethics and Germanic racial characteristics.

Spreading Sexual Disease

Amongst the various methods of seduction that the Jewish girl-hunter is wont to employ—preferably as a last resource, when he sees that he will not otherwise attain his object—is that of "betrothal" or "engagement." It is simply incredible how the prospect of a "ring on the finger" operates so passionately on the disposition of simple and innocent women. But the power of this method is known only too well by the Jewish snarer.

> Two commercial travelers—a German and a Jew—were gossiping in an inn about another hotel…and doubtless considered that no one overheard them.
> "I recollect," remarked the Jew, "that I once went there years ago. Quite an interesting incident was the cause of this. I had 'picked up' an extremely pretty girl in the course of my railway journey. She was scarcely more than a school girl. After a time, she came to confide in me, and we became engaged…" "Engaged?" asked the other, astounded. "Well,

> yes, what one calls engaged," continued the Jew, in a tone of amused indifference. "I gave her a ring—I always carry several cheap little rings with me for this purpose. I then persuaded her to get out with me at the station ... by telling her that we must formalize our betrothal!" concluded the Jew, laughing, "and we then spent the night together in the hotel."
>
> "And what was the end of it all?" asked the other. "God only knows," replied the Jew, in his nasal, indifferent tone of voice. "She continued her journey the next morning. It is a pity, for she was a nice, little thing…"

The Jew also does not hesitate to promise marriage, if it is necessary to make a formal promise in order to gain his purpose; he knows that, in any case, the matter cannot affect him seriously. As soon as he wishes to get rid of the girl, all that he must do is to acknowledge himself a Jew, and to declare with feigned distress that his family are bitterly opposed to his marriage with a Christian. Under the supposition that the relatives of the girl also, would refuse, in all probability, to hear of her union with a Jew, he plays the role of a man afflicted with misfortune, and parts from the woman, whom he has deceived, assuring her that he will never forget, for the rest of his life, his one true love affair—only to begin the same game with another woman the next day. German girls, for the most part, are confiding and naive enough to accept such miserable subterfuge as something genuine, frequently even to defend the impostor against the accusations of others, and actually to carry an affectionate remembrance of him.

That section of the German Press that occupies itself especially with social matters, remarked, after describing a number of cases of this kind:

> Is any lawsuit of a disgraceful nature ever heard of in any law court throughout the whole world, without Jews being either directly or indirectly involved, whether as seducer, keeper, inciter, or in some such unsavory capacity? Wherever it may be—we always find that it is the Jew who is the most daring seducer, and to whom no one's virtue, no one's beauty, no one's honor is sacred, when it is a question of the gratification of his lust. One is even inclined to believe that it is not merely sensuality that impels him to this, but that he experiences a devilish and malignant joy in undermining moral femininity, and in dishonoring those who would otherwise have been the respected wives of German men.

Shameless as he is by nature, he makes use of the circumstance that 'desire awakens desire,' especially when it is displayed, brazen-facedly—without the slightest trace of shame—for all to see. In sexual life, the animal appeals to the animal; and it is precisely in this respect where the lowest and most animal nature finds the best opportunity to display its power. Therefore, there is nothing to be astonished at in the fact that an animal desire, proclaimed without the slightest restraint, must make an irresistible effect upon a weak and impressionable nature.

And there is still another psychological factor which cannot be left out of account: an absolute lack of shame, openly advertised, deadens the sense of shame in others, and arouses shamelessness. One thing is quite certain, and that is that one feels far less shame in the presence of the Jew than in the presence of any other man. Why do the peasant, the mechanic, yes, even the landowner, the officer, and the clergyman, when they get into money difficulties, apply to a Jew rather than to a friend, a bank, or a loan office? "No one feels ashamed in the presence of a Jew!" This frequently heard phrase solves many riddles. And as a matter of fact, one has many a transaction with the Jew that one would anxiously conceal from the eyes and ears of other men; one does not feel ashamed in the presence of the Jew because the Jew does not know what shame is.

And to this cause also must be attributed the extraordinary faculty for bribery possessed by the Jews, "moral nihilism," i.e. the renunciation of any higher standards than those of money and enjoyment. This is proclaimed with such unflappable assurance by the Jew that he can degrade the sentiments of others to his own low level.

This forms the base for the fearfully corruptive force exerted by the Jew, also with respect to femininity. The Jew allows no other feeling to come to the surface in his vicinity than a lust for enjoyment and profit. Is it then essential that he should possess any particular or special power for this purpose? By no means! Wherever the lowest and crudest instincts appear unrestrained, it is impossible for anything higher and more refined to hold its own. The erroneous doctrine of the victory of what is better in the "free interplay of forces," leads in reality, step by step, to an absurdity.

Furthermore, it is extremely useful to the Jews that the superstition concerning the particularity and favorableness of the "People of God" is inculcated into us from childhood onward, and it is precisely the female disposition that clings more tenaciously to all superstition than the man's sober sensibility.

And in addition to this, our women are given an entirely wrong idea of what constitutes the ideal man. On the stage, the role of the lover is played, for the most part, by Jewish youths; in our romantic literature that is now completely Judaized, the hero of the story is almost always a Jew, while the role of the duffer, the dupe, of the altruistic seeker for the ideal, is assigned to the German. Is it to be wondered at, then, if the misguided taste and bewildered fancy of our young girls see in every half-grown, black-headed Jew-boy, the hero of a romance, and are "enchanted" by his appearance? The general German folly that makes a special point of admiring everything that is un-German and alien, also plays its part. We have, as a matter of fact, for decades encouraged a culture of that which is oriental in the higher branches of literature, in the ladies' journals and fashion papers, in art...

It is, however, not only the honor and moral purity of German women that are at stake; their physical health is likewise endangered. Whether it is that the peculiar nature of the Jew exhausts the female body to an unusual degree, or whether it is that physiological circumstances, connected with the act of circumcision, play some part—it is sufficient to state the fact that women accustomed to have sexual intercourse with Jews suffer from a variety of uterine disorders, and remain barren. Yes, one can go so far as to say: women who have been accustomed to sexual intercourse with Jews are lost to the other race. And, if enquiry is being made at the present moment to find out the causes of the decline in the birthrate, there ought to be no delay in directing attention to the influence of this racial alien in our midst, who ruins women, not only morally but physically, and who threatens, together with widespread efforts to check conception, to become always more and more injurious to the community.

It is not difficult to conclude from all this that the Jewish race is the principal carrier of sexual disease amongst other nations; in fact, it could hardly be otherwise, considering how unbridled their sensuality is. And

Chapter 16 – The Influence of the Jews upon Womankind

even when he is afflicted with an infectious disorder, the Jew will still not restrain his lust. One recalls the disclosures of young Jews, according to which a fiendish kind of rapture is experienced by them in seducing—despite their diseased condition—what is, in all probability, an innocent girl. A terrible picture of such devilish cynicism was revealed during a judicial proceeding in 1904:

> The trader Julius Klippstein, married man and proprietor of a moneylending business that he carried on under the name of Jacob Weg, was brought up before a jury in the Law Courts at Munich. He was charged with perjury, and with incitement to perjury. Klippstein had attempted to induce the wife of a postman, who was under examination on account of some other misdemeanor, and was one of his customers, to deny under oath the fact that Klippstein was, in the course of his business, in the habit of having immoral relations with her. Klippstein denied the fact. The woman, however, eventually confessed, despite the present of money that had been promised to her.
>
> The examination of Klippstein now brought to light that it was a regular part of the daily proceedings for him to make immodest proposals to the female customers. The State Attorney discovered that no less than 35 women and girls had come to their ruin through Klippstein. They all appeared in court as witnesses. Their joint evidence furnished the material for a terrible history; some cases were little removed from rape. Klippstein proceeded to sell up the goods and belongings of certain women who resisted his advances. He only postponed execution, and granted a longer period for payment when the women yielded to his wishes. These unfortunate beings consisted, for the most part, of the wives and daughters of workmen and small officials.
>
> Due to his licentious mode of living, Klippstein suffered continuously from a revolting disorder that he communicated, moreover, to the victims of his lust. His wife was infected by him, and had to undergo a severe operation; the cook in his own household, with whom he also had relations, suffered from the same disorder—and the same was the case with his seventeen-year-old son, who had taken his father as

an example. Klippstein was sentenced to one and a half years (!) imprisonment.

The social democratic *Münchener Post*, one of the few papers that published this story as a public warning, stated also: "During the retirement of the jury, the accused was busily muttering Hebrew prayers in his cell. Various divorce proceedings are a further consequence of this case."

The *Deutsche Handels-Wacht* also had something to report concerning the personality of the accused:

> Julius Klippstein had already been arrested and detained on a charge of rape in his former domicile, Giessen, but managed to secure an acquittal. After moving to Munich, he had carried on his business scarcely for a year, when he entered into an "arrangement" with his creditors, whereby the latter incurred a loss of 25,000 marks. He then embarked on a fresh career of debauchery that simply beggared description. "If you are nice to me," he was known to say to his female employees, "you will have a good time; but if not, I will make your life hell."
>
> A girl employed at the counter, who had energetically resisted his advances, and had, on that account, been disgracefully abused by Klippstein, complained to the bookkeeper of the business, who told Klippstein, straight to his face, that he ought to be locked up. This, however, did not trouble that 'man of honor' in the least.
>
> His customers, both girls and women, were assailed in the same way as the servants of his household and the employees in his business. He compelled many of them, as mentioned above, to yield to his wishes, by threatening to seize and sell up the last of their belongings. Some things that happened cannot even be hinted at.

The paper adds:

> Naturally we shall at once be accused of unfairly suggesting that an isolated incident is evidence of a general trend, but we feel ourselves compelled to say that the case of Klippstein is more or less typical of certain kinds of business.

Chapter 16 – The Influence of the Jews upon Womankind

At the same time, *The Hammer* made the following remarks:

> It would be mock modesty to forbid the public examination and discussion of such disquieting monstrosities as these. A danger lurks in the gloom of concealment, the effects of which are inconceivable as regards their range and extent. Anyone who has affection for his nation must open his nation's eyes to such horrors. The great, public press has taken no notice whatever of these unheard-of occurrences—not even that portion that is fond of stepping to the front as the special guardian of national morality and rights, and which otherwise makes a huge fuss over every trifling scandal.
>
> A remarkable confusion of moral conceptions dominates our dear public. When some rough words are spoken to a few recruits, and an exceptional blockhead amongst them happens to get a smack on the head, all the newspapers work themselves up into a state of fury, and inflame public opinion for weeks with the 'incident,' and the Reichstag occupies session after session with a discussion of such occurrences. But when it is a question of criminal acts of the basest description, and the honor and health of numerous women and girls are at stake, everything is enveloped in silence.
>
> Why didn't Herr Bebel, who is so ready to play the part of a moral censor in his book *The Woman*, discharge some of his moral wrath in this particular direction? Aren't the majority of victims the wives and daughters of workmen and minor officials? We would very much like to have an answer to these questions.

Traffic in Girls

The Hebrew has almost made a principle of degrading woman, both in illustration and text, as well as in speech and action. He dominates the stage and cinema with his insolent lasciviousness. Shops where the most shameless books and pictures are sold, are kept by Jews—mostly under a Christian pseudonym—who are also purveyors of the worst kind of devices for preventing conception and procuring abortion. So it is scarcely a surprise that the profoundest disregard for mankind in general, and especially for young unmarried women, as well as the degradation of commerce to its lowest conceivable plane, should proceed from the Jew. I refer here to what is known as the "White Slave Trade," and in particular to the traffic in young girls. It signifies the most disgraceful degeneration of the business instinct: *trade in living human flesh*, sale of souls, for the sake of foul profit. It was reserved for Hebrewdom to develop this vile business, systematically and on a grand scale, until it grew into a vast organization that embraces half the world.

Even in olden times, the slave trade was already a Jewish specialty. With good reason did the eminent Polish painter Henryk Siemiradzki depict the two slave dealers, in his celebrated picture of ancient Roman life "The Girl or the Vase" (1878), with unmistakably Hebraic features. Even in Carolingian times, the slave trade was preponderantly in the hands of the Jews.[7] Thus, in conformity with the original state of affairs, dealers in girls of the present day are, almost without exception, Jews; and this is admitted by the Jews themselves. During a conference held in London, in March 1910, protesting against the traffic in women, *The Jewish Chronicle* of 2 April 1910 acknowledged that "the Jews in this particular sphere of activity far outnumbered all the other 'dealers'," and added; "the Jewish trafficker in women is the most terrible of all profiteers out of human vice; if the Jew could only be eliminated, the traffic in women would shrink, and would become comparatively insignificant."

If avarice and greed for profit occasionally tempt the man of Aryan race to engage in businesses of a doubtful nature, and if his sensuality also calls for many a victim, it is improbable that a man of genuine Aryan race has ever descended to such cold-blooded commercialism and malicious subtlety as is required to carry on the "White Slave Traffic;" if such has been the case, it is an instance of moral abortion.[8] Only by means of the Talmudic perception that regards all non-Jews as beasts, and more particularly so the women who are not Jewish, is it possible to find an explanation for the cold-blooded behavior of the Hebrews towards women, whom they treat as articles of merchandise. One is justified in asserting that the extent to which the Jew avails himself of cold calculation and cunning disguise, in order to entice young and unsuspecting girls into his trap—for the most part either by betrothing himself to them, or by promising them marriage or a good situation in order to induce them to run away from their parents'

---

[7] See Dürr and Klett (*History of the World* II, page 56).
[8] One must not allow oneself to be misled into regarding an unquestioned Hebrew as not being a Jew, merely because his name sounds genuinely German. In publishing the names of malefactors, the Press is deceit itself. Every day it succeeds in "misprinting" an unmistakably Jewish name so that it assumes the form of a genuine German one.

home, and then, after "his passion has lost its novel force," handing them over like ordinary merchandise to another, and surrendering them to ruin—would be practically impossible in the case of any man of Aryan descent.

The Jew is always ready for the purpose of screening the pernicious activity of his fellow Jew, and so it is in this particular case. All the efforts of charitable women and social workers on behalf of the miserable victims of White Slave Traffic are rendered, for all practical purposes, null and void from the start by the fact that Jews place themselves at the head of these organizations. In this way, every genuine investigation is held up.[9] For it is the aim and object of the Jews, always and everywhere, to weaken, emasculate, or to divert toward non-Jews any accusation that might prejudice a Jew, until the gravest affair fades away into insignificance or is transformed into a comedy.

The literature on this subject is copious enough to preclude any necessity here of going into the more intimate details of this sorrowful business. One account alone, taken from actual life, is sufficiently eloquent to reveal all the ignominy of the conditions, and to provide testimony as to the long period throughout which this shameful trade has been conducted.

Otto Glagau's *Kulturkämpfer* of 1880 contains the following description of Rio de Janeiro (from the pen of a former German Consul):

> Could anything cause us deeper shame, when we visit the wonderful capital of Brazil, than to observe that German and Austrian girls compose one of the largest portions of local prostitutes? Whole streets are occupied by them, and from open windows, in the most shameless fashion, they endeavor, in their native tongue, to entice passing men to visit them; and even in the numerous pleasure resorts of the same city, one is pestered with their importunities.
>
> The majority of them are very young, and it can be proved that they have not emigrated of their own accord, in order to earn money in a foreign country, in this unclean

---

[9] Here is an instance worth mentioning as significant of women's work in this direction. There is an association in Munich, presided over by Princess Sulkowska, and called "The German League for Combating the Traffic in Women." The committee includes a number of ladies and three men as well: the publisher of the society's journal, and two Jews—the General-Superintendent, D. Possart, and Oscar Tietz. The secretary, who acts also as editor, signs himself Robert Heymann, and makes a third Jew. The experienced reader can at once detect that the purpose is to prevent, at all cost, any exposure of Jews.

fashion, but are the unfortunate victims of Jewish procurers and procuresses, who have earned an undisguised traffic in German girls to Rio for several years.[10] This eventually assumed such dimensions, and operated so alarmingly upon the already very feeble morality of the Brazilian capital, that the local government was forced finally to interfere, and to order the deportation of the Jewish procurers, who posed, for the most part, as dealers in jewelry and precious metals, but whose principal source of income was the traffic in women.

In Rio de Janeiro, in the month of December, the following persons were "moved on": Markus Shomer, Moritz Silbermann, Markus Weinbach, Tebel Silbermann, Moses Silberstein, Moritz Eisenberg, Johann Freund, Adolf Bernstein, Tobias Saphir, Hermann Ficheler, Gerson Baum, Markus Schwarz, Hermann Beitel, Markus Freeman, Samuel Auster, Karl Bukowitz, and Abraham Robins. They drove in carriages to the place of embarkation, and engaged first-class cabins on the steamer "Equator," which was to take them to Buenos Aires; they were enabled to travel in this style out of the iniquitous profits which they had pocketed in Rio. However, on arrival in Buenos Aires, the unclean company were disagreeably surprised to find that the police had boarded the vessel, and had protested against their landing; consequently, these "uncles" will again make old Europe joyous with their presence.

According to the newspapers of Rio de Janeiro later on, 23 more Jews who had been convicted of traffic in girls were again ordered to leave the country. Simultaneously their unfortunate victims were relieved by the authorities of any obligation with regard to repayment of any monetary advances that had been made to them by the Jews, for the purpose of paying their passages and other inevitable expenses. This measure enabled the women to withdraw themselves from the dens of vice…

But, praiseworthy as the measures taken by the Brazilian Government undoubtedly are, the evil is far from being extirpated, and will soon break out again in a new form. Complete

---

[10] To such an extent is this traffic a Jewish specialty, that the brothel keepers are officially and openly spoken of as *os caftens*. In New York, matters have reached such a pitch that the brothel business has been converted into a Trust! At the head of this "Trust" is a Jew called Goldberg. See *The Hammer* No. 267 (August 1913).

suppression is only possible if the procurers are attacked here in Germany and Austria, where they obtain their victims. In order to ascertain their names, it would be necessary for the German police to communicate with the authorities at Rio de Janeiro, so that the latter could institute an official examination of the unfortunate girls who have become the prey of the vilest form of greed.

The following notice, taken from the *Tägliche Rundschau* of 24 July 1913, will serve as proof that these conditions have not altered but have, if anything, grown worse:

> **Abduction of 4,000 girls**. The Russian [i.e. Jewish] "White Slave" trafficker, Jakubowitsch, who was arrested the day before yesterday in Hamburg, is regarded as the business principal of the entire trade in women that is carried on in the east of Europe. Several thousand cases alone have been brought home to him. According to reliable statistics, more than 4,000 girls have been passed through German ports for this purpose, over several years.

Even though a "League for Combating White Slave Traffic" has been instituted, even though harsher measures have been ordained by the government, even though every year a few procurers and procuresses are arrested—who are always and exclusively Jews—the hateful business still flourishes, to the shame of "moral" Europe. This is an infamous reminder of the feebleness of will, sickly tolerance, and last but not least, of the uncontrolled *dread of the Jews* that possess the majority of our "cultured" men and women, up to the highest circles, and which sap any collective effort at its very inception.[11] The power of infatuating the female mind, possessed and exerted by the Jewish commercial competitor, appears, indeed, to verge on the supernatural. It is all the more necessary, then, to expose this power, and to warn all people of its dangerous nature.

---

[11] Our consideration for the Jew is carried to an incomprehensible extreme. To realize this, one has only to recall with what precaution and indulgence everyone treated the name of a Doctor Sternberg, the Jewish lover of the accused, in the Hedwig Müller criminal proceeding. Counsel for the defense, witnesses, reporters and even the judge—all united their efforts in this direction. Experienced newspaper readers know that, for several decades, whenever the names in a questionable case are suppressed in any of our papers, Jews are invariably the evildoers.

Chapter 17
The Jews and the World War

The wars of the Aryan nations have always served to enrich and strengthen Judah. Reference to this fact has been made many times in the course of this book. By usurious behavior in connection with army contracts, by financial maneuvers with various securities, and by raising and depressing the rate of exchange, the Jews have always known how to make profit out of the agony and need of the various nations. Jewish families that became rich and ennobled are almost always indebted for their ascension to wartime profiteering, and in this respect the *Semi-Gotha* contains some interesting disclosures.[1]

The World War of 1914-1918 also showed us Hebrewdom in a state of feverish activity. This time, once again, they were the most important army contractors, the most daring manipulators of prices, and the most cunning clandestine dealers, and hence formed the most powerful business rings, and absorbed incredible profits. By their behavior they contributed, to a large extent, to the defeat of the Central Powers; one may even go so far as to say: *the Jews have emerged as the real victors from this monstrous war of nations.*

Directly after the outbreak of war, the Hebrews Walther Rathenau and Albert Ballin took over the organization of the economic side of the war—ostensibly in the interests of the nation, but in reality to secure the lion's share of the army contracts for their racial comrades, and to create almost a Jewish monopoly of the entire trade, not only in Germany itself, but with neutral foreign countries as well.[2]

An industrialist who visited the Prussian War Ministry in September 1914 in order to present an offer, displayed his amazement when he found installed in this high office, not, as he had expected, officers and military officials, but preponderantly Jews. Rathenau sat in a large room, at an enormous secretarial writing table, and gave out army contracts. Around him were seated, almost without exception, Jewish clerks and Jewish businessmen. Seeing his shipping enterprise temporarily paralyzed by the war,

---

[1] *Semi-Gotha: Register of Ennobled Jewish Families*. Kyffhäuser Press (1912).
[2] Ed.: Rathenau (1867-1922) was a Jewish-German industrialist and politician. Ballin (1857-1918) was a Jewish-German shipping magnate. Rathenau was assassinated in 1922; Ballin died by suicide in 1918.

Ballin offered himself to the Imperial Government as a voluntary organizer and business expert; he migrated with his entire staff of officials and clerks to Berlin, and organized the Central Purchase Company (ZEG) and other Jewish undertakings.

The feeble government under Kaiser Wilhelm II that had always formerly favored Jews in all important positions, allowed this to happen, to its embarrassment and perplexity. And if, during the war, any fact rose conspicuously to the surface that, until then, had only been perceptible to those who could see deeply, and which even then appeared incredible to German visionaries, it was a fact that, since the beginning of Wilhelm II's reign, the Jews had been the real rulers of the German Empire. For the last 15 years, those in immediate personal contact with the Kaiser were Hebrew financiers, Hebrew manufacturers, and Hebrew merchants—men like Emil and Walter Rathenau, Albert Ballin, Paul von Schwabach, James Simon, Fritz Friedländer-Fuld, Goldberger, Herbert Gutmann, Hulschinsky, Katzenstein etc.[3]

The old legend that the Kaiser was under the influence of the high nobility and of the Junkers, living east of the Elbe, was only a Jewish ruse to deceive the nation as to the real state of affairs, and to lower the Kaiser himself in the estimation of his people. It is quite true that the Kaiser, for the last decades, went mainly to the Jews for advice, who flattered his weaknesses and contributed much to the follies that led finally to the World War, and to the collapse of Germany. The German Nobility were as good as banished from the Berlin Court.

Hymns of praise have been sung to one of the Rathenaus in the press, conducted by his racial brethren, on account of his supposed services in connection with the organization of the wartime economy—without which it is pretended that the war could never have been carried on. He arranged that he should be designated, behind the scenes, as "Chief of Economic General Staff," the man to whom German victories were really to be attributed. As a matter of fact, Rathenau created by means of his "war companies," which exceeded 300, an absurdly complicated apparatus that disordered the economy and made things more difficult for the entire country, and transferred, by a kind of jugglery, all the power and the advantages into the Jews' hands. I do not hesitate to maintain, and can furnish convincing proof, that Rathenau's "war companies" contributed, in large part, to Germany's defeat. They did not facilitate German economic life but, on the contrary, disturbed and interrupted it—for reasons that I cannot discuss here. This particular subject, as well as the general attitude of the Jews

---

[3] Compare Rud. Martin: *Deutsche Machthaber* (German Potentates).

throughout the war, calls for special treatment in a book devoted to that subject alone, and I hope that an opportunity to accomplish this will soon present itself.

Here, I mention some grave facts for which valid documentary evidence is forthcoming: The activity of the ZEG has, in many cases, rendered the importing of the necessities of life from abroad more difficult than it was before. And furthermore: A particularly glaring instance is that of the War Grain Department; its grains have been sent backwards and forwards, from one end of the Empire to the other, time after time, in such an absolutely crazy manner that they have spoiled before reaching the hands of the consumers. Simultaneously the railways were burdened, in an unheard-of manner, beyond their capacity, and the cost of the commodities unnecessarily increased by heavy freight charges. What extraordinarily uneconomical business was perpetrated by the ZEG buyers in Holland, Denmark, and other countries can be easily ascertained by referring to the numerous and instructive instances given in the *Hammer* publications from 1915 to 1918.[4] The annual volumes 1915 to 1919 of the trade paper *Deutscher Müller* in Leipzig, contain numerous examples of the favoritism shown to the great mills owned by Jews, and of the crazy transport, backwards and forwards, of grain and flour by the Grain Dept.

It would be a great mistake to see in all this merely blunders in organization and disposition. Closer observation discloses that malevolence prevailed.

The Hebrews' attitude is only comprehensible by attributing to it their deep aversion for all that is German, for the German form of government, and for militarism. Victory was begrudged to the German Empire. It is beyond all doubt that the Jews hate the Germans more than they hate any other nation—simply because German idealism is the natural antithesis to the Jewish chandala-disposition. It is also quite obvious that the majority of Jews sympathized with our enemies and were on their side, especially with England. Influential Jewish newspapers, such as the *Frankfurter Zeitung*, *Berliner Tageblatt*, the Vienna *Neue Freie Presse*, and many others also knew well how to glorify the Western Power at the expense of the German people, whom they characterized as a horde of reactionaries, and of whom they could never say anything bad enough. It is this kind of newspaper that has carried on a steady campaign, for decades, with the definite object of

---

[4] These were collected and published under the title: "Complaints Against the ZEG." Further, compare "The ZEG and the Jewish Business Monopoly." *Hammer* No. 377, 1 March 1918.

rendering everything connected to Germany despicable in the eyes of foreign countries. They did so by circulating as widely as possible, occasional scandalous incidents, such as the Eulenberg lawsuit, various military excesses etc., and by suggesting that the German Nation was addicted to a revolting vice, has procured for it the equally revolting term of abuse *Boche*—a word that cannot be reproduced in the German language, for it denotes someone who is addicted to indulgence in unnatural lust, namely, a desire for young boys.[5]

The crime that the Hebrews have committed against the German people by their unprecedented war-usury, by their invention of the clandestine and secret method of trading (known as *Schieber und Kettenhandel*), by raising the prices of all the necessaries of life, and thereby enriching themselves to an immeasurable extent, can hardly be estimated. All these matters call for a searching investigation at the appropriate time and place.

Here it is only necessary to call attention to the fact that, alone in the case of army supplies, a disproportionate increase in prices immediately occurred, because—thanks to Jewish influence—direct delivery from the producers was evaded, and the orders were assigned to Jewish commission merchants, agents, and middlemen. It created the impression that the people of Judah had made a contract with the German government, from the very beginning of the war, that they should receive the lion's share of army contracts. The cases are too numerous where German contractors, manufacturers, merchants, trade associations, guilds, etc., have been "turned down," whilst, later on, Jewish middlemen have secured the contracts at considerably higher prices. In this way, the delivery of important supplies was frequently entrusted to dealers who were inexperienced in that particular kind of business, and who had no technical knowledge of the goods required; it sufficed that they were Jews.

The Hebrews were seldom to be found in the trenches, but were more at home in the depots, the offices, the garrisons, and the war-trading companies. In consequence of the numerous complaints that were made about this even in the Reichstag—statistics were taken, but never published; presumably because they would disgrace even Judah.

The Revolution of 1918—the object of which was certainly not to assist the honest working class to obtain its fair share of political influence, but rather to enable the Jews to do away with the hated Monarchy and the military organization—was principally the work of Jews. The Masonic

---

[5] It is quite possible that the expression is derived from the Hebrew word *Bocher* (boy).

Lodge at Milan—Latin Freemasonry is completely under Semitic direction—announced in a circular dated 30 July 1914 that the object of the Lodges was to introduce an age "free from thrones and altars." That is to say: the overthrow of all princes and the removal of all non-Jewish religions. Jewry has been working at this task, openly and in secret, for decades. And they have very nearly succeeded in their aim.

The ill-advised working class, instigated by the Jews, has allowed itself to become a tool, in order to promote interests that are entirely Jewish. The destruction of all national feeling amongst the working people, and the actual turning to contempt of everything German, are the work of a subtle Jewish press campaign. Throughout all the years of war, confidence in an ultimate German victory was steadily sapped by the influence that the Jewish press exerted upon the public frame of mind, and the attempt was made to lay the entire blame for the war on German shoulders. The collapse of our front was the result of sheer treachery. A person who enjoyed the fullest confidence of the *Hammer*, reported that a Jewish soldier had declared in July 1918: "Germany will not be victorious, for we (Jews) will make the revolution before the end of the war comes." The independent Social Democrat, Karlheinz Vater, admitted at Magdeburg that, since January 1918, his party had carried on propaganda at the front, inciting to desertion and mutiny. Thus, the German people are indebted for the collapse and the annihilating peace conditions to those malicious forces that, even within Germany, played into the hands of her enemies outside. And this process was aided by the blindness and trustfulness of the German people themselves. It is as if the old prophecy in the cloister of Lehnin in Brandenburg fulfilled itself:

Israel infandum scelus audet, morte piandum.
(Israel dares to commit an unspeakable crime, worthy of death.)

Chapter 18
Concluding Words

Whoever weighs up all the facts that have been displayed in the course of this work will understand how frivolous and superficial those words are that, clothed in the semblance of humaneness and tolerance, speak of an adaptation and blending of the Jews with the cultured Aryan nations. Only an incomprehensible detachment from real life can excuse such fantasy. The entire humanitarian assimilative idea shatters miserably at first contact with the profound seriousness of racial heredity. The illusion that all contrasts could be balanced, as it were, by men living in closer contact with one another, and by so-called civilization, rests on a doctrinaire interpretation that is contradicted by the hard facts of actual life at every turn.

Jewry is something that moves and acts beyond the sphere of the natural laws of life; it is something hostile to life, something unnatural, something demonical.

Even the nominally scientific doctrine of 'that which is better and stronger will conquer' is out of place here. A selective combat of this kind is only efficacious and warranted when beings of kindred stock, provided with the same natural weapons, strive against one another for the mastery. No one will claim that an unrestricted sphere of action should be granted to the bacilli that cause disease, or that one should not oppose devastating pestilences with precautionary measures; no one will contend that the cholera bacillus is a 'better' and a 'stronger' being than a human because the former is able to destroy the latter.

This doctrine of a 'free play of all forces' requires rational restraint, for the very reason that diseases work by infection, but that health does not. A single rotten apple in a barrel will easily transfer its corruption to a hundred sound ones, but even a thousand sound apples cannot heal a rotten one. Here, it is a case not of selective combat and superiority, but of shielding what is healthy against infective illness, of warding off national poison. Intelligence demands that all corrupting and infecting forces must be kept at a distance from healthy life, and must be suppressed by all possible means. To avoid what is poisonous is the first precautionary law of life: "Find out what is good for your body, and avoid what is bad for it."

Jewry, however, is a symptom of disease within humanity. This is a fact that even the Hebrew Heinrich Heine admits, for he calls it "the plague brought from the valley of the Nile".[1] The Hebrew is the *Untermensch* who has passed into a condition of spiritual and moral rottenness, who carries disintegration and corruption with him wherever he is allowed to go. He is himself fully aware of this peculiar property, as the following outburst of the Hebrew, Dr. Kurt Münzer, shows. He has written a novel—*The Road to Zion* (1907*)*—which has been suppressed on account of its disgustingly naturalistic contents. In this book, he makes the hero of his story speak as follows:

> Not only have we Jews degenerated in this manner, and are at the end of a civilization that is used up and sucked dry; we have ruined the blood of all races in Europe—perhaps we infected them in the first instance. Generally speaking, everything is under Jewish influence in the present day. Our ideas animate everything; our spirit dominates the world. We are the masters; for what is power in the present day is the direct offspring of our genius. However much we are hated, however much we are hunted down and persecuted, our enemies can only triumph over our frail bodies. We are no longer to be expelled. We have eaten into the nations, have tainted and dishonored the races, have broken their power, and, with our death-culture, have brought staleness and decay into everything.

Münzer also tries, in the usual way, to represent the Jews' war of annihilation against humanity as a justified act of revenge, under the pretext that the Jew has been unjustly despised and persecuted. He portrays the Jew as being insulted and spurned; he portrays him as ducking, dodging, and twisting; and then adds in the same strain:

> But behind it all, glows triumph at the surreptitious victory. The world has been Judaized, and has decomposed into the Jewish mode of thinking and into Jewish vice. That was revenge!

"The surreptitious victory!" The phrase aptly describes the situation—involuntarily. Only by surreptitious falsehood and deceit has the Hebrew attained to his power. But surreptitious victory is no victory—just as little

---

[1] Ed.: In his poem "The New Jewish Hospital at Hamburg" (1843). In original: *Das schlimmste von den dreien ist das letzte [Judentume] / Das tausendjährige Familienübel / Die aus dem Niltal mitgeschleppte Plage / Der altägyptisch ungesunde Glauben.*

as the success of a thief is a proof of his power and superiority. Anyone who, as a guest in a house, abuses the trust placed in him and robs his host, has not thereby gained a victory, but has, on the contrary, committed an act of villainy. The Jewish "victory" is a parallel case.

Now, it seems to me that the triumph is somewhat premature. It is certainly true that the dull masses in civilized countries have been infected, both with the Jewish mode of thinking and with the poisonous blood bacillus of the Hebrew. It is also true that certain higher classes of our society, who, devoid of instinct, have dallied and fraternized to such an extent with the destroyer of nations that they have fallen victims to the corruption, are beyond rescue. But a sound core still lives in our nation, one that has, so far, avoided the foreign poison. And even if a tremendous collapse is impending over the imbecile masses who have been Judaized both in body and soul—over those masses who crowd together in the great cities—our nationality will grow young once again and renew itself out of the unspoiled reserves who live on the land.

I hope that our nation will adopt Lagarde's standard, something that he expresses so well in his *Deutsche Schriften* (German Writings): "Every Jew who is burdensome to us is a serious reproach to the genuineness and veracity of our life. Germany must be German, and be full of Germans, full of itself like an egg... [T]hen there will be no room for Palestine."

This is perfectly true: The nations of antiquity have collapsed under racial degeneration and Judaization, without any proper foreboding of what was gradually happening to them. We, however, have learned from history, and have discovered the source of racial destruction. Now, for the first time, the Jew is being unmasked and recognized for exactly what he is, and now, for the first time, the secret of Jewry is being pitilessly unveiled. For many decades, intelligent men have been on the lookout, carefully observing every movement of this enemy. They have seen completely through him, have calculated his next moves in advance, and have begun, as quietly and unobtrusively as possible, to protect the most important positions against destruction. No one now has the power to arrest the collapse of our muddy surface culture—collapse of that structure of fraud, erected by Jewish speculation, collapse even of the Judaized system of government.[2] But

---

[2] These words were written in the year 1913, and have since proved themselves true. [Ed.: 1913 was of course prior to World War One, a time when Kaiser Wilhelm was still (nominally) in power. After defeat in the war, and the emergence of the Jewish-dominated Weimar government, Germany was in greater danger of collapse at the hands of the Jews. And indeed, as Fritsch issued this revised text in 1922, German hyperinflation was only a year away.]

one may well hope that the unspoiled elements will escape in an ark, as it were, from the deluge, and will land on a purified soil, to build up a new and better life—in a German world, free from Jews.

Theodor Fritsch
Leipzig, August 1922

Postscript

The contents of the present book have not been altered since the second edition in 1913. In the meantime, the movement directed against Jewry has developed to an undreamed-of extent. Whatever I have written here, in the separate chapters, as characteristic of the Jew, still retains its validity. It has not been refuted by more recent events; but rather, on the contrary, has been confirmed in all that is essential. Moreover, a new and extensive literature has appeared that supplements that which is given here.

The most remarkable literary event in this particular domain is the appearance of a book written by the American, Henry Ford, the great and widely-known motorcar manufacturer. The title of this work is: *The International Jew: The World's Foremost Problem* (1920-1922). Millions of copies of this book are dispersed throughout English-speaking countries, and there is also a strong demand for the German edition. The discriminating and careful manner in which the author introduces the American public to this question, which was entirely new to most people, is masterly and works irresistibly. In particular, the accounts in the second volume present an engrossing picture of the machinations of Jewish High Finance during the World War that later stands revealed as the indubitable work of the Jewish "Golden International."

The discovery of the so-called *Protocols of the Elders of Zion*, which in truth represent the program of political action of the secret confederations of the Jews, is of further great importance. The Jewish plans that are revealed therein display such demonical malice that the uninitiated reader might well believe them to be a fabrication. Jewry is straining every nerve to refute the genuineness of these "protocols;" what, however, speaks most strongly for their authenticity is the circumstance that, not only during the war but even now, Jewry unmistakably acts in full accordance with the program laid down. (The essential points in these "protocols" are also repeated in Ford's book).

At the present moment, Jewry is endeavoring, by means of the government organs at its disposal, to stifle the ever-swelling anti-Jewish movement.³ It hopes, principally by means of an artificial and disproportionate increase of prices on the paper market, to render impossible any further publication of those books, periodicals, and newspapers that are hostile to the Jews—the paper trade lies under the control of Hartmann, a Hungarian Hebrew, who lives in Germany. All this, however, cannot prevent the spark of perception that has fallen into the national soul, from continuing to glimmer, and from bursting, one day, into a clear flame. Already, far down into the working class, insight is dawning that the pernicious effects of the degenerate capitalist system can be referred mainly to Jewish machinations, and that it is precisely from that quarter that the greatest danger threatens the freedom of nations. The awful events in Russia have made it clear to everyone what Jewish tyranny means.

The movement against the predomination of Jewry is no longer confined to Germany; it has taken root in all civilized lands. Anti-Jewish periodicals and books are being published in England, France, and the United States, and also in Poland, Hungary, and Sweden. And a "White International," a league of all honorable nations to clear a way for the departure of Jewry, is now in the process of formation.⁴

Peace and quietude will not return to humanity until the enemy of humanity has been completely unmasked, and has been warned to keep within his own boundaries. We are, however, on the right road to accomplish this.

---

³ Numerous patriotic and German-national associations have been dissolved and banned.
⁴ Ed.: Nothing seems to have come from this movement.

APPENDIX

Editor: This material is the remainder of the original Chapter 10. As noted in the main text, it is largely tangential to the main thrust of the book, and so I have elected to move it here.

The installment or hire-purchase system

In nearly all the larger cities, there are business firms who, by means of brisk advertising, offer a special deal. They are prepared to part with their goods on receiving a small down payment, provided that the purchaser pledges himself, in writing, to pay off the debt by regular—generally weekly—installments. On account of the apparently wonderful offer, this kind of business secures many customers, especially among lower officials and the more needy of the working class. People without any means look upon these firms almost as benefactors, and as noble-hearted philanthropists because, for instance, they hand over an entire suite of furniture to a young couple, anxious to get married, with only an agreement to pay a small weekly installment. This type of businessman knows well how to advertise himself as a friend of mankind. As a matter of fact, there lurks behind this particular method of conducting business, an unparalleled usury—one that the law, as it now stands, finds extremely difficult to deal with.

The next point is that the goods that are offered have been hastily made out of inferior material; but in spite of this, their price is high. The willing purchaser, however, pays little heed to the high price for the simple reason that he does not have to pay it at once; he imagines that the comfortable method of payment renders a dispute about the price unnecessary, for it becomes an easy matter to produce the money when payments are spread over a considerable time. Accordingly, he signs the contract laid before him, with a light heart, quite heedless of the snare in which he is entangling himself. It is stated in the contract, amongst other conditions, that the seller is entitled to regain possession of the goods that have been delivered, without refunding any of the money that he has already received, if the buyer does not pay each installment punctually.[1] The buyer, who has every intention of paying regularly out of his income, is naturally unable to realize that such could ever be the case, and unhesitatingly signs

---

[1] Recent legislation interferes to a considerable extent with the easy operation of contracts of this nature.

his name to the document. But unfortunately, it only too often happens that the buyer—perhaps through loss of his situation, perhaps through ill-health or misfortune—is one day unable to meet his obligations, and suddenly he finds himself robbed—not only of the articles of furniture that he has taken on this "hire-purchase" system, but also of all the installments that he has already paid, and which are irretrievably lost.

An appeal to the legal system seldom succeeds because the written contract has been drawn up in such a manner that, from a legal viewpoint, the seller is completely within his rights. Year after year, large sums of money are sacrificed in this way by people of scanty means, who live, so to speak, from hand to mouth. It can scarcely be a pure accident that these "payment by installment" businesses are, almost without exception, owned by Jews; they are among the most objectionable inventions that the Hebrew has bestowed upon the modern age. The whole operation is based on a well-thought-out plan; it is an important part of a great system to rob the people of their money, according to a carefully conceived and prearranged scheme. The Hebrew is not content with depriving people of the money in their pockets; he forces them to pledge their future earnings. The anticipation of future profits is entirely the product of the speculative Jewish mind, something that conveys the taint of unreality into economic life, building it up, so to speak, on thin air. Any situation founded upon such future values must, of necessity, undergo shipwreck as soon as the slightest hitch occurs in the tranquil and natural development of affairs. It is truthfully said in Goethe's *Faust*: "The Jew will not spare you, for he creates anticipations."

We learn that 27 of these great "hire purchase" or "payment by installment" businesses in Germany are united under one control—which is to say, belong to one company. Its chairman or managing director is said to be one Leskowitz of Dresden. It is further maintained that his yearly income amounts to 800,000 marks. Enormous as this may sound, it is by no means improbable, especially if one takes into consideration that very high prices must be paid for all the goods. And furthermore, the goods that have been confiscated and taken back as a result of failure to pay an installment, are "touched-up" a little, and immediately sold again to a new customer.

What a plight of the community and its legislation when it is unable to check barefaced plundering of its poorest members by such a system of thinly-disguised usury. Would we not be in far better shape by substituting a healthy sense of fairness for the innumerable laws that prove worthless, and which are easily evaded by expert cheaters?

The Department Stores

The origin of the department store is the eastern "bazaar" which, already more than a century ago, was represented in this land by the country "general store." Both of these satisfied an obvious need. But even in this direction, an alien and degrading feature began to make itself visible in the sound development of trade, in the shape of the 50, 25, and 10 cent bazaars. These were caricatures of the originals that were started by the Jews soon after the establishment of the freedom of industry. It is worth noting that the first department stores arose in grand style in that most pleasure-loving of all world cities—Paris. They did so in order to provide the world of frivolous women with a convenient establishment or depot where the hundreds of requirements of an elegant lady could be satisfied under one roof. Their field of activity was then extended into the United States in order to make it possible for the population there, who—though dwelling in the smaller towns and in the open country, separated from one another by vast distances and mostly cut off from trade—still wished to be "up to date." The Hebrews have introduced their imitation bazaars into our larger cities that were already amply supplied with shopping facilities, without any other justification than that of speculation, based upon the love of comfort, a mania for enjoyment, confusion of thought, and the absence of any critical faculty that characterizes most people. Not in one single case are our department stores necessary in the sense that the eastern bazaars, general stores, and the American department stores are necessary. And it is worthy of note that in many countries—for instance, Brazil—the erection of these great department stores is forbidden in the interests of sound, straightforward commerce, and therefore in the interests of the community at large.

Thus the great, dazzling, central shopping establishments found in all our large cities, and into which the department stores gradually develop, owe their existence entirely to a deliberate violation of the practices of sound commerce that forces a way for itself, regardless of everything and everyone. It is undeniable that these establishments belong to the most remarkable creations of modern times, and it is quite comprehensible why the buying public seems to lose its head over these novelties, and is powerfully attracted by the real or apparent advantages of these establishments. Everyone speaks of these supposed advantages because the stores themselves have taken very good care to advertise them. It is not so well known, however, that these great bazaars find it necessary to make use of a number of cleverly conceived maneuvers in order to attract their public, and to secure a good profit, despite the apparent cheapness of their wares. Chief among these maneuvers is to dazzle the customer and generally bewildering the senses with an extravagant and varied display of goods. Further, they enlist the arts of persuasion and cajolery to such an extent as to make it almost impossible, or at least very difficult, for the customer to leave the establishment without having purchased something, whether he actually needs it or not. A number of special tricks have also been invented to mislead the customers on the one side, and to ingeniously exploit the manufacturers and merchants on the other. A few examples of these tricks are given below.

Tricks to Deceive Customers

"*Articles to Entice*." The department stores have found that the best means to attract customers is to offer certain articles of little intrinsic value at surprisingly low prices—so low, in fact, that they don't allow for any profit, or are maybe even below the actual cost of goods. They sell many such articles for less than the factory price—fully aware that by so doing they are brilliantly advertising themselves. What does it matter after all, if a few pennies are lost each time that reels of cotton, hairpins, goldfish, gloves, buttons, glasses etc. are sold! Customers are drawn in by the enticing prices, and temptation is placed in their way to purchase other articles that they are less able to estimate the value of. And thus the great emporium is richly recompensed for its small initial loss.

Moreover, it is the intention to create the impression amongst buyers that, in a business where certain articles are so cheap, everything must necessarily be cheap. But they are not. This is one of the most effective deceptions practiced by the great department stores. In the case of the larger and more costly goods that are only occasionally purchased, and which the ordinary layman is not experienced enough to judge their value, considerably higher prices are charged than would be the case if the item had been purchased at a genuine business of the usual kind—that is, businesses that specialize in the sale of one kind of goods.

Also, it is worth remarking that articles intended to act as a bait are always objects that have but little value in a household, and for that reason, are not widely purchased. However, if anyone tries to buy more of the bait items than usual, he is almost invariably met with the answer that the stock is "sold out."

"*Display articles.*" In the windows of the great department stores, we occasionally see larger items that cause astonishment due to their exceptional cheapness. As far as can be seen, these articles are made of good material and the workmanship is sound. When attempting to buy one of these articles, one is usually shown something of similar appearance but of inferior quality. If the customer detects the difference, he is led to understand that all the better quality has been sold. If he then demands the article that is displayed in the window, he is told that it has been sold already, but that the purchaser has given permission for it to remain on display until a new consignment arrives. Certainly the law concerning unclean competition provides some remedy against tricks of this kind, but the customer scarcely ever invokes it, and if he does, seldom with success. The rule is that one simply does not obtain the desired article at the stated price.

"*Mixing of goods.*" Amongst a number of cheap goods such as articles of clothing, linen, crockery, etc., several articles of a better quality are introduced. These better articles are, for obvious reasons, placed on top of the heap, and are handed, for quick inspection, to likely purchasers. If the buyer takes one, the salesman tries to substitute the inferior article or, if a large quantity is involved, to mix the inferior with the better.

"*Deception and Exchange articles.*" The department stores buy a parcel of goods of superior quality from a manufacturer of good reputation, and armed with a sample of these, order articles deceptively similar in appearance but made of inferior material to be manufactured at another factory. As they then alternately sell the superior and inferior stocks—but mostly the latter—they can then evade the reproach that they deal in inferior goods. Whenever a dispute arises, they simply produce one of the better articles, and assure the customer that this is their normal quality, and that the inferior specimen complained of has been introduced amongst the better goods "by accident."

Here is one example proven to be true: A business in question had bought a large quantity of well-made lace, at a factory price of 10 cents per meter. It then also ordered two inferior qualities of lace, of the same pattern, at prices of 6 and 3 cents per meter. The spools of these three different qualities of lace—that all appear to the ordinary observer to be of the same quality—are placed side by side, and are all offered for sale at the same price of 9 cents per meter. It is easy to understand that the salesmen received instructions to sell as much as possible from the spool that contained the cheapest lace. It was only when a customer entered who displayed a certain amount of criticism, and appeared to understand something about the matter, that lace was taken from the superior spool. The lady who, by chance, happened to receive a piece of the best lace for 9 cents would naturally continue to sing the praises of the superiority and cheapness of the article in question amongst the whole circle of her acquaintances; in this way, this particular store recovered by the good advertisement far more than the value of the single penny that had been actually lost in the transaction.

"*Prices that confuse and mislead.*" The great department stores often attempt, by marking articles at unusual prices, to create the impression that their calculations are made with the greatest nicety, and that they are satisfied with a very meager profit. But this is also a delusion, because amongst the articles marked 98 cents, there are many that can be bought in genuine business for 75 or 80 cents.

The *Konfektionär*, which is the official organ of the union of department stores and warehouses, recently gave its readers the following good advice:

> The smaller articles must often be sold at cost, and sometimes even for less, in order for a higher price to be charged for the larger ones. If a lady is allowed to purchase gloves or soap for a few pennies below the usual price, she is there and then convinced that all articles in that same business-house are cheap, and continues, with complete confidence, to purchase coats and silken garments.

In the course of a legal action taken by the department store Stein against the Association of Commerce and Industry, a pronouncement was made by the Prussian Court of Appeals, when reversing the judgement of 14 November 1907, as follows:

> It is a matter of common knowledge to those engaged in law, that the department stores endeavor to attract large numbers of customers by offering for sale, at absurdly low prices, those particular goods that are in daily use or consumption by the masses. But when other goods are sold, far higher prices are demanded than are charged by the small and moderately-sized shops that specialize in the particular kind of goods concerned.

When a large Berlin department store went so far recently as to offer pre-stamped, 5-cent postcards for 4 cents, it was obvious that the intention was to entice customers into the establishment and to force other articles upon them. Ultimately, the reduced price for the postcards was only granted to those who could prove that they had purchased other goods. But the intuition was also present to create the bewildering impression that this department stores was making the impossible possible, and was actually in a position to sell the government postcards cheaper than the postal authorities themselves could. The success of this questionable kind of business depends, to a large extent, on the suggestion that this store, by some incredible means or magic, could actually sell goods cheaper than those who manufactured them. It is certainly only the most thoughtless person who can allow themselves to be fooled by such unbusinesslike tricks; it can therefore be regarded as a speculation in stupidity. Whoever allows himself to be enticed by these department stores tricks is foolish indeed.

Injury Done to the Producers

From the practices just described, one can see how the department stores generally favor the production of inferior goods, and this reacts very negatively on certain branches of manufacture. The procedure is usually as follows: The department store buyer puts in an appearance at the factory office, and holding a certain item in his hand, he says: "I will order large quantities of this article every year if you can produce it at 20 to 25 percent cheaper. It does not matter if the workmanship and the material are inferior, but the appearance must be the same." When a respectable manufacturer declines to accept this invitation, the buyer threatens to take his order to some other firm. Many a manufacturer, apprehensive of being squeezed out of the market, ends up consenting and produces the inferior goods that are desired. One further consequence of the increasing manufacture of inferior goods is that the production of high-quality goods tends to diminish.

An expert in the manufacture of porcelain reports:

> Our factory has worked for years at a loss simply because the demand for a good class of ware that is worth its price, is gradually falling off. The department stores buy only 'fourth selection' and flawed goods—which is to say, garbage. They then mix several good pieces among the lot; in the case of plates, for instance, laying them on the top of the others, and the public buys this rubbish unsuspectingly. A solid line of

goods, however, waits in vain for a buyer. There is nothing left but to resign oneself to the manufacture of artificially produced refuse. On the other hand, wages keep on rising, so that it is no longer possible to make the business pay, and this entire branch of industry goes from bad to worse.

Numerous factories in other branches of trade have also allowed themselves to be coerced into manufacturing rubbish, especially for the department stores, and have been ruined in the process. It was the invariable habit of the department store buyer to try to beat the price down each time he gave a fresh order, until there was no longer any possibility for the producer to make even the least profit. The customers for the better class of wares had, however, disappeared in the meantime, so there was no option except to discontinue business.

When a sausage manufacturer was asked how he could deliver his sausages so cheaply to the department stores that they could be sold for 12 cents, when the same sausages were 15 cents everywhere else, he answered laughing: "Just measure the things! They are certainly a fifth cheaper, but they are also a quarter shorter."

The purchasing public has no idea whatsoever of such proceedings— or at least behaves as if it had no such idea. The public is bewitched by the fascinating and bewildering life of the great department stores, and does not pause to consider to what an extent the entire economic life is being undermined by such a questionable form of development. For not only is industry reduced to producing rubbish, but also those sound businesses in the towns that confine themselves to the sale of high-class specialties are being ruined because the department stores are gradually depriving them of their customers. In the neighborhood of the department stores, one good business after another disappears; in Berlin, for instance, in the year 1913, no less than 18,000 separate shops were standing empty. Development of this kind can only end in a gigantic economic catastrophe; and we shall be indebted for this to the magnificence of the department stores, as well as to the incredible shortsightedness of the public that allows itself to be enticed into such traps, and which stifles every feeling of responsibility with arguments that are prompted solely by its own laziness and vanity.

Reduced quality in all types of articles for trade. Given that the department stores prefer to have large quantities of nearly-identical goods, the try, as far as they can, to reduce the number of the various samples and types. The whole of the art industry suffers especially thereby, as it prefers to give free reign to both fashion and personal taste. The department stores like to have a suitable sample reproduced a thousand, or even a million times, and this naturally causes other samples to be forced out of the market. The art industry loses its individuality; all becomes mass-manufacture for mass-taste. Inferior material is almost invariably introduced where the above happens, and the art industry suffers degradation and cheapening in every respect.

The French political economist, Trepreau, characterizes the development in the following words:

> This change is causing the taste for what is good and beautiful, that formerly earned such a good reputation for French trade, to disappear. In its place is the mass production of rubbish that is degrading our industry, and the sequel of which will be the disappearance of all specialties of artistic handicraft in the immediate future.

In the case of jam and preserves, for example, the factories were compelled to reduce prices and to produce special lines of preserves for the department stores alone, whereby not only did the quality suffer but the difference between gross and net weight was increased by improper filling. Many textile fabrics are reduced, not only with regard to the quality of the yarn and the tightness of the mesh, but actually with regard to the breadth, customary in the trade. Thus, velvet was woven 42 centimeters instead of 50 centimeters wide—a fact that escapes a hasty inspection. To what an extent the contents of the balls and skeins of yarn, thread, etc., mostly stated in English yards instead of in meters, differs from what it ought to be, is seldom ascertained; and in this case, the price difference is considerable.

But enough; the manufacturers, whether they like it or not, are compelled to help the department stores to deceive the public, although they destroy their own business in doing so.

The Overpowering and Monopolization of all Economic Means

A further danger menaces our economic and social relations, arising from the circumstance that the department stores, by gradually concentrating retail trade into their hands, almost have a monopoly. This can make it as bad in the future for the buying public as for the manufacturers. As soon as the department stores have driven the majority of competing shops out of business, they will no longer find it necessary to entice customers with cheap prices because the public will simply be compelled to buy many things from them on account of the total disappearance of the competition—businesses that confined themselves to one kind of trade and specialized in it. When this time comes, the department stores will raise prices as high as they like, and this will be made all the easier for them, as they have already formed themselves into a trust, and are codifying their rules and regulations. There is no doubt that the buying public will eventually have to pay the piper for the apparent favors that it enjoys today.

At the present day, the great department stores exert a kind of monopoly-domination over the manufacturers. They claim the right to take all kinds of discounts that the manufacturers are powerless to resist, as they are placed more or less at the mercy of these great undertakings, who can give or withhold orders. When a special tax of 2% was imposed on the department stores in Prussia, they immediately passed it on to the manufacturers and merchants, by deducting 2% from all their accounts, even before the tax actually came into force. Thus it is clear how the monopolizing nature of these great stores, which is steadily increasing, is creating and inflicting a slate of servile dependency upon the manufacturers. This in turn will gravely endanger both economic and civic freedom—to say nothing of objections from a moral viewpoint. And it is not only the employers who suffer, but the employees are threatened with the same evils and to the same extent. All those who patronize the stores should make a note of this.

As a matter of fact, the department stores and the great banks that work in close alliance with them are obtaining—thanks to the continually progressing concentration of economic life—a dominating power that gives cause for the gravest apprehension. They have the power to crush every smaller competing business, and to make the manufacturers and producers absolutely dependent on them. This means nothing less than steering a direct course towards an economic "might makes right," which is an end to every conception of justice and morality. Every kind of compulsion that hurts the feeling of justice and wounds social sensibility must, of necessity, lead to an undermining of public morality, and finally to anarchy; consequently it cannot be tolerated in any well-organized community. Since the great department stores already form an international trust, they are in a position to subject the citizens of any country to international machinations, and to interfere to such a degree with the means for upholding authority that they seriously menace the economic freedom and independence of the inhabitants.

This calls for objection and opposition. The state cannot sanction that private persons or companies should have a monopoly of commerce, and consequently of profiteering. But this is precisely what any further development of the department stores system will lead to. Least of all, however, can an economic predominance of such a nature be tolerated when it endeavors to attain its ends by questionable means, when it makes use of trickery and deceit, and thereby endangers public wellbeing.

Moral and Physical Harm

The great department stores endanger not only the economic existence of the smaller and moderate sized businesses, as well as the steady and regular production of goods, but are harmful to public morality. It is a well-known fact that, side by side with the evolution of the great stores, certain new and disquieting features have made their appearance in the public's moral attitude. A new category of offenses has come into being: the seductive influence leading to shop-lifting, the pathological appearance of that class of theft that is peculiar to the big stores. Experience shows that this particular type of larceny is not confined to the poorer class of people and professional thieves, but is practiced by individuals drawn from all stations of life, and more especially by women, even when they belong to the most prosperous levels of society.

The phenomenon arises from the peculiar nature of business as conducted in the great stores. Everything is designed to excite greediness, to bewilder and to ensnare. The whirl of business and the multitude of impressions raise excitement to such an extent that the senses become quite confused. Weak characters succumb entirely to these influences, and lose control of their willpower. They are tempted, when they feel that they are not observed, to appropriate something, and steal occasionally even from their fellow customers. They are, however, nearly always caught, for the proprietors of the department stores, well aware of the insidious charm of their "shows," and keep a special staff of detectives to watch those whom they attract. Numerous cases have already occurred where ladies of good standing have been escorted into a private office, and have been subjected to the indignity of a personal search. It is easy to imagine what scandals develop out of such incidents.

But even if it does not lead quite so far as punishable offenses, the influence upon the character of the public of the peculiar method of trading introduced by the department stores is altogether bad. This is due to the simple reason that it induces many to buy more than their circumstances warrant, and to spend money on useless things. The whole system connected with this method of trading is designed to create the impression on the customers that they are guilty of neglect if they do not at once recognize and utilize the opportunity to make a cheap purchase, or in other words, a bargain. The cheap rubbish, made to look like something better, seduces simple people into buying articles quite unsuited to their position in life; by so doing, they accustom themselves to a mode of living that far exceeds what their circumstances and means justify. One of the great department stores ran an extended advertisement with reference to one of their brands of cheap champagne: "Champagne must become a popular drink!"—a phrase that one of the Social Democratic members of the Reichstag actually made his own particular slogan.

The demoralization that arises out of the peculiar method of business extends not only to the buying public but even more to the staff or personnel of the department stores, to the salesmen and saleswomen who labor under the steady und unvarying influence of the lax morale prevalent in these establishments, and who are compelled to help to deceive and overreach the public.

The physical injury caused by the unceasing strain of the service is considerable, and this acts on the character. Paul Berthold says:

> The store assistants live in unhealthy surroundings, in badly-ventilated apartments that are crowded with people. In most of the great department stores, the number of cases of illness and of actual death is appalling—so much so, that those who work for several years in these establishments without acquiring tuberculosis are the exceptions.

In addition, moral perils arise from other causes. Dr H. Lambrecht, Director of the Ministry for Public Works in Brussels, deserves recognition for having published a memorandum concerning "Stores and Cooperative Societies," containing a number of facts dealing with these matters—facts which are all the more striking for having been scientifically corroborated. He makes the following remarks with reference to this subject:

> This penning-in of a number of young females, and making them absolutely dependent on a person of the opposite sex, whether the latter may happen to be the shop-walker, inspector, or manager, constitutes already a gross moral danger that is all the more marked, when one takes into consideration that the saleswomen are drawn from the very class that is

most susceptible to the enticement of luxury and social pleasures.

He goes on to express his opinion about the questionable "friendships" that the great department stores offer both sexes so many opportunities of making, and which are utilized, not only by the salesmen and the saleswomen, but also by the customers. We have neither space nor time to refer further to the chapter dealing with this delicate subject. Lambrecht continues:

> The danger, however, is still further increased by the inadequate payment of the young girls employed, by bad advice, and by bad example. In these great businesses, in each of which several hundred people are employed, some of the older ones always find the means to dress themselves better than the others, and to visit the theaters and the restaurants after business hours, and soon the little girl apprentice, with her salary of 20 marks a month, allows herself to be deceived by what she imagines to be the brilliant prospect in store for her.

J. Hennigsen of Hamburg, after portraying the questionable moral relations that evolve out of the department stores system, remarks:

> I am convinced that if all this could only be published, far and wide, no German woman who still preserved a spark of sympathy with her fellow-women, would ever set foot again in one of these "stores."

And Baroness Brincard, after describing the same conditions, observes:

> Generally speaking, women are sympathetic beings, whose hearts are touched by all suffering. Therefore they do not act intentionally when they profit grossly from the misery and distress of other women; but unfortunately it is just the women of the well-to-do classes, who know nothing of these matters, who neither see nor think...

The great department stores are responsible for the production of a new nervous disease, a fact that Emile Zola has portrayed in his book *Au Bonheur des Dames*. The French physician, Dr. Dubuisson, has chosen as a theme for his book (*Les voleuses des grands magasins*) the injurious effect that the department stores have upon neurotic people; he says:

> It is impossible, even for people of the strongest constitutions, to spend any considerable time in these gigantic establishments without experiencing a peculiar feeling of nervous debility—of mental languor and bewilderment.

In the case of neurotic people, this condition amounts to a complete confusion of the senses that, to a certain extent, deprives them of self-control, bringing mental and moral disaster.

Dr. Laquer, in *Thieving at the Stores* says:

> Thieving at the great department stores is very extensively carried on, and it is a matter of urgency that this fact should be made widely known, especially as children are taking a large part in it. The unguarded display of goods without any compulsion to buy, is a great temptation to those who are deficient in will-power; for this reason alone, it should be restricted. Whether this deficiency in will-power, when brought face to face with the allurements of the great department stores, is to be regarded as a malady, must be decided by the evidence of medical experts in the Law Courts...

In any case, the department stores contribute enormously to undermining the morality of a generation, whose conscience is already blunted, and multiply to a serious extent the already-numerous social evils. The rulers in the State ought to seriously consider whether the trivial advantages of making one's purchases under these luxurious conditions are sufficiently valuable to be placed in the scales against the economic and moral welfare of the population. And, before everything else, if it is consistent with the duty of those who are in authority to see that justice is enforced and that the interests of the commonwealth are guarded, that the brute force of money, combined with boundless selfishness, should be established as a system to enslave the whole nation. The evasion of our politicians, who maintain that these results of modern life are inevitable, and must be "surmounted," is equivalent to the consolation, given to a man who is unable to swim, that, in any case, he would also have to learn how not to drown.

Bonuses for Those Employed and the Cost Involved in Carrying on This Method of Trading

How thoroughly unsound are the business principles of the great department stores is shown by the evidence of Dr. Josef Lux, who maintains that many of the department stores have different prices for certain customers and for certain times of the day.

A salesman, who had been employed in a department store, informs us that the employees were instructed to exploit the weaknesses and inattentiveness of the public. A leading principle was that, if possible, no one should be allowed to leave the building without making a purchase. If a certain article was too expensive for a customer, after several ingenious attempts had been made to persuade him or her to take something else, the same article would be produced again at a lower price under the pretext that it was of a different quality. Further, that salesmen were instructed, if the opportunity presented itself, to charge *more* than the goods had actually been priced at. In this case, they receive special bonus for the excess profits that they have obtained.

It is well-known how often employees at department stores are tempted to steal goods. The Law Courts are incessantly engaged with cases of this kind. Several years ago in the Berlin Courts, in one case alone, 54 salesmen and saleswomen, as well as the head of a department at the same store, received sentences.

The idea that the working expenses of the department stores are lower than those of other businesses is erroneous. The peculiar conditions under which these great businesses are worked call for all kinds of arrangements that can be dispensed with in sound businesses.

In order to protect themselves in some measure against thefts, both by employees and customers, most of the great department stores engage and maintain a number of detectives, secret agents, inspectors, and searchers, whose business it is to keep both the public and the staff under continual observation and control. A number of the staff, as well as of the customers, are detained daily at the exits, and are conducted to a room where they must divest themselves of their clothing in order to be thoroughly searched. The moral effects of this bodily examination need only be hinted at. It is by no means excluded that a perfectly innocent customer might have suspicion deliberately directed against her, and would consequently be exposed to a search of this kind.

In any case, the department stores are bound to maintain a large staff of people whose sole duty consists in dealing with the moral damage that follows, and this, of course, increases the expenses enormously. If one also takes into account the continuous and costly advertising that the department stores are quite unable to do without, it ought to be sufficiently clear that these modern undertakings cannot spell progress from an economic point of view, and that they are not at all in the position to deliver genuine goods at lower prices than other businesses. They are only able to keep themselves going by deceiving the public, and by lowering the quality of goods.

Moreover, they have a devastating effect upon the economic existence of the middle class, and, in this respect also, bring again a whole row of social evils. Trepreau ascribes the appalling falling off in the number of marriages in France to the herding-together of the unmarried of both sexes in the enormous business barracks that are called "business emporiums."

Ironically, women and girls never think that, by supporting the department stores, they are sinning against their own sex. If one only pauses for a moment to consider that, owing to the growing power of the great capitalistic department stores, it becomes almost impossible for a middle-class man to establish his own business. Marriage thus becomes more and more remote for many men, and more and more women are consequently driven to seek some means of making their own livelihood. One is finally bound to admit that, by reason of the development of the department stores system, the situation of women becomes precarious. Thus it is women themselves who help to destroy their own social position when they give their business to the great stores.

* * * * *

Lambrecht thus sums up the result of his investigations: The system of concentration in retail trade offers no social advantages that are not far outbalanced by other great disadvantages. The latter are leading towards a social condition full of danger, and which must be regarded as less advantageous and desirable when compared with the soundness and many-sidedness of the smaller businesses, each of which confines itself to one special branch of trade. Regarded from the social point of view, it is the ethical forces, and not the economic, that must decide the issue.

In the past, many older civilizations have gone to ruin because they would not recognize this truth about the accumulation of all wealth in a few hands, and the consequent impoverishment of the masses. What leads to decay cannot be called progress. For us, however, material self-enrichment must not be carried on to the detriment of morality, and the general welfare must not be sacrificed in order that profiteering shall flourish.

The mission of a truly moral system of government remains unaltered, viz, to respect and protect the economically weak man, who, at the same time, can well be the *best* man when judged from the physical and moral point of view. A particularly valuable social quality of the middle class is moderation in all its needs and requirements, even in its aspirations after honors and riches; only in this case can there be a fairly good distribution of prosperity, and a cheerful slate of wellbeing be made possible for the community. The entire mechanism of acquisition that has been placed at the absolute disposal of an unrestrained lust for gain has not increased either the health, or the safety, or the happiness of individuals.

The social consequences of an evolution along these lines are: monotony, degeneration, and a gradual disappearance of the aesthetic sense and taste; degradation of personality and of the individual, and lack of an appropriate field of activity; suppression of the artistic industry. This whole series of appearances are the forerunners and symptoms of the decay of a nation and of its culture.

It is almost superfluous to add that the great department stores, in all parts of the world, are almost exclusively in the hands of Hebrews, and that it is in this particular domain that the Jewish business spirit celebrates its questionable triumphs.

* * * * *

A media that represents every political party, and is always at the service of the great department stores thanks to their advertising dollars, has, up until now, helped to present these modern bazaars of rubbish in the most favorable light. It has, in any case, refrained altogether from exposing the terrible nature of the economic, social, and moral damage that is inseparably connected with the management and working of these great emporiums. Thus, for the sake of money, a grave crime is perpetrated against our nation.

When people, in the attempt to justify their patronage of these establishments, offer the excuse that it is "so convenient" to do their shopping at the department stores, they should be reminded that convenience is a property or quality that ultimately can be used to justify any kind of indolence and carelessness, and that it becomes an absolute vice when it is referred to as an excuse for supporting dubious undertakings. This much-praised convenience is inseparably bound up with an incalculable expenditure of time, and with many other drawbacks as well, so that in reality, double as much inconvenience is experienced as if one had made the purchases in separate shops. The dawdling about in the department stores is already recognized as one of the modern vices that the Hebrew knows so well how to foster.

If all the facts that have been portrayed above were only sufficiently known, the great department stores would soon lose their fascinating splendor in the eyes of all thoughtful people. Most of all, it is to be hoped that the conscience will awake, and will ask itself the question, if it is consonant with decency and morality to support, with their custom, these questionable emporiums of trash, and thus to condemn whole classes of our nation to economic and moral ruin. It is fully time that the customers realized at last their social responsibility. Whoever, for the sake of a paltry and often merely an apparent advantage, supports businesses founded on questionable principles, whoever shows favor to an unwholesome and immoral development, must not be surprised when the consequences of his ill-considered trading finally turn against him. The morbid principle, spreading always further and further, endangers the social order and moral welfare, and helps to establish conditions that most seriously menace social and national stability.

Our cultured people have opportunity enough to observe and deplore the growing laxity of public morals; it never seems to occur to them, however, that they themselves have helped to undermine the spirit that makes for order and morality, by the support that they give to these questionable business undertakings that pander solely to fashion. It is more especially the possessing and cultured classes who ought to be conscious of their social duties, and who ought not to give their custom and support to these dubious trading concerns, and thereby to set a bad example to those below them in the social scale. The principle of the great department stores is uneconomic, antisocial, and immoral; and out of these great lanterns of modern times, erected to attract and dazzle, issues a spirit that threatens to poison and demoralize all society from top to bottom; the spirit greedy for gain at any cost, the spirit of vain boastfulness and of pleasure-seeking, the spirit of frivolity, of bodily and spiritual sickness—in fact, of megalomania.

Whoever has regard for our nation and its future, whoever has not already made it a habit to barter his moral consciousness for momentary enjoyment and momentary advantage, ought now to understand clearly, in which direction we are bound, if we continue to give our support to lax morality in business affairs. All offense against good sense and morality, by destroying both state and society, attacks finally both us and our posterity.

BIBLIOGRAPHY

Bischoff, E. 2023. *The Book of the Shulchan Aruch*. Clemens & Blair.
Dalton, T. 2011. "A most subterranean conspiracy," in *Nietzsche: Thoughts and Perspectives*. Black Front Press.
Dalton, T. 2019. *The Jewish Hand in the World Wars*. Castle Hill.
Dalton, T. 2020. *Debating the Holocaust: A New Look at Both Sides* (4th ed.). Castle Hill.
Dalton, T. 2020b. *Eternal Strangers: Critical Views of Jews and Judaism*. Castle Hill.
Dalton, T. 2020c. "Christianity: The great Jewish hoax." Online: www.nationalvanguard.org
Dalton, T., ed. 2022. *Classic Essays on the Jewish Question*. Clemens & Blair.
Dalton, T. 2023. *The Steep Climb: Essays on the Jewish Question*. Clemens & Blair.
Delaney, C. 2012. *Columbus and the Quest for Jerusalem*. Free Press.
Disraeli, B. 1844/1976. *Endymion*. AMS Press.
Fishberg, M. 1911. *The Jews: A Study of Race and Environment*. Walter Scott.
Gobineau, A. 1853/1967. *The Inequality of Human Races*. H. Fertig.
Luther, M. 2020. *On the Jews and Their Lies* (T. Dalton, ed.). Clemens & Blair.
Marx, K. 1843/1978. "On the Jewish question," in *The Marx-Engels Reader*. Norton.
Mommsen, T. 1856/1957. *History of Rome*. Free Press.
Sombart, W. 1911/1951. *The Jews and Modern Capitalism*. Free Press.
Wiesenthal, S. 1972. *Sails of Hope*. Macmillan.

INDEX

advertising 5, 88-89
Agence Havas 123
Agencia Stefania 123
agriculture 39, 174, 178, 180
Alberti, Conrad 134, 199
America 64-66, 108, 123
Andree, Richard 37n6, 153n1, 177n5
Aryans 27, 86, 106, 109, 143, 154, 172, 177, 188, 214, 219, 225
Ashkenazi Jews 170-171
Associated Press 123
Augsburg 89
Ausrottung 42

Ballin, Albert 219-220
Barbarossa, Frederick 125
Behr, Georg 49
Berlin 85, 88, 182, 195, 200n5
Bible
    Esther, Book of 16, 197
    Genesis, Book of 69, 125, 151, 183
    John, Gospel of 61
    Old Testament 41-44, 114n1, 115, 128, 143-144, 149-151, 155, 167, 173-174, 204
Bischoff, Erich 44n2, 48n4, 195n2, 199n4
Bismarck, Otto von 110, 122, 153
Blacks *see* Negroes
Bleichröder, Gerson von 123
Bordeaux (France) 185
Brandenburg 85, 87
Breslau 132
Bruno, Giordano 153
Buxton, Thomas 31

chandala 148
Charlemagne 125

Chawrusse 35, 75-76, 176
Christ *see* Jesus
coal (resource) 10
Columbus, Christopher 64

De Torres, Luis 64
Delaney, Carol 64n1
Dingelstedt, Franz von 101
Disraeli, Benjamin 2-3
Dühring, Eugen 153, 179

Ecker, Jakob 49
Eisenmenger, Johann 49
Elkhan, Moses 68
Engels, Ernst 82n7
Englaender, Sigmund 121
environmental damage 9-10
Erasmus von Erbach 18
Esther, Book of 16, 197

Feuerbach, Ludwig von 141, 153
Fichte, Johann 51, 131-132, 153, 155
fideicommissum 12
Fishberg, Maurice 178n8
Ford, Henry 228
Frankfurt 87
Frederick the Great 51, 153
Fromer, Jacob 145

Gans, Eduard 156
George V, King 121
George, King of Greece 127
German race, origin 171
Gilani, Abdul *see* Jilani, Abd al
Gildemeister, Johann 49
Glagau, Otto 81-82, 215
Gobineau, Arthur de 177
God 42, 60, 95, 110, 141-145, 150, 164, 179

Goethe, Wolfgang von 103, 111-112
gold 7
Goldstein, Moritz 52n8
Gotha 18
Goy (Goyim) 42, 45-46, 99, 110, 139
Graetz, Heinrich 150-151
Greece, ancient 4

Hamid, Abdul 126
Hannover 87
Hansemann, David 83
Hebbel, Christian 101-102
Heine, Heinrich 146n2, 225-226
Heine, Salomon 83
Herder, Johann 153, 177
Herod, King 182
Hertz, Friedrich 154

iron ore (resource) 10-11
Israel 66n3

Jehovah *see* God
Jesus 43, 61-62
Jews
    and human trafficking 213-217
    and prostitution 195, 215-216
    and the press 136-137, 191, 223
    as "chosen" 41, 148
    as a hydra 118
    as a race 1-3, 150, 153-168
    as a religion 1
    as anti-Nature 160-161
    as bacillus of decomposition 93
    as Khazars 170
    as mental cripples 167
    as parasites 146, 181
    Ashkenazi 170-171, 185
    effect on women 187-217
    Marranos 170
    Sephardic 170, 185
    wealth 7, 184
    world rule 7, 42, 184
Jilani, Abd al 183
John, Gospel of 61
Josephus 182

Kellermann, Bernard 196
Khazars 170
Klatzkin, Jacob 55-57
Klüber, Johann 50
Kohl, J. C. 37
Kol Nidre prayer 47-48
Königsberg 87
Kortum, Ernst von 127

Laffan Bureau 123
Lagarde, Paul de 61, 144, 153, 184, 227
Langenfeldt, Theodor von 37-38
Lasker, Eduard 81
Lassalle, Ferdinand 39n8
Law, John 79
Lessing, Gotthold 190
Liszt, Franz 153
loan capital 13-15, 134-136
Lopez, Roderigo 78
Lowe, Charles 122
Ludwig of Bavaria 17n3
Luschan, Felix von 171
Luther, Martin 53-54, 60, 180-181

Maimon, Bernhard 125-127
Mainz 85
Marlborough, Duke of (John Churchill) 78
Marranos 170
Marx, Karl 39, 95, 167
Maximilian I, Emperor 125
Medina, Solomon de 78
Meding, Oscar 121
Metternich, Klemens von 31
Meyer, Paul 197-198
Meyer, R. H. 32-33
miscegenation 194, 227

Moltke, Helmut von 51-52
Mommsen, Theodor 93n5
Münzer, Kurt 226

Napoleon I 153
Nebuzaradan 180-181
Negroes 189
Nordau, Max 195
Nossig, Alfred 58

Otto II, Emperor 125

Pereire brothers 83
Philo 182
Poland 37-38, 51-52, 68
Posen 25
"Protocols of Elders of Zion" 228

qahal 177n5

Rathenau, Walther 219-220
Reuter, Herbert von 123
Reuter, Paul 121
Reuters News Bureau 121-123
Rohling, August 49
Rothschild, Amschel Mayer 167
Rothschild, House of 29-34, 79-81
Rothschild, Nathan Meyer 78
Rudolf I, King 125

Scherb, F. 30
Schneider, Louis 123
Schopenhauer, Arthur 153
Schröder, Richard 72n7, 132n10
Schwabach, Paul von 123, 220
Scott, Walter 190
Sephardic Jews 170
Shulchan Aruch 48, 57, 151-152
Siemiradzki, Henryk 214
Simon, James 220
Social Democracy 30
Strabo 182
Süss-Oppenheimer, Joseph 79

Tacitus 148
Talleyrand-Perigord, Charles 67
Talmud 43-51, 57, 110, 114, 128, 139-140, 150-151, 176, 195, 198, 204-205
Toulouse 85
Treitschke, Heinrich von 93n5

United States *see* America
urbanization 11-12
usury 15-18, 41-43, 69, 149-150, 173-178

Vater, Karlheinz 223
Vernichtung 42
Voltaire 153

Wagner, Richard 153
Wahrmund, Adolf 36n5, 43, 52-53, 128, 153, 169, 179
Waterloo, Battle of 78
Wellhausen, Julius 179
Wellington, Duke of (Arthur Wellesley) 31
Wiesenthal, Simon 64n1
Wilhelm II, Kaiser 220
William I of Hesse 30
William III, King 78
Witte, Emil 121, 124
Wolff Telegraphic Bureau 121-124
Wolff, Bernhard 121-123

Yahweh *see* God

Zöllner, J. K. 205-206

www.ingramcontent.com/pod-product-compliance
Ingram Content Group UK Ltd.
Pitfield, Milton Keynes, MK11 3LW, UK
UKHW020245240426
12048UKWH00026B/1610